The State of the World Atlas

The State of the World Atlas
Michael Kidron & Ronald Segal
A Pluto Press project

 Heinemann **London**

First published 1981 by Pan Books Ltd.
Cavaye Place, London SW10 9PG
and simultaneously in hardback by
Heinemann Educational Books Ltd,
22 Bedford Square, London WC1B 3HH
ISBN 0 435 35495 7

Concept and text copyright © Michael Kidron and Ronald Segal 1981
Maps copyright © Pluto Press Limited 1981

Artwork for maps created by Irene Bates, Andrea Fairbrass,
Phyllis Hoyle, Rex Nicholls, Kate Swanston, Malcolm Swanston,
Alan Turner and Ian Wakefield of Swanston & Associates,
Derby, England

Layout and other design by Marsha Austin

Editor and production coordinator: Anne Benewick

Introduction and notes typeset by Latimer Trend & Company Ltd,
Plymouth, England

Film origination by David Brin Limited, London EC1R 0JH
Printed and bound in Hong Kong by
Mandarin Offset International (HK) Limited

Contents

Introduction

The State of the World Atlas stems from the rich tradition of political atlases, born out of war or the threat of war, and out of the widespread interest that this excited in military strategy and deployment. In time the tradition came to embrace economic, social and cultural factors; reflecting and promoting the diffusion of knowledge about the world at large which has accompanied the spread of mass education, new forms of communication and international travel.

Like the others in their time, this atlas seeks to fulfil a need for information and interpretation. It identifies the major topics of public concern. It provides a frame of reference for the changing pattern of events. It explains connections that are obscure in themselves or have been deliberately obscured. And it does all this as graphically as possible, in our belief that the information so provided is more easily grasped in this way than through texts and tables.

But this atlas does rather more than its predecessors. It endeavours to be truly international: not only in showing the world-wide incidence of this or that condition or event, but in associating that incidence with an underlying structure – the self-perpetuating system of sovereign states preoccupied with aggrandisement and conflict. While it is true that the state has in its time been an instrument for the extension of personal liberty and for much material progress, it has also been an instrument of personal oppression, collective violence and economic waste. It is our contention that the destructive aspects of the state have come crucially to exceed the constructive ones.

The first section of this atlas shows how states have proliferated in the last few decades and how, with their rival claims, they are reaching out to possess the last uninhabited land mass, the high seas and the sky. The maps then turn to the military preoccupations of the state and the squandering of resources on war, the threat of war, and preparations to meet the threat of war.

The power of states rests on more than arms alone. We show how unequally states are endowed with natural and developed resources, how they employ those endowments and how they are related to the power of private industry and finance. We then consider the impact of all this on labour, on society in general and on the environment, before tracing the symptoms of crisis and identifying some of the mounting challenges to the system.

The great mass of information presented in these maps comes from governments and international agencies, whose statistics often constitute the only available source. Some states, lacking the means or the will to provide accurate statistics, may have published mere approximations – as for infant mortality rates, used in *Map 45: Bill of Health* which contain substantial ingredients of wishful thinking. In other cases, states provide no information at all, or may refuse to make public information they plainly have. The USSR and related states, for example, do not reveal figures for gold and foreign currency reserves. And in some cases, information for some states could be obtained only on a basis which would encourage misleading comparisons. In many of these, we have preferred to leave gaps.

On the understanding that all statistics may be suspect, we have used in this atlas those that we believe are valid enough for broad comparison. Band sizes have been adopted and moving averages used both to isolate certain trends and to reduce dependence on the accuracy of particular statistics. Where possible, the extreme range of statistical events has been given in the keys to the maps. And if reservations are still considered necessary, these are made in the relevant notes.

Some statistics had to be rejected altogether, a fact best exemplified by *Map 52: The Unemployment Time Bomb*, for which an International Labour Office projection was eventually used, in the form of a chart. Not only do the official unemployment rates reported by many poor states bear no recognizable relation to reality, but the existence, reported to us, of strictly confidential and alarming statistics for unemployment in advanced industrial states, confirmed our already deep suspicion of even the best figures publicly provided.

Some generally accepted statistics are marred by conceptual flaws. Gross national product (GNP) is a common measure and is used in several maps. Yet in largely agricultural societies it conveys only roughly, if at all, the value of subsistence production; and in largely industrialized societies it ignores the value of the domestic labour that confines the lives of so many women. Because it involves the use of a national currency, currently the US dollar, as an international standard, it requires further qualification. Even under conditions of monetary stability, a national currency is sig-nificantly affected by both the performance of the related national economy and by shifts in international investment. In a period of floating exchange rates, when the value of the dollar standard in other currencies moves constantly and often sharply, the distortions are enormous.

Two further observations on the use of statistics are necessary. That the very choice of which figures to collect must involve the bias of those who choose them may be exemplified by *Map 45: Bill of Health*. The provision of hospital beds is a measure of medical care that ignores traditional forms of medical treatment, available in many societies, but for which there is no statistical index. The availability of information also imposed limitations. Whereas we had hoped to include a map on the progress of the movement for women's liberation, we had to limit ourselves for lack of a more explicit measure to a comparison of abortion rights (see *Map 63: 'Our Bodies Our Selves'*).

In a number of instances, maps have been based on a degree of personal judgement. For example, information for *Map 42: The Force of Labour*, came out of intensive discussions with leading international trade union officials. Wherever possible, their judgement was checked by others. On occasion, however (for example *Map 28: Military Government* and *Map 34: Religions of Rule*), we had to fall back on our own assessment, in the light of incomplete, ambiguous or contradictory information.

Some maps, such as *Map 64: The Student Sixties* or *Map 65: Urban Heavings in the Seventies*, are the result of extensive culling of newspaper reports. And still others have been augmented in this way: *Map 32: Refugees* or *Map 44: Our Daily Bread*. Such a method presents practical limitations and had to be confined to newspapers in the major European languages.

The projection used throughout is Winkel's Tripel, an 'equal-area' projection which provides a familiar view of our spherical world. For reasons of space and scale, and because detailed information is rarely available for them, some tiny island states appear on very few maps, notably *Map 2: The Proliferation of States*, and *Map 5: The State Invades the Sea*. State boundaries conform to those used in *The Times Atlas of the World*. State names have been given on the maps in their shorter and more commonly used form: for full designations, see the list of states which follows the maps.

A project such as this could not have made the journey from concept to publication without help from many people and their resources of energy, knowledge and talent. We must, first and foremost, thank Anne Benewick, our editor, creative intermediary and production coordinator at Pluto Press. We must thank Malcolm Swanston of Swanston & Associates, who prepared the artwork for the maps, and Marsha Austin who prepared the layouts, for their keen understanding of our purposes, their inventiveness and skills. We must thank Nina Kidron of Pluto Press whose judgement and ingenuity were crucial to the publication. And we must thank Richard Kuper of Pluto Press and David Kewley of Pan Books for their continued advice and support.
    Too many people, in too many places to be listed, have responded readily to requests for guidance, information and reassurance. We are grateful to all of them. And, not least, we wish to thank each other, for mutual encouragement and understanding.

Michael Kidron
Ronald Segal
August 1980

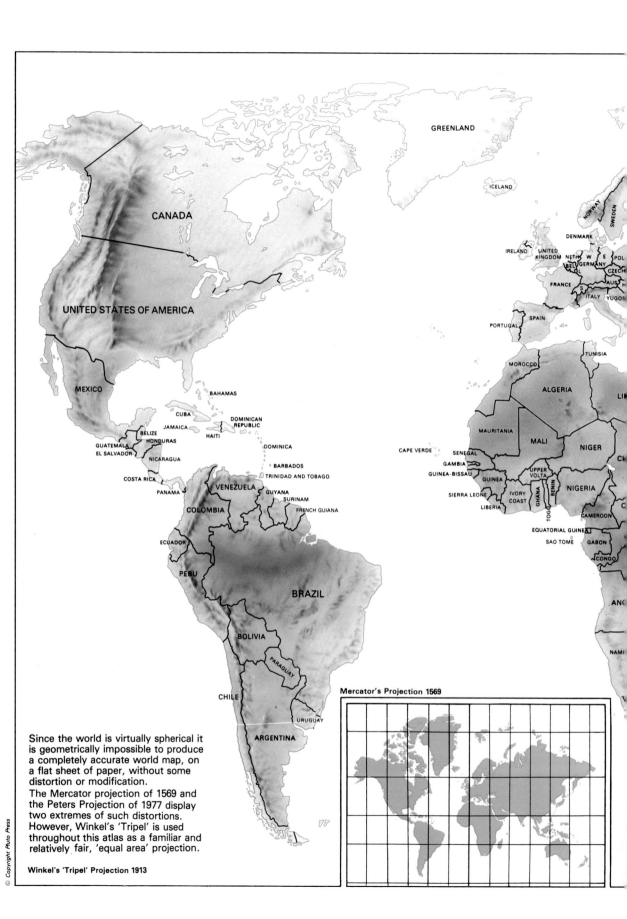

GREENLAND

ICELAND

NORWAY

SWEDEN

CANADA

DENMARK

IRELAND UNITED KINGDOM NETH W E POL
BEL GERMANY CZECH
FRANCE AUS
ITALY YUGOS

UNITED STATES OF AMERICA

PORTUGAL SPAIN

TUNISIA

MOROCCO

MEXICO

BAHAMAS

ALGERIA LIB

CUBA

DOMINICAN
REPUBLIC

JAMAICA

HAITI

BELIZE
HONDURAS

GUATEMALA
EL SALVADOR

DOMINICA

MAURITANIA

MALI

NIGER

CAPE VERDE SENEGAL

GAMBIA

NICARAGUA

BARBADOS

GUINEA-BISSAU

CH

COSTA RICA

TRINIDAD AND TOBAGO

GUINEA

UPPER
VOLTA

PANAMA

VENEZUELA

GUYANA

SIERRA LEONE

IVORY
COAST

NIGERIA

SURINAM

LIBERIA

GHANA

BENIN

COLOMBIA

FRENCH GUIANA

TOGO

CAMEROON

C

ECUADOR

EQUATORIAL GUINEA

SAO TOME

GABON

PERU

BRAZIL

CONGO

ANG

BOLIVIA

NAMI

PARAGUAY

Mercator's Projection 1569

CHILE

URUGUAY

Since the world is virtually spherical it
is geometrically impossible to produce
a completely accurate world map, on
a flat sheet of paper, without some
distortion or modification.

ARGENTINA

The Mercator projection of 1569 and
the Peters Projection of 1977 display
two extremes of such distortions.
However, Winkel's 'Tripel' is used
throughout this atlas as a familiar and
relatively fair, 'equal area' projection.

Winkel's 'Tripel' Projection 1913

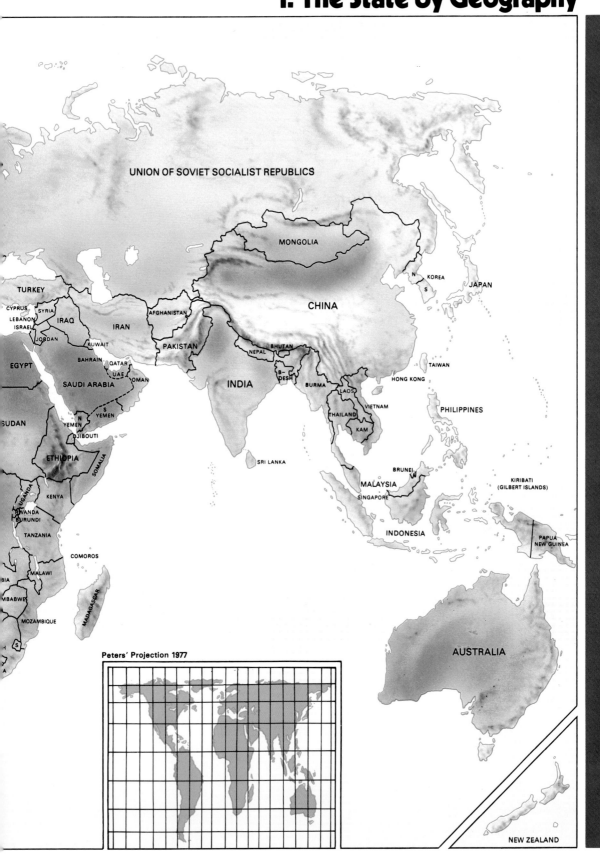

UNION OF SOVIET SOCIALIST REPUBLICS

MONGOLIA

KOREA
N
S
JAPAN

TURKEY

CYPRUS
SYRIA
LEBANON
ISRAEL
IRAQ
JORDAN
KUWAIT
AFGHANISTAN

CHINA

IRAN

PAKISTAN

NEPAL
BHUTAN

TAIWAN

EGYPT

BAHRAIN
QATAR
UAE
OMAN

SAUDI ARABIA

B-
DESH

HONG KONG

INDIA

BURMA

LAOS

SUDAN

N
YEMEN
S
YEMEN

DJIBOUTI

VIETNAM

THAILAND

PHILIPPINES

KAM

ETHIOPIA

SOMALIA

SRI LANKA

BRUNEI
W

KIRIBATI
(GILBERT ISLANDS)

UGANDA

KENYA

MALAYSIA

SINGAPORE

RWANDA
BURUNDI

TANZANIA

INDONESIA

PAPUA
NEW GUINEA

COMOROS

BIA

MALAWI

MADAGASCAR

MBABWE

MOZAMBIQUE

S

AUSTRALIA

Peters' Projection 1977

NEW ZEALAND

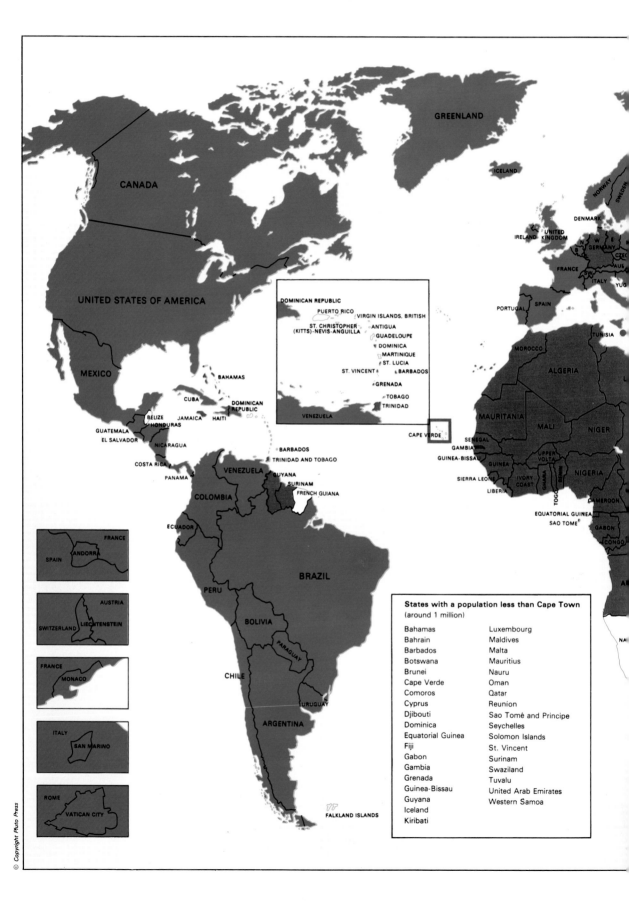

GREENLAND

ICELAND

NORWAY

SWEDEN

CANADA

DENMARK

IRELAND UNITED
KINGDOM

N   W
GERMANY

CZEC

FRANCE

AUS

ITALY   YUG

UNITED STATES OF AMERICA

PORTUGAL   SPAIN

DOMINICAN REPUBLIC

PUERTO RICO

VIRGIN ISLANDS, BRITISH

ST. CHRISTOPHER   ANTIGUA
(KITTS)-NEVIS-ANGUILLA   GUADELOUPE

DOMINICA

MARTINIQUE

ST. LUCIA

ST. VINCENT   BARBADOS

GRENADA

TOBAGO

TRINIDAD

VENEZUELA

TUNISIA

MOROCCO

ALGERIA

MEXICO

BAHAMAS

CUBA

DOMINICAN
REPUBLIC

BELIZE   JAMAICA   HAITI
HONDURAS

GUATEMALA
EL SALVADOR

NICARAGUA

COSTA RICA

PANAMA

BARBADOS

TRINIDAD AND TOBAGO

VENEZUELA   GUYANA

SURINAM

FRENCH GUIANA

COLOMBIA

ECUADOR

CAPE VERDE

MAURITANIA   MALI   NIGER

SENEGAL
GAMBIA

GUINEA-BISSAU

GUINEA

UPPER
VOLTA

SIERRA LEONE   IVORY
COAST

LIBERIA

NIGERIA

TOGO

GHANA

BENIN

CAMEROON

EQUATORIAL GUINEA
SAO TOME

GABON

CONGO

FRANCE

SPAIN   ANDORRA

AUSTRIA

SWITZERLAND   LIECHTENSTEIN

FRANCE

MONACO

ITALY

SAN MARINO

ROME

VATICAN CITY

BRAZIL

PERU

BOLIVIA

PARAGUAY

CHILE

URUGUAY

ARGENTINA

FALKLAND ISLANDS

NA

States with a population less than Cape Town
(around 1 million)

Bahamas	Luxembourg
Bahrain	Maldives
Barbados	Malta
Botswana	Mauritius
Brunei	Nauru
Cape Verde	Oman
Comoros	Qatar
Cyprus	Reunion
Djibouti	Sao Tomé and Principe
Dominica	Seychelles
Equatorial Guinea	Solomon Islands
Fiji	St. Vincent
Gabon	Surinam
Gambia	Swaziland
Grenada	Tuvalu
Guinea-Bissau	United Arab Emirates
Guyana	Western Samoa
Iceland	
Kiribati	

2. The Proliferation of States

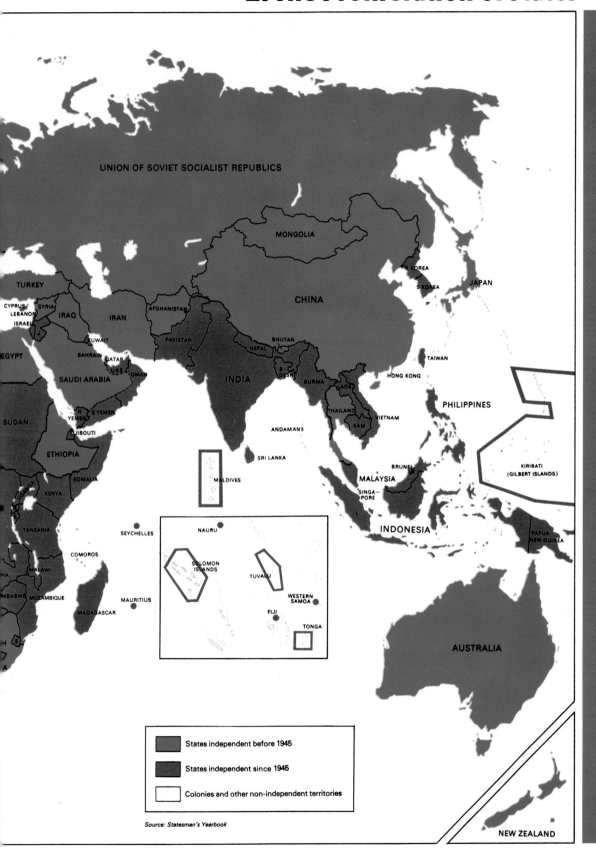

UNION OF SOVIET SOCIALIST REPUBLICS

MONGOLIA

N KOREA

JAPAN

S KOREA

TURKEY

CYPRUS
LEBANON
SYRIA
ISRAEL
IRAQ
IRAN
AFGHANISTAN
CHINA

KUWAIT

EGYPT

BAHRAIN
QATAR
UAE
OMAN
SAUDI ARABIA
PAKISTAN
NEPAL
BHUTAN
TAIWAN

INDIA
B-
DESH
BURMA
HONG KONG

N
YEMEN
S YEMEN

SUDAN

DJIBOUTI
LAOS
PHILIPPINES

THAILAND
VIETNAM

ETHIOPIA
ANDAMAN
KAM

SOMALIA
SRI LANKA

UGANDA

KENYA
MALDIVES
BRUNEI
KIRIBATI
(GILBERT ISLANDS)

MALAYSIA

SINGA-
PORE

TANZANIA

SEYCHELLES
NAURU

COMOROS

MALAWI
INDONESIA

PAPUA
NEW GUINEA

MBABWE
MOZAMBIQUE
SOLOMON
ISLANDS
TUVALU

MADAGASCAR
MAURITIUS
WESTERN
SAMOA

FIJI

TONGA

AUSTRALIA

	States independent before 1945
	States independent since 1945
	Colonies and other non-independent territories

Source: Statesman's Yearbook

NEW ZEALAND

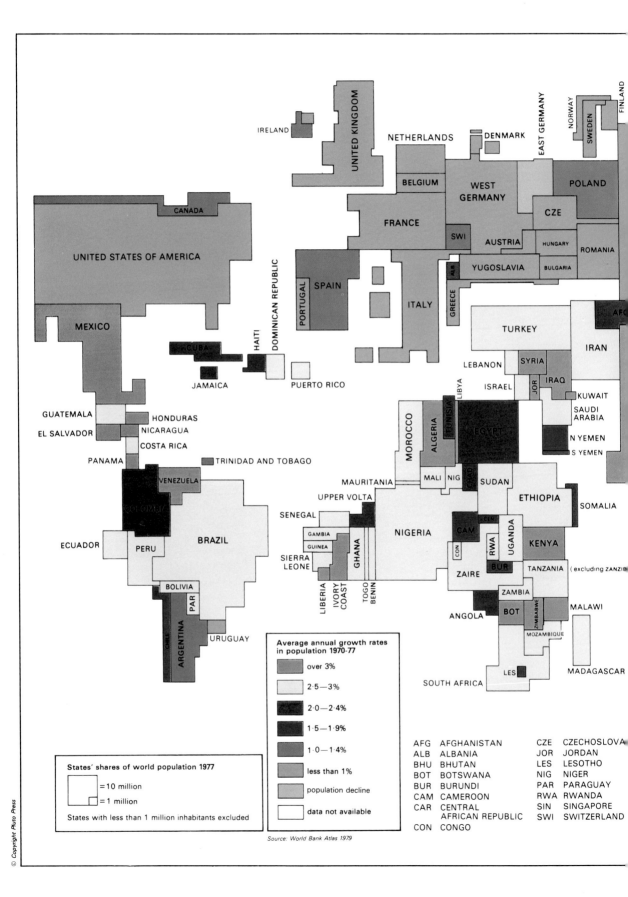

IRELAND

UNITED KINGDOM

NETHERLANDS

DENMARK

EAST GERMANY

NORWAY

SWEDEN

FINLAND

BELGIUM

WEST GERMANY

POLAND

CANADA

FRANCE

CZE

SWI

AUSTRIA

HUNGARY

ROMANIA

UNITED STATES OF AMERICA

DOMINICAN REPUBLIC

ALB

YUGOSLAVIA

BULGARIA

PORTUGAL

SPAIN

ITALY

GREECE

MEXICO

TURKEY

IRAN

AFG

HAITI

LEBANON

SYRIA

IRAQ

CUBA

ISRAEL

JOR

KUWAIT

JAMAICA

PUERTO RICO

SAUDI ARABIA

N YEMEN

S YEMEN

GUATEMALA

HONDURAS

MOROCCO

ALGERIA

TUNISIA

LIBYA

EGYPT

EL SALVADOR

NICARAGUA

COSTA RICA

PANAMA

TRINIDAD AND TOBAGO

MAURITANIA

MALI

NIG

CHAD

SUDAN

ETHIOPIA

SOMALIA

VENEZUELA

UPPER VOLTA

COLOMBIA

SENEGAL

NIGERIA

CAM

CEN

UGANDA

KENYA

ECUADOR

PERU

BRAZIL

GAMBIA

GUINEA

GHANA

CON

RWA

BUR

TANZANIA

(excluding ZANZIB)

SIERRA LEONE

LIBERIA

IVORY COAST

TOGO

BENIN

ZAIRE

BOLIVIA

PAR

ZAMBIA

ZIMBABWE

MALAWI

ANGOLA

BOT

MOZAMBIQUE

ARGENTINA

CHILE

URUGUAY

LES

MADAGASCAR

SOUTH AFRICA

Average annual growth rates in population 1970-77

- over 3%
- 2·5—3%
- 2·0—2·4%
- 1·5—1·9%
- 1·0—1·4%
- less than 1%
- population decline
- data not available

States' shares of world population 1977

☐ = 10 million

▫ = 1 million

States with less than 1 million inhabitants excluded

AFG	AFGHANISTAN	CZE	CZECHOSLOVA
ALB	ALBANIA	JOR	JORDAN
BHU	BHUTAN	LES	LESOTHO
BOT	BOTSWANA	NIG	NIGER
BUR	BURUNDI	PAR	PARAGUAY
CAM	CAMEROON	RWA	RWANDA
CAR	CENTRAL	SIN	SINGAPORE
	AFRICAN REPUBLIC	SWI	SWITZERLAND
CON	CONGO		

Source: World Bank Atlas 1979

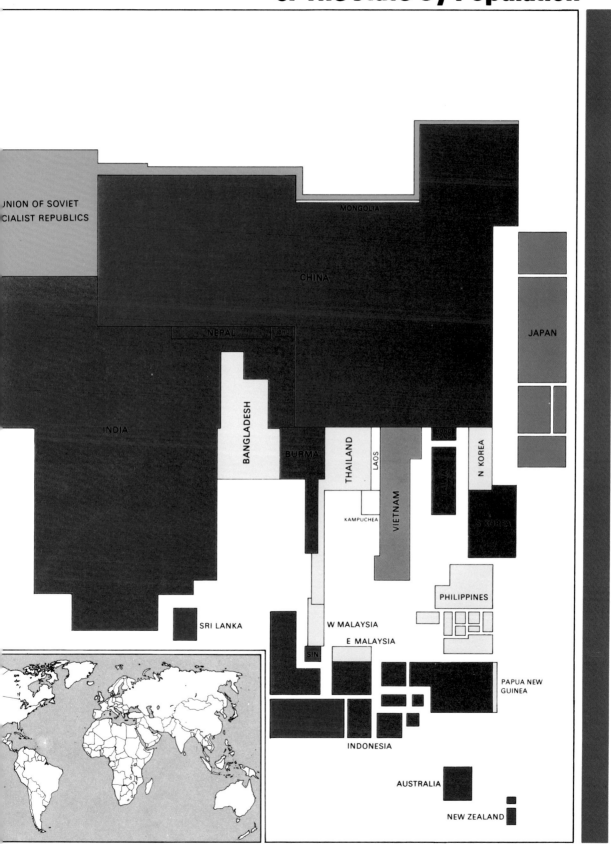

Antarctica and Its Neighbours

Pacific Ocean

CHILE   ARGENTINA   URUGUAY   BRAZIL
Buenos Aires

Antarctic Circle

Bellinghausen Sea

Amundsen Sea

Weddell Sea

NEW ZEALAND
Christchurch

Ross Sea

Atlantic Ocean

+ South Pole

ANTARCTICA

Melbourne

Cape Town

AUSTRALIA

Indian Ocean

SOUTH
AFRICA

NAMIBIA

LESOTHO

Territorial Claims:
A Difference of Opinion

Belgium, Japan, South Africa and the USSR do not
formally recognise any claims; the USA and the
USSR 'reserve their rights' and the USA has
rejected all existing claims.

Resources of the
Antarctic seas

Antarctic krill

Antarctic cod

Antarctic icefish

Minke whale

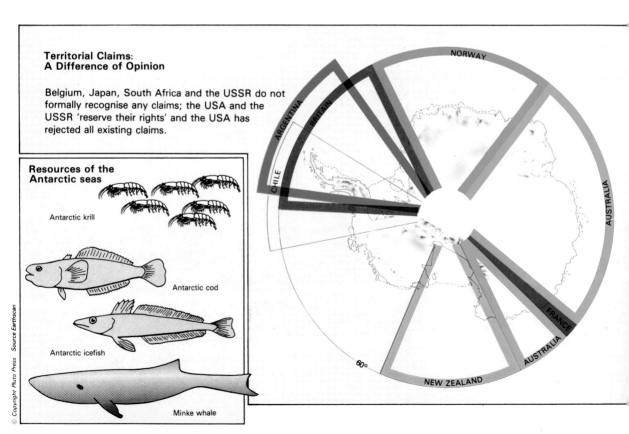

NORWAY

CHILE   ARGENTINA   BRITAIN

AUSTRALIA

FRANCE

AUSTRALIA

60°

NEW ZEALAND

4. The State Invades Antarctica

The Lure of Wealth

Antarctica, one hundred million years ago, showing what were until then continuous mountain ranges: the Transantarctic Mountains connected to the Andes in South America; the Central Antarctic Mountains connected to the Rand in South Africa and to mineral rich areas in Australia.

Metallic minerals already located in Antarctica include chromium (Cr), nickel (Ni), cobalt (Co), copper (Cu), gold (Au), silver (Ag), manganese (Mu), molybdenum (Mo), iron (Fe), titanium (Ti), platinum (Pt), lead (Pb), zinc (Zu), tin (Su), uranium (U). There are also vast reserves of coal and deposits of oil and natural gas: for the present, uneconomic to exploit.

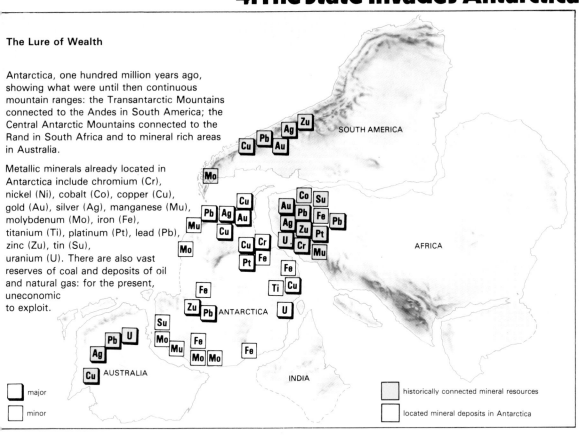

The settlers

Scientific stations south of the 60th parallel, 1979

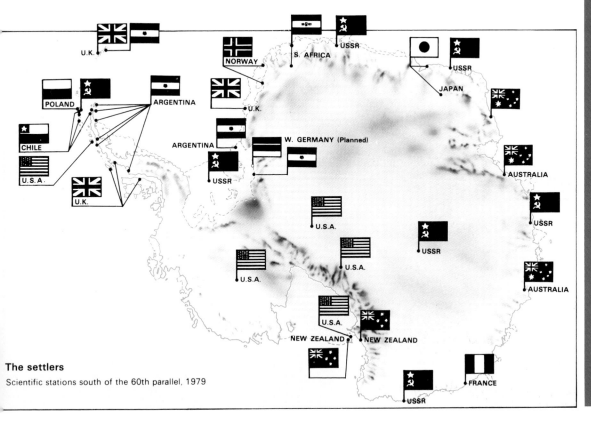

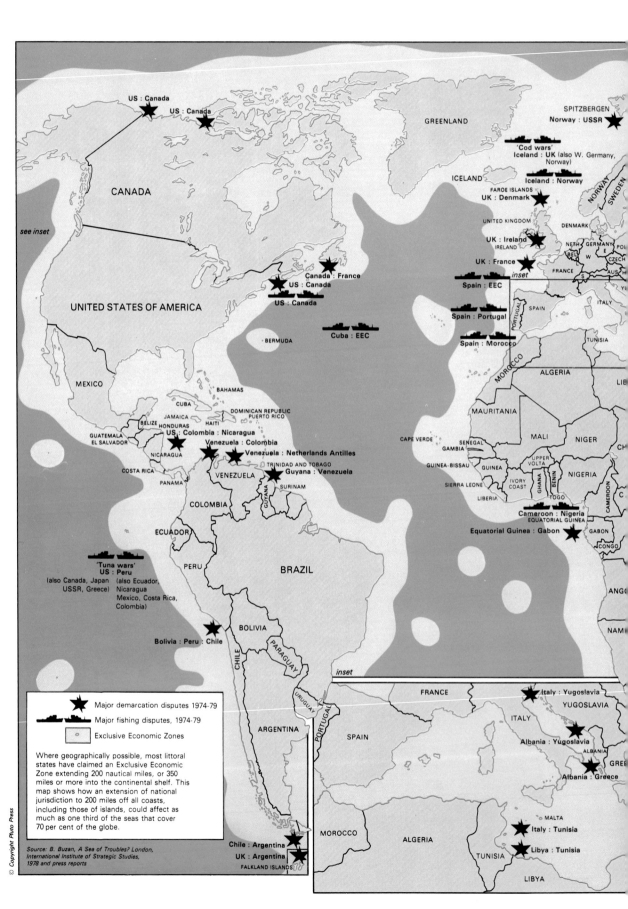

US : Canada

US : Canada

SPITZBERGEN
Norway : USSR

GREENLAND

'Cod wars'
Iceland : UK (also W. Germany,
Norway)

ICELAND

Iceland : Norway

FAROE ISLANDS
UK : Denmark

CANADA

NORWAY

SWEDEN

UNITED KINGDOM

DENMARK

UK : Ireland
IRELAND

NETH. GERMANY POL
BEL

see inset

UK : France
FRANCE

inset

CZECH.
AUS

Canada : France
US : Canada

UNITED STATES OF AMERICA

Spain : EEC

SPAIN

ITALY

PORTUGAL

US : Canada

Spain : Portugal

TUNISIA

BERMUDA

Cuba : EEC

Spain : Morocco

MOROCCO

ALGERIA

LIB

MEXICO

BAHAMAS

CUBA

MAURITANIA

MALI

NIGER

CH

DOMINICAN REPUBLIC
PUERTO RICO

JAMAICA

CAPE VERDE

HAITI

SENEGAL
GAMBIA

BELIZE

HONDURAS

US : Colombia : Nicaragua

GUATEMALA
EL SALVADOR

Venezuela : Colombia

GUINEA-BISSAU

UPPER
VOLTA

GUINEA

NIGERIA

NICARAGUA

Venezuela : Netherlands Antilles

IVORY
COAST

GHANA

BENIN

TRINIDAD AND TOBAGO

COSTA RICA

PANAMA

VENEZUELA

Guyana : Venezuela

SIERRA LEONE
LIBERIA

TOGO

CAMEROON

C

SURINAM

COLOMBIA

Cameroon : Nigeria
EQUATORIAL GUINEA

ECUADOR

Equatorial Guinea : Gabon

GABON

CONGO

'Tuna wars'
US : Peru

PERU

BRAZIL

(also Canada, Japan
USSR, Greece)

(also Ecuador,
Nicaragua
Mexico, Costa Rica,
Colombia)

BOLIVIA

ANG

NAM

Bolivia : Peru : Chile

CHILE

PARAGUAY

inset

FRANCE

Italy : Yugoslavia

URUGUAY

YUGOSLAVIA

Major demarcation disputes 1974-79

ITALY

Major fishing disputes, 1974-79

SPAIN

Albania : Yugoslavia

ALBANIA

Exclusive Economic Zones

ARGENTINA

PORTUGAL

GRE

Albania : Greece

Where geographically possible, most littoral
states have claimed an Exclusive Economic
Zone extending 200 nautical miles, or 350
miles or more into the continental shelf. This
map shows how an extension of national
jurisdiction to 200 miles off all coasts,
including those of islands, could affect as
much as one third of the seas that cover
70 per cent of the globe.

MALTA

Italy : Tunisia

Source: B. Buzan, A Sea of Troubles? London,
International Institute of Strategic Studies,
1978 and press reports

Chile : Argentina

MOROCCO

ALGERIA

Libya : Tunisia

UK : Argentina

LIBYA

FALKLAND ISLANDS

TUNISIA

R : Norway

rway : USSR

UNION OF SOVIET SOCIALIST REPUBLICS

MONGOLIA

USSR : Japan

N KOREA

JAPAN

S

N. Korea : S. Korea

N. Korea : S. Korea : Japan : USSR

TURKEY

CYPRUS

LEBANON SYRIA

ISRAEL JOR

IRAQ

IRAN

AFGHANISTAN

CHINA

Iran : Iraq

Iraq : Kuwait

Iran : UAE

KUWAIT

QATAR

PAKISTAN

NEPAL

BHUTAN

B
DESH

BURMA

China : Taiwan

TAIWAN

HONG KONG

EGYPT

UNITED ARAB EMIRATES

SAUDI ARABIA

OMAN

INDIA

China : Vietnam

LAOS

N
YEMEN

S
YEMEN

India : Taiwan

Thailand : Taiwan

THAILAND

KAMP

VIETNAM

PHILIPPINES

SUDAN

DJIBOUTI

Thailand : Kampuchea

Vietnam : Kampuchea

China : Vietnam : Thailand : Philippines

ETHIOPIA

India : Sri Lanka

SRI LANKA

Japan : India

USSR

S. Korea

W

SOMALIA

MALDIVE

MALAYSIA

Philippines : Indonesia

KENYA

Somalia : Kenya

SEYCHELLES

SINGAPORE

Taiwan : Indonesia

TANZANIA

COMOROS

INDONESIA

PAPUA
NEW
GUINEA

MADAGASCAR

inset

UNION OF SOVIET SOCIALIST REPUBLICS

CANADA

US : Canada

MOZAMBIQUE

MBABWE

MALAWI

MONGOLIA

N KOREA

S

JAPAN

US : Canada

UNITED STATES OF AMERICA

US : Panama

CHINA

TAIWAN

MEXICO

Japan : US

CUBA

BELIZE

HONDURAS

GUATEMALA NICARAGUA

EL SALVADOR

COSTA RICA

PANAMA

COLOMBIA

PHILIPPINES

France : Mexico

ECUADOR

Tuvalu : Kiribati

PAPUA NEW GUINEA

US : UK

TURKEY

INDONESIA

Papua New Guinea : Bougainville

PERU

Greece : Turkey

NZ : US

CYPRUS

Solomon Is : Shortland Is

LEBANON

Taiwan : Australia

FIJI

CHILE

ISRAEL

JORDAN

AUSTRALIA

l : Egypt : Jordan : Saudi Arabia

NEW ZEALAND

ARGENTINA

EGYPT

One year's launching of satellites

Of the 159 satellites launched in 1978, 119 were Soviet (mainly short-lived), 30 American (longer-lived), 4 Japanese, 2 Western European, and one each Chinese, Czechoslovak, Canadian and NATO.

Of the total, probably 112 were military (91 Soviet, 19 American 1 Chinese and 1 NATO), which brought the number of military satellites ever launched to 1603, three-quarters of all artificial satellites. Over half the military satellites are for surveillance, a quarter for military communications and the rest for geodesy, navigation, early warning of attack and meteorology.

1978 saw two more Russian firsts in space: the launching of a primitive hunter-killer satellite in May, and the crash, in the Canadian Northwest, of Kosmos 945, which contaminated a large area with radioactive debris.

Tyuratam

Lop Nor

Tanegashima

tsk

Cape Kennedy ●

Vandenberg ●

Sources: COSPAR Information Bulletin SIPRI, World Armaments and Disarmaments Yearbook 1979

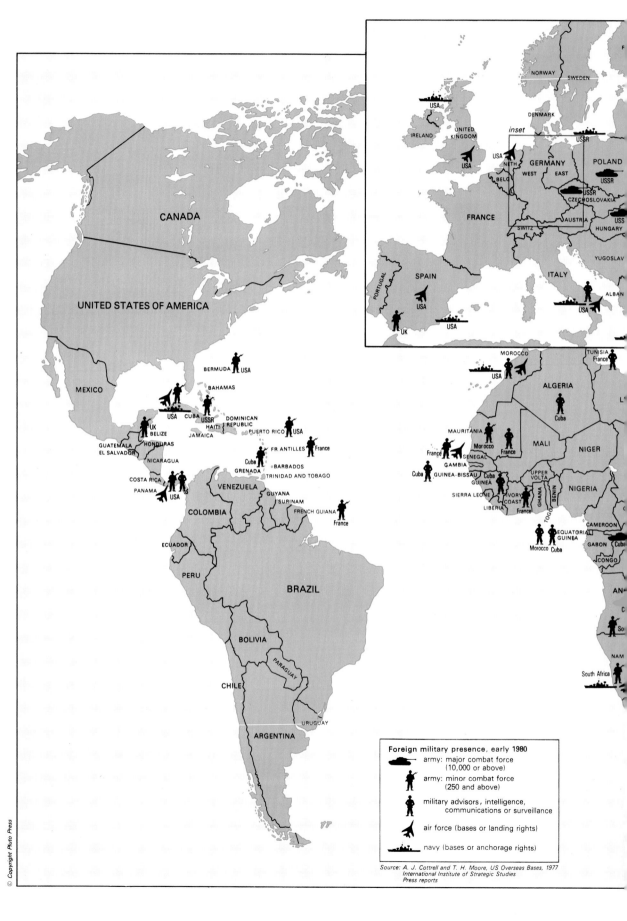

NORWAY
SWEDEN
IRELAND
UNITED KINGDOM
USA
USA
DENMARK
inset
USSR
USSR
NETH.
USA
GERMANY
WEST EAST
POLAND
USSR
BELG.
FRANCE
CZECHOSLOVAKIA
USSR
AUSTRIA
USS
SWITZ.
HUNGARY
YUGOSLAV
PORTUGAL
SPAIN
USA
ITALY
ALBAN
UK
USA
USA

CANADA

UNITED STATES OF AMERICA

MEXICO

BERMUDA USA
BAHAMAS
USA CUBA
USSR
HAITI
DOMINICAN REPUBLIC
UK BELIZE
PUERTO RICO USA
JAMAICA
GUATEMALA
EL SALVADOR
HONDURAS
NICARAGUA
FR ANTILLES France
COSTA RICA
PANAMA
USA
Cuba BARBADOS
GRENADA
TRINIDAD AND TOBAGO
VENEZUELA
GUYANA
SURINAM
COLOMBIA
FRENCH GUIANA
France
ECUADOR
PERU
BRAZIL
BOLIVIA
PARAGUAY
CHILE
URUGUAY
ARGENTINA

MOROCCO
TUNISIA
France
USA
ALGERIA
Cuba
MAURITANIA
Morocco
MALI
NIGER
France
Senegal
GAMBIA
France
Cuba
GUINEA-BISSAU
Cuba
GUINEA
UPPER VOLTA
SIERRA LEONE
IVORY COAST
GHANA
BENIN
NIGERIA
LIBERIA
France
TOGO
CAMEROON
EQUATORIAL GUINEA
GABON
Cuba
Morocco Cuba
CONGO
AN
C
So
NAM
South Africa

Foreign military presence, early 1980

- army: major combat force (10,000 or above)
- army: minor combat force (250 and above)
- military advisors, intelligence, communications or surveillance
- air force (bases or landing rights)
- navy (bases or anchorage rights)

Source: A. J. Cottrell and T. H. Moore, US Overseas Bases, 1977
International Institute of Strategic Studies
Press reports

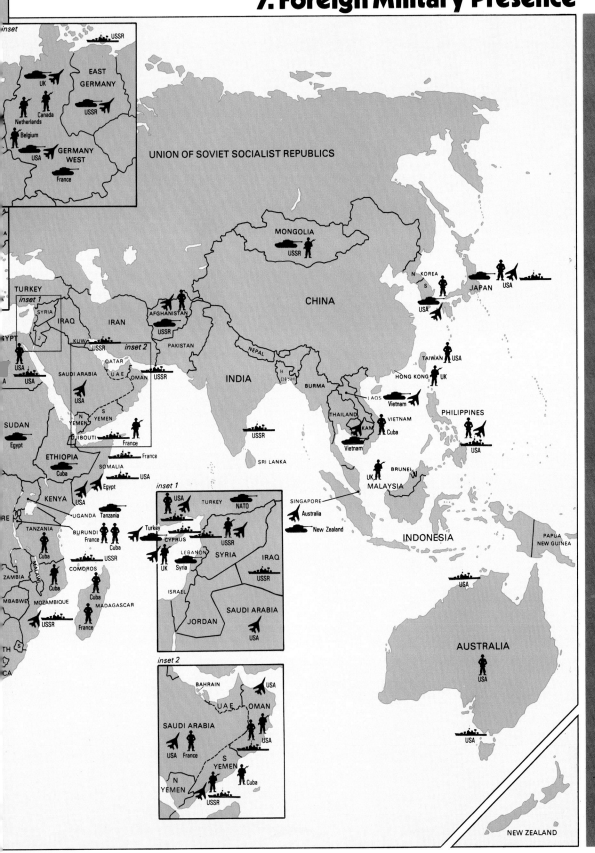

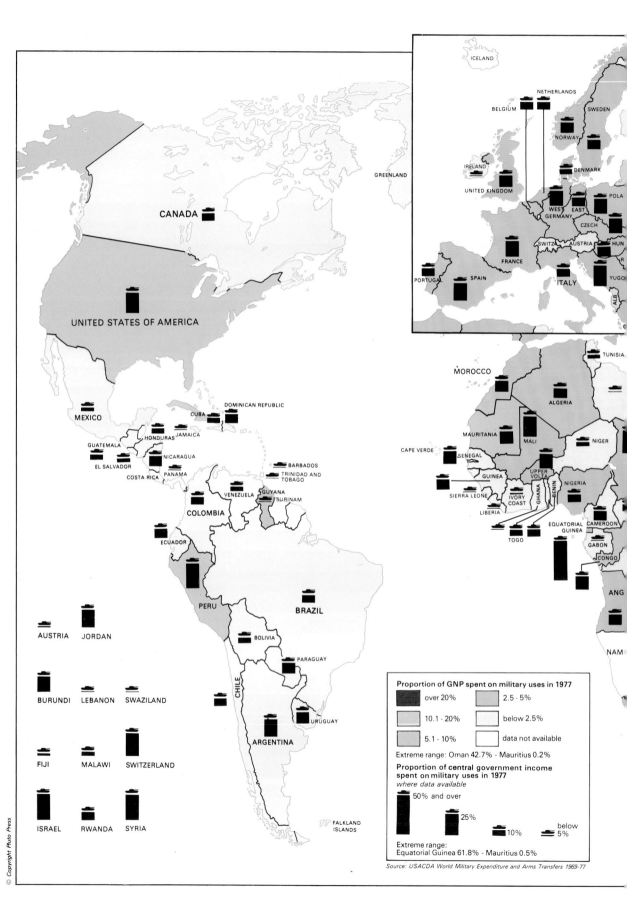

ICELAND

NETHERLANDS
BELGIUM
SWEDEN
NORWAY
IRELAND
DENMARK
UNITED KINGDOM
POLA
WEST
EAST
GERMANY
CZECH
HUN
SWITZ
AUSTRIA
FRANCE
YUGO
PORTUGAL
SPAIN
ITALY
ALB

GREENLAND

CANADA

UNITED STATES OF AMERICA

MEXICO
CUBA
DOMINICAN REPUBLIC
JAMAICA
HONDURAS
GUATEMALA
NICARAGUA
EL SALVADOR
BARBADOS
COSTA RICA
PANAMA
TRINIDAD AND TOBAGO
VENEZUELA
GUYANA
COLOMBIA
SURINAM

ECUADOR

PERU

BRAZIL

AUSTRIA JORDAN

BOLIVIA

PARAGUAY

CHILE

URUGUAY

BURUNDI LEBANON SWAZILAND

ARGENTINA

FIJI MALAWI SWITZERLAND

FALKLAND ISLANDS

ISRAEL RWANDA SYRIA

TUNISIA
MOROCCO
ALGERIA
MAURITANIA
MALI
NIGER
CAPE VERDE
SENEGAL
GUINEA
UPPER VOLTA
SIERRA LEONE
IVORY COAST
GHANA
BENIN
NIGERIA
LIBERIA
EQUATORIAL GUINEA
CAMEROON
TOGO
GABON
CONGO

ANG

NAM

Proportion of GNP spent on military uses in 1977

over 20%	2.5 - 5%
10.1 - 20%	below 2.5%
5.1 - 10%	data not available

Extreme range: Oman 42.7% - Mauritius 0.2%

Proportion of central government income spent on military uses in 1977
where data available

50% and over

25%

10%

below 5%

Extreme range:
Equatorial Guinea 61.8% - Mauritius 0.5%

Source: USACDA World Military Expenditure and Arms Transfers 1969-77

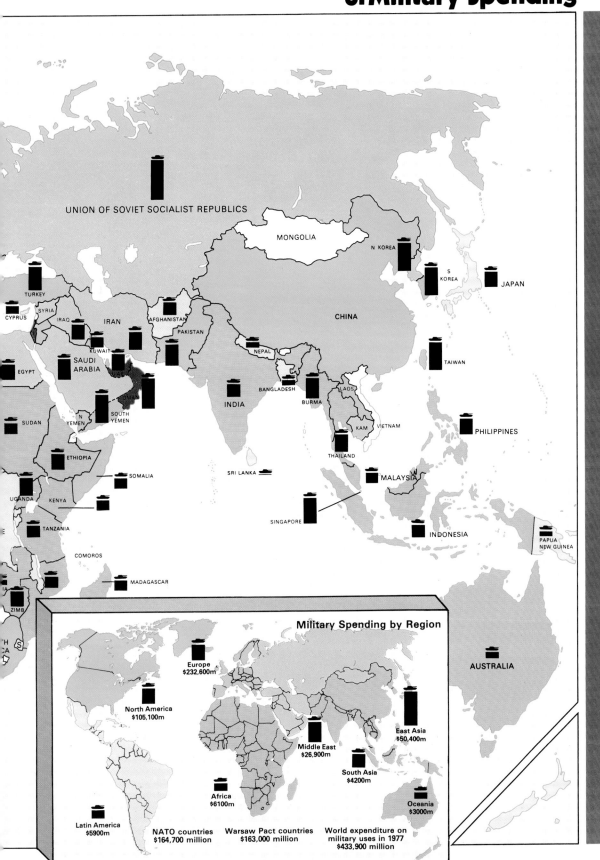

UNION OF SOVIET SOCIALIST REPUBLICS

MONGOLIA

N KOREA

S KOREA

JAPAN

TURKEY

CYPRUS

SYRIA

IRAQ

IRAN

AFGHANISTAN

PAKISTAN

CHINA

KUWAIT

SAUDI ARABIA

UAE

OMAN

NEPAL

TAIWAN

EGYPT

SUDAN

N YEMEN

SOUTH YEMEN

INDIA

BANGLADESH

BURMA

LAOS

KAM

VIETNAM

PHILIPPINES

ETHIOPIA

SOMALIA

SRI LANKA

THAILAND

UGANDA

KENYA

MALAYSIA

TANZANIA

COMOROS

SINGAPORE

INDONESIA

PAPUA NEW GUINEA

MADAGASCAR

ZIMB

AUSTRALIA

Military Spending by Region

Europe
$232,600m

North America
$105,100m

Middle East
$26,900m

East Asia
$50,400m

South Asia
$4200m

Africa
$6100m

Oceania
$3000m

Latin America
$5900m

NATO countries
$164,700 million

Warsaw Pact countries
$163,000 million

World expenditure on
military uses in 1977
$433,900 million

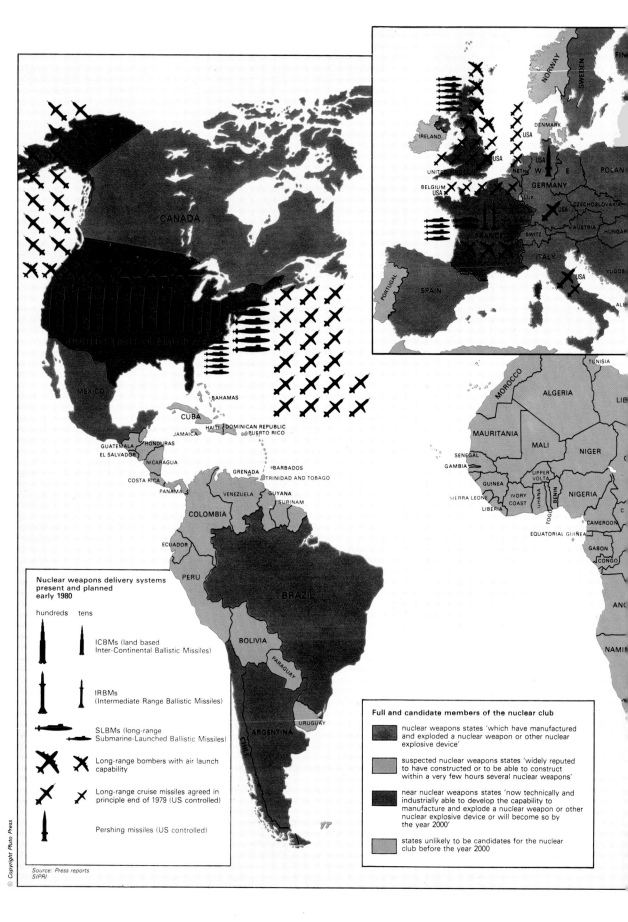

Nuclear weapons delivery systems present and planned early 1980

hundreds	tens	
		ICBMs (land based Inter-Continental Ballistic Missiles)
		IRBMs (Intermediate Range Ballistic Missiles)
		SLBMs (long-range Submarine-Launched Ballistic Missiles)
		Long-range bombers with air launch capability
		Long-range cruise missiles agreed in principle end of 1979 (US controlled)
		Pershing missiles (US controlled)

Source: Press reports
SIPRI

Full and candidate members of the nuclear club

nuclear weapons states 'which have manufactured and exploded a nuclear weapon or other nuclear explosive device'

suspected nuclear weapons states 'widely reputed to have constructed or to be able to construct within a very few hours several nuclear weapons'

near nuclear weapons states 'now technically and industrially able to develop the capability to manufacture and explode a nuclear weapon or other nuclear explosive device or will become so by the year 2000'

states unlikely to be candidates for the nuclear club before the year 2000

UNION OF SOVIET SOCIALIST REPUBLICS

MONGOLIA

N KOREA
S

JAPAN

TURKEY

CYPRUS SYRIA
LEBANON
ISRAEL
IRAQ
IRAN
AFGHANISTAN

KUWAIT
PAKISTAN
CHINA
2 ICBM

EGYPT

BAHRAIN
QATAR
U.A.E.
OMAN

NEPAL
B
DESH
TAIWAN
HONG KONG

SAUDI
ARABIA

INDIA
BURMA
LAOS

N
YEMEN
S
YEMEN

SUDAN

VIETNAM

PHILIPPINES

ETHIOPIA
SOMALIA

KENYA

KAM

UGANDA

SRI LANKA

TANZANIA

MALAYSIA
SINGAPORE
W

INDONESIA

PAPUA
NEW GUINEA

MALAWI

MBABWE

MADAGASCAR

MOZAMBIQUE

AUSTRALIA

Kill capacity
Areas of destruction: from the Hiroshima bomb to the ICBM of the mid 1980s

Hiroshima

Hiroshima

Hiroshima

Hiroshima bomb
3 sq. miles

current US ICBMs
50 sq. miles

US ICBMs for mid 1980s
290 sq. miles

NEW ZEALAND

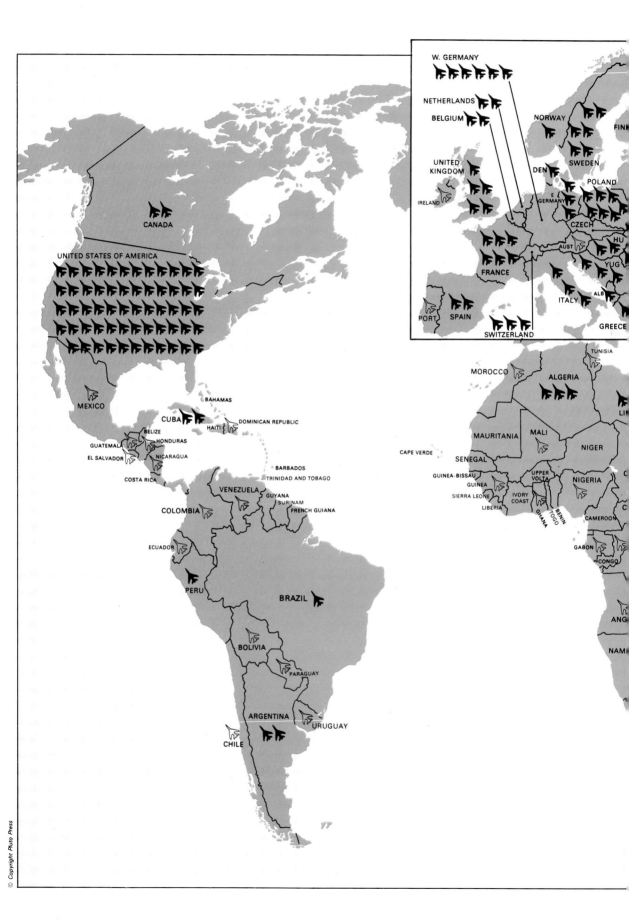

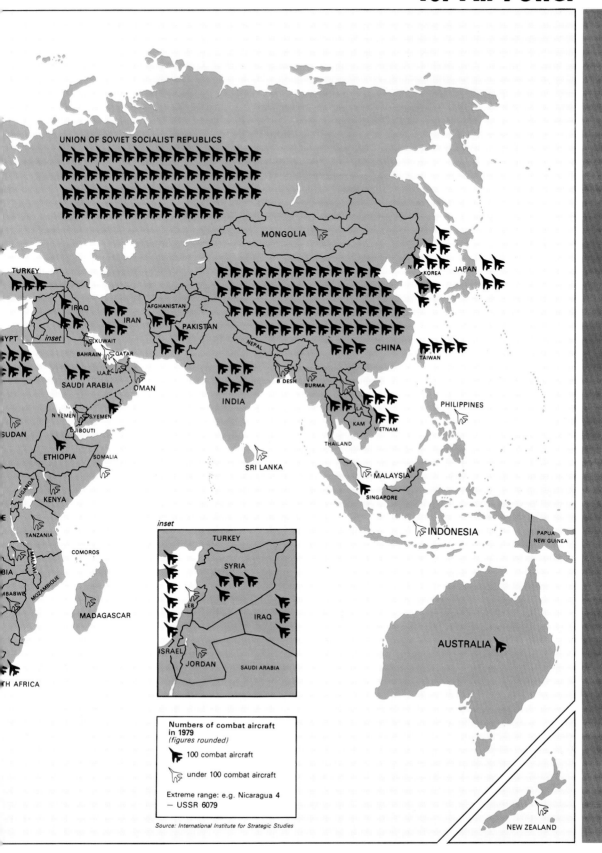

UNION OF SOVIET SOCIALIST REPUBLICS

MONGOLIA

TURKEY

IRAQ

IRAN

AFGHANISTAN

PAKISTAN

KUWAIT

BAHRAIN QATAR

U.A.E.

SAUDI ARABIA

OMAN

N YEMEN S.YEMEN

DJIBOUTI

SUDAN

ETHIOPIA

SOMALIA

UGANDA

KENYA

TANZANIA

COMOROS

MADAGASCAR

MOZAMBIQUE

TH AFRICA

YPT

inset

NEPAL

B DESH BURMA

INDIA

SRI LANKA

THAILAND

LA

KAM

VIETNAM

MALAYSIA

SINGAPORE

INDONESIA

CHINA

N KOREA

S

JAPAN

TAIWAN

PHILIPPINES

PAPUA NEW GUINEA

AUSTRALIA

NEW ZEALAND

inset

TURKEY

SYRIA

LEB

ISRAEL

JORDAN

IRAQ

SAUDI ARABIA

Numbers of combat aircraft in 1979
(figures rounded)

100 combat aircraft

under 100 combat aircraft

Extreme range: e.g. Nicaragua 4
— USSR 6079

Source: International Institute for Strategic Studies

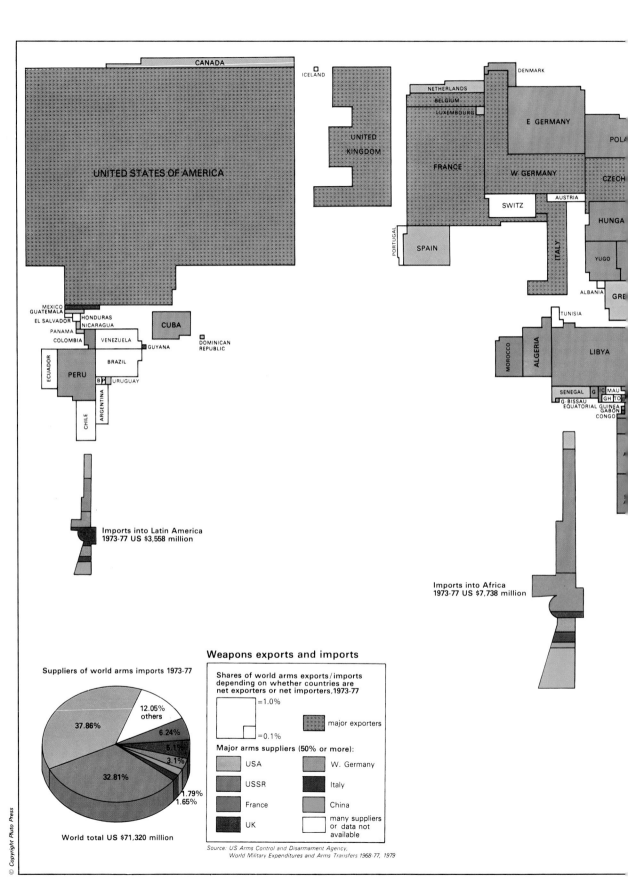

CANADA

ICELAND

UNITED STATES OF AMERICA

DENMARK

NETHERLANDS

BELGIUM

LUXEMBOURG

E GERMANY

POLA

UNITED KINGDOM

FRANCE

W. GERMANY

CZECH

SWITZ

AUSTRIA

HUNGA

PORTUGAL

SPAIN

ITALY

YUGO

ALBANIA

GRE

MEXICO

GUATEMALA

EL SALVADOR

HONDURAS

NICARAGUA

PANAMA

COLOMBIA

VENEZUELA

CUBA

GUYANA

DOMINICAN REPUBLIC

TUNISIA

MOROCCO

ALGERIA

LIBYA

ECUADOR

PERU

BRAZIL

B

URUGUAY

ARGENTINA

CHILE

SENEGAL

G. BISSAU

EQUATORIAL GUINEA

GABON

CONGO

G IC MAU

GH TO

**Imports into Latin America
1973-77 US $3,558 million**

**Imports into Africa
1973-77 US $7,738 million**

Weapons exports and imports

Suppliers of world arms imports 1973-77

12.05%
others

37.86%

6.24%

5.1%

3.1%

32.81%

1.79%

1.65%

World total US $71,320 million

Shares of world arms exports/imports
depending on whether countries are
net exporters or net importers, 1973-77

=1.0%

=0.1%

major exporters

Major arms suppliers (50% or more):

USA	W. Germany
USSR	Italy
France	China
UK	many suppliers or data not available

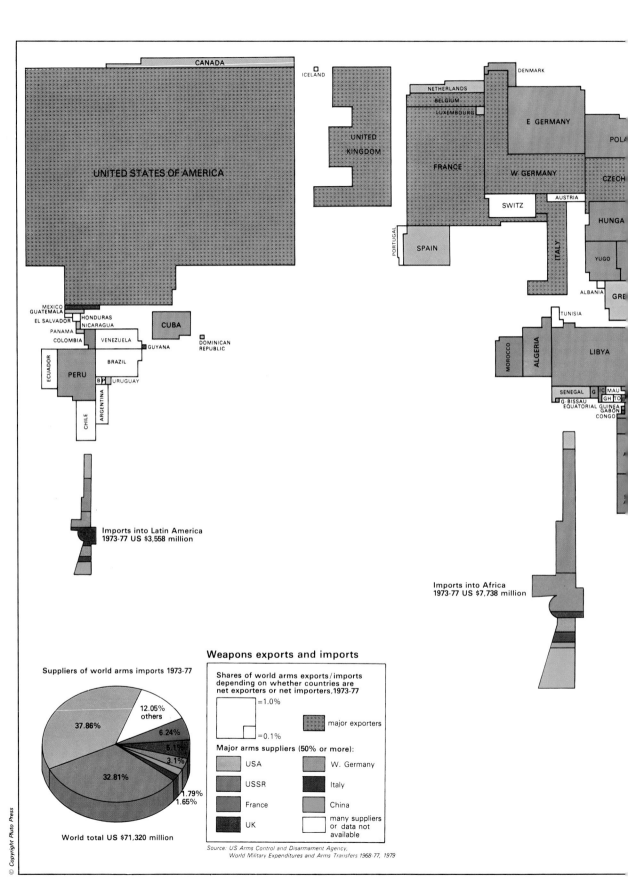

Source: US Arms Control and Disarmament Agency,
World Military Expenditures and Arms Transfers 1968-77, 1979

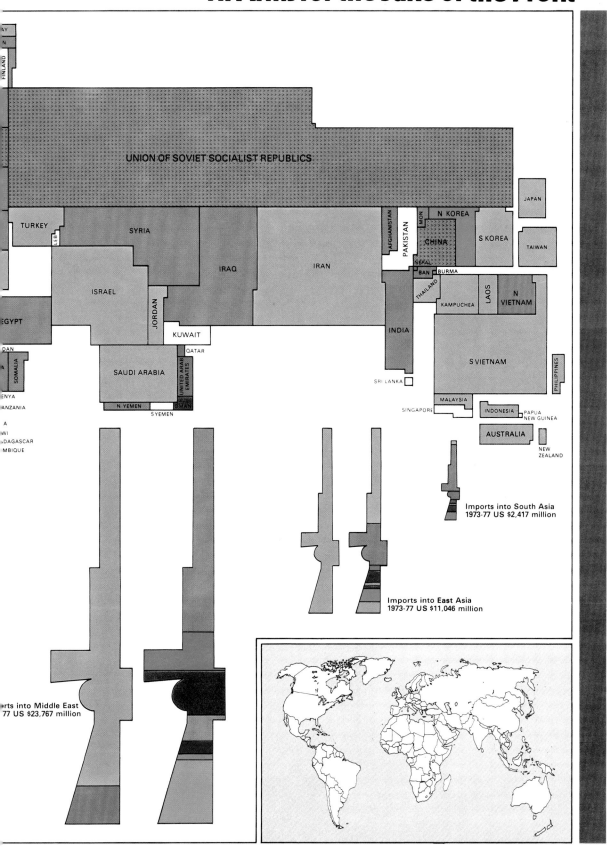

UNION OF SOVIET SOCIALIST REPUBLICS

FINLAND

TURKEY
LEB
SYRIA

ISRAEL
JORDAN
IRAQ
IRAN

EGYPT
KUWAIT
QATAR
AFGHANISTAN
PAKISTAN
NEPAL
BAN
INDIA
CHINA
MON
N KOREA
S KOREA
JAPAN
TAIWAN
BURMA
THAILAND
KAMPUCHEA
LAOS
N VIETNAM

DAN
SOMALIA
SAUDI ARABIA
UNITED ARAB EMIRATES
OMAN
N YEMEN
S YEMEN

ENYA
ANZANIA
A
WI
DAGASCAR
MBIQUE

SRI LANKA
S VIETNAM
PHILIPPINES

SINGAPORE
MALAYSIA
INDONESIA
PAPUA NEW GUINEA

AUSTRALIA
NEW ZEALAND

Imports into South Asia
1973-77 US $2,417 million

Imports into East Asia
1973-77 US $11,046 million

rts into Middle East
77 US $23,767 million

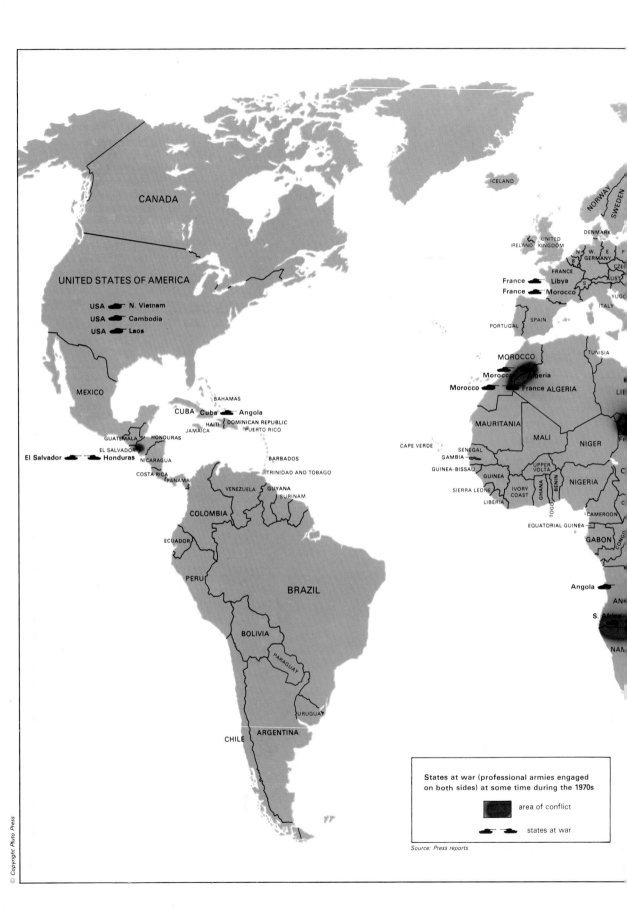

CANADA

UNITED STATES OF AMERICA

USA ⬤ N. Vietnam
USA ⬤ Cambodia
USA ⬤ Laos

MEXICO

BAHAMAS

CUBA   Cuba ⬤ Angola

HAITI   DOMINICAN REPUBLIC
JAMAICA   PUERTO RICO

GUATEMALA   HONDURAS
EL SALVADOR
El Salvador ⬤ ⬤ Honduras
NICARAGUA

COSTA RICA
PANAMA

BARBADOS

TRINIDAD AND TOBAGO

VENEZUELA   GUYANA
SURINAM

COLOMBIA

ECUADOR

PERU

BRAZIL

BOLIVIA

PARAGUAY

URUGUAY

CHILE   ARGENTINA

ICELAND

NORWAY   SWEDEN

DENMARK

IRELAND   UNITED
KINGDOM
N.   W.   E
GERMANY   P
S   CZEC
FRANCE   AUST
YUGO
ITALY

France ⬤ Libya
France ⬤ Morocco

PORTUGAL   SPAIN

MOROCCO   TUNISIA

Morocco⬤geria
Morocco ⬤   France ALGERIA   LIE

MAURITANIA   MALI   NIGER

CAPE VERDE
SENEGAL   Fr
GAMBIA
GUINEA-BISSAU   GUINEA   UPPER
VOLTA   NIGERIA   C
SIERRA LEONE   IVORY
COAST   BENIN
LIBERIA   GHANA
TOGO

CAMEROON

EQUATORIAL GUINEA

GABON   CONGO

Angola ⬤   AN

S. Afr

NAM

**States at war (professional armies engaged
on both sides) at some time during the 1970s**

⬛ area of conflict

⬤ ⬤ states at war

Source: Press reports

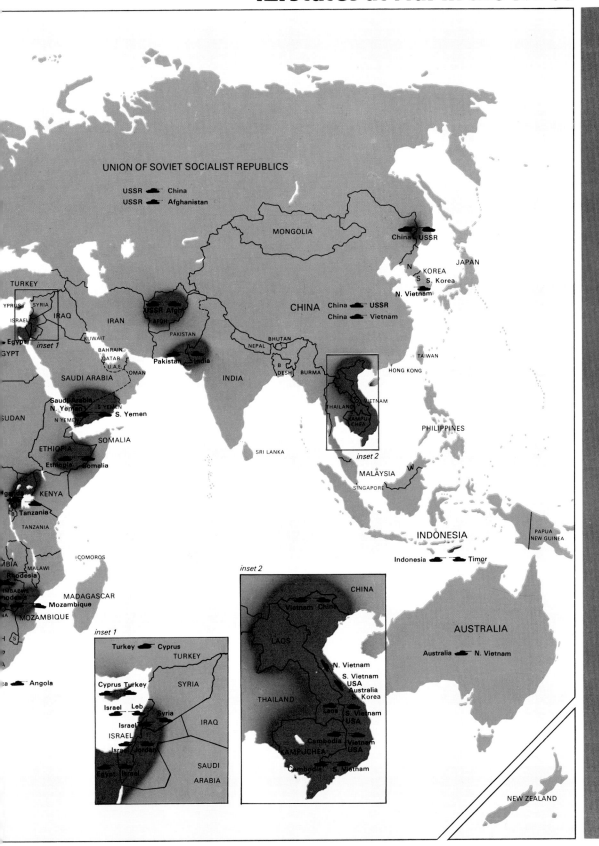

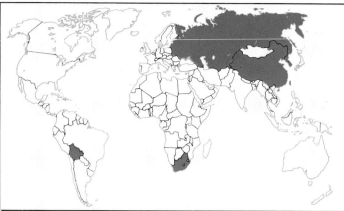

Antimony
World production 1976:
69,700 metric tons

Countries with 5 per cent
of more of world
production 1976:

Bolivia	21.9 per cent
China	17.2 per cent
South Africa	16.48 per cent
USSR	11 per cent

Total produced by
top four countries:
66.58 per cent

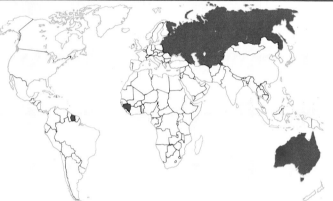

Bauxite
World production 1976:
73,800 thousand metric
tons

Countries with 5 per cent
or more of world
production 1976:

Australia	26.69 per cent
Guinea	13.9 per cent
Jamaica	14.19 per cent
Surinam	6.2 per cent
USSR	6.2 per cent

Total produced by
top five countries:
67.28 per cent

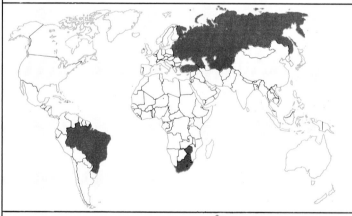

Chrome
World production 1976:
4030 thousand metric tons

Countries with 5 per cent
or more of world
production 1976:

Albania	8.4 per cent
Brazil	8.3 per cent
South Africa	26.97 per cent
Turkey	8.7 per cent
USSR	21.8 per cent
Zimbabwe	7.56 per cent

Total produced by
top six countries:
81.73 per cent

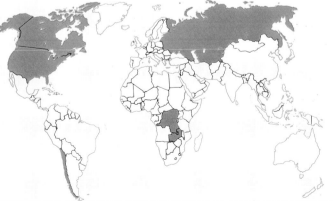

Copper
World production 1976:
8000 thousand metric tons

Countries with 5 per cent
or more of world
production 1976:

Canada	9.13 per cent
Chile	12.66 per cent
USSR	14.1 per cent
USA	18.2 per cent
Zaire	5.54 per cent
Zambia	10.62 per cent

Total produced by
top six countries:
70.25 per cent

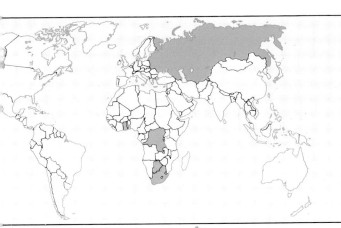

Diamonds
(Gems and industrial
diamonds combined)
World production 1976:
38,100 thousand metric carats

Countries with 5 per cent
or more of world production 1976:

Botswana	6.19 per cent
Ghana	5.99 per cent
South Africa	18.43 per cent
USSR	25.98 per cent
Zaire	31 per cent

South Africa is by far the biggest
producer of gem stones

Total produced by
top five countries:
87.59 per cent

Iron Ore
World production 1976:
263,799 thousand metric
tons

Countries with 5 per cent
or more of world
production 1976:

Liberia	5.3 per cent
Sweden	7.2 per cent
USSR	49.6 per cent
USA	19 per cent

Total produced by
top four countries:
81.1 per cent

Lead
World production 1976:
3330 thousand metric tons

Countries with 5 per cent
or more of world
production 1976:

Australia	11.9 per cent
Canada	7.69 per cent
Peru	5.49 per cent
USSR	14.1 per cent
USA	16.6 per cent

Total produced by
top five countries:
55.78 per cent

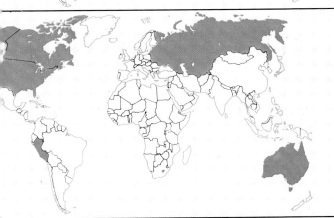

Manganese
World production 1976:
9840 thousand metric tons

Countries with 5 per cent
or more of world
production 1976:

Australia	7.7 per cent
Brazil	12.88 per cent
Gabon	11.11 per cent
India	6.76 per cent
South Africa	24.48 per cent
USSR	30.4 per cent

Total produced by
top six countries:
93.4 per cent

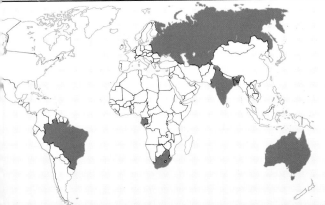

Source: *UN Statistical Yearbook 1978*

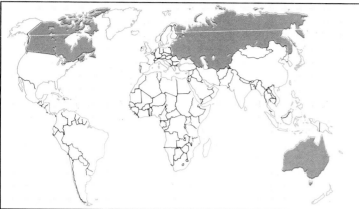

Nickel

World production 1976:
803,900 metric tons

Countries with 5 per cent
or more of world
production 1976:

Australia	10 per cent
Canada	29.5 per cent
New Caledonia	
(Fr colony)	14.79 per cent
USSR	19.9 per cent

Total produced by
top four countries:
74.64 per cent

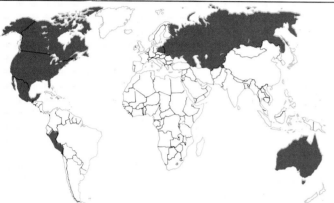

Silver

World production 1976:
9690 metric tons
Countries with 5 per cent
or more of world
production 1976:

Australia	7.45 per cent
Canada	13.2 per cent
Mexico	13.68 per cent
Peru	12.13 per cent
Poland	5.15 per cent
USSR	14.13 per cent
USA	11 per cent

Total produced by
top seven countries:
76.7 per cent

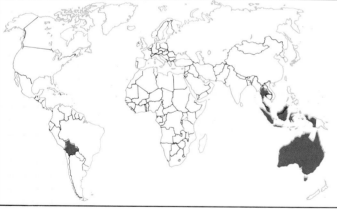

Tin

World production 1976:
179,800 metric tons
Countries with 5 per cent
or more of world
production 1976:

Australia	5.78 per cent
Bolivia	16.86 per cent
Indonesia	13 per cent
Malaysia	35.26 per cent
Thailand	11.37 per cent

Total produced by
top five countries:
82.27 per cent

Zinc

World production 1976:
5520 thousand metric tons
Countries with 5 per cent
or more of world
production 1976:

Australia	8.68 per cent
Canada	17.79 per cent
Peru	8.27 per cent
USSR	13 per cent
USA	7.96 per cent

Total produced by
top five countries:
55.7 per cent

14. The World Mineral Powers

The World Mineral Powers

All countries with 5 per
cent or more of at least four
major minerals, 1976

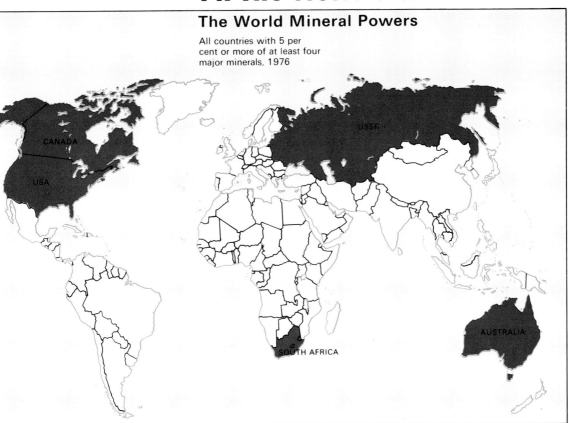

Uranium
World production 1976
(excluding USSR, Eastern
Europe, China)
22,293 metric tons
Countries with 5 per cent
or more of world
production 1976:

Canada	21.75 per cent
France	9.25 per cent
Niger	6.54 per cent
South Africa	15.3 per cent
USA	43.95 per cent

Total produced by
top five countries:
96.79 per cent

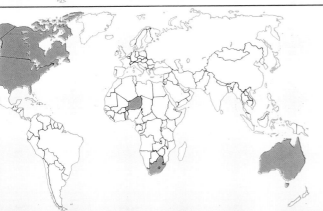

Uranium reserves
January 1978

World reserves at a market
price of less than US$30 a lb.
(excluding USSR, Eastern
Europe, China): 1650 thousand
metric tons

Countries with 5 per cent
or more of world reserves:

Australia	17.5 per cent
Canada	10.12 per cent
Niger	9.69 per cent
South Africa	18.54 per cent
USA	31.69 per cent

Total produced by top five
countries: 87.54 per cent

Source: *UN Statistical Yearbook 1978*

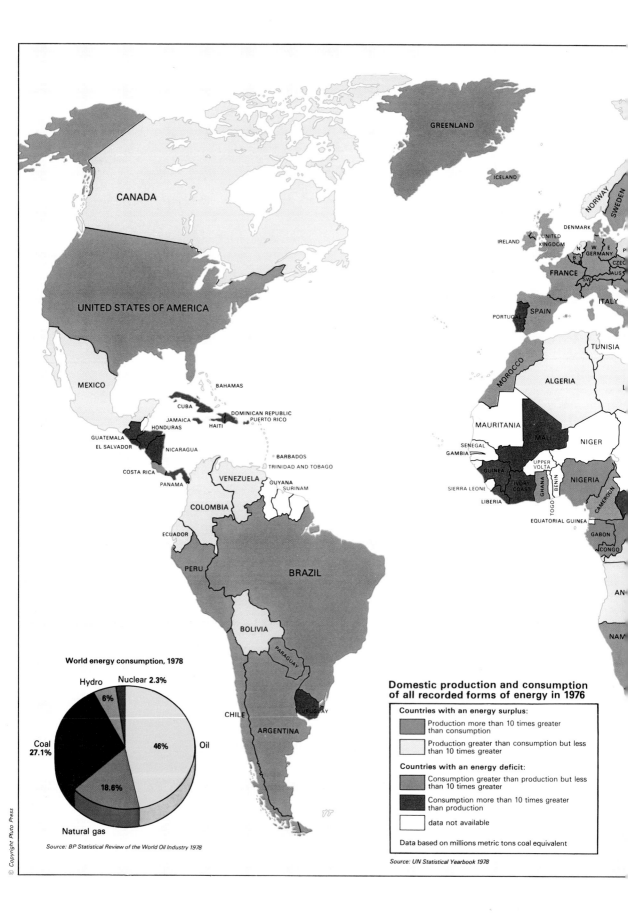

GREENLAND

ICELAND

NORWAY

SWEDEN

DENMARK

IRELAND

UNITED KINGDOM

N GERMANY W E P

CZEC

FRANCE SW AUS

ITALY

CANADA

UNITED STATES OF AMERICA

PORTUGAL SPAIN

TUNISIA

MOROCCO

ALGERIA

L

MEXICO

BAHAMAS

CUBA

JAMAICA HONDURAS

DOMINICAN REPUBLIC
PUERTO RICO

HAITI

MAURITANIA

SENEGAL

GAMBIA

MALI

NIGER

GUATEMALA
EL SALVADOR

NICARAGUA

BARBADOS

GUINEA

UPPER
VOLTA

COSTA RICA

PANAMA

VENEZUELA

TRINIDAD AND TOBAGO

GUYANA
SURINAM

SIERRA LEONE

LIBERIA

IVORY
COAST

GHANA

BENIN

TOGO

NIGERIA

CAMEROON

COLOMBIA

EQUATORIAL GUINEA

ECUADOR

GABON

CONGO

PERU

BRAZIL

AN

BOLIVIA

PARAGUAY

NAM

World energy consumption, 1978

Hydro   Nuclear **2.3%**
6%

Coal
27.1%

46%   Oil

18.6%

CHILE

URUGUAY

ARGENTINA

Natural gas

Source: BP Statistical Review of the World Oil Industry 1978

**Domestic production and consumption
of all recorded forms of energy in 1976**

Countries with an energy surplus:

Production more than 10 times greater
than consumption

Production greater than consumption but less
than 10 times greater

Countries with an energy deficit:

Consumption greater than production but less
than 10 times greater

Consumption more than 10 times greater
than production

data not available

Data based on millions metric tons coal equivalent

Source: UN Statistical Yearbook 1978

15. Energy Power

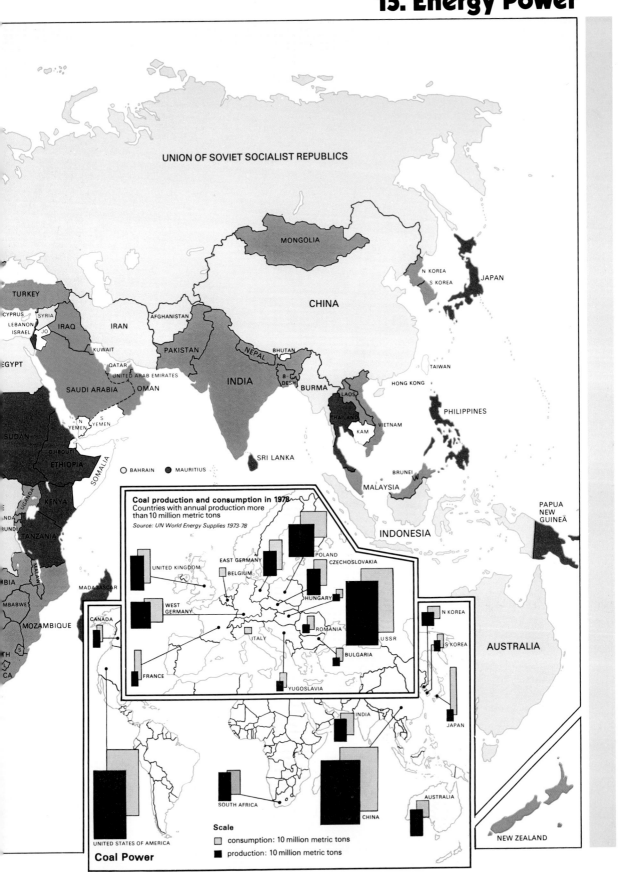

UNION OF SOVIET SOCIALIST REPUBLICS

MONGOLIA

N KOREA
S KOREA
JAPAN

CHINA

TURKEY
CYPRUS
LEBANON
ISRAEL
SYRIA
JO
IRAQ
IRAN
AFGHANISTAN
KUWAIT
PAKISTAN
NEPAL
BHUTAN
QATAR
UNITED ARAB EMIRATES
SAUDI ARABIA
OMAN
INDIA
B'DESH
BURMA

TAIWAN

HONG KONG

EGYPT

N
YEMEN
S
YEMEN

LAOS
THAILAND
KAM
VIETNAM

PHILIPPINES

SUDAN
DJIBOUTI
ETHIOPIA
SOMALIA

SRI LANKA

○ BAHRAIN   ● MAURITIUS

BRUNEI

UGANDA
KENYA
NDA
RUNDI
TANZANIA

MALAYSIA

INDONESIA

PAPUA
NEW
GUINEA

MADAGASCAR

BIA
MBABWE
MOZAMBIQUE

MALAWI

Coal production and consumption in 1978
Countries with annual production more
than 10 million metric tons
Source: UN World Energy Supplies 1973-78

UNITED KINGDOM
EAST GERMANY
BELGIUM
POLAND
CZECHOSLOVAKIA
HUNGARY
WEST
GERMANY
ITALY
ROMANIA
USSR
BULGARIA
FRANCE
YUGOSLAVIA

N KOREA

S KOREA

AUSTRALIA

CANADA

INDIA

JAPAN

SOUTH AFRICA

AUSTRALIA

CHINA

UNITED STATES OF AMERICA

NEW ZEALAND

Coal Power

Scale

☐ consumption: 10 million metric tons

■ production: 10 million metric tons

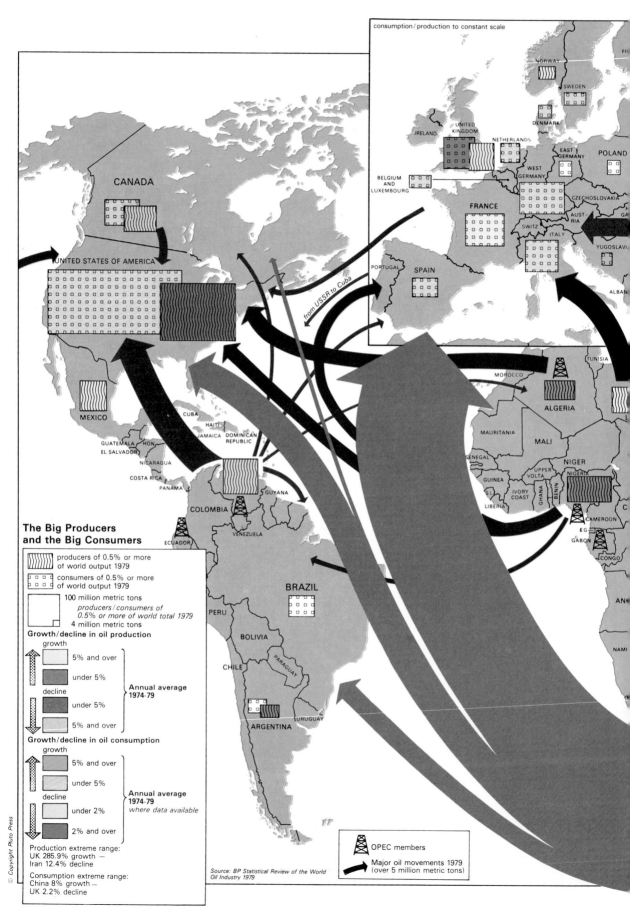

consumption/production to constant scale

CANADA

UNITED STATES OF AMERICA

MEXICO

CUBA
HAITI
JAMAICA
DOMINICAN
REPUBLIC
GUATEMALA HON
EL SALVADOR
NICARAGUA
COSTA RICA
PANAMA

GUYANA

COLOMBIA

VENEZUELA

ECUADOR

PERU

BRAZIL

BOLIVIA

PARAGUAY

CHILE

URUGUAY

ARGENTINA

from USSR to Cuba

NORWAY
SWEDEN
IRELAND
UNITED
KINGDOM
DENMARK
NETHERLANDS
EAST
GERMANY
POLAND
BELGIUM
AND
LUXEMBOURG
WEST
GERMANY
CZECHOSLOVAKIA
FRANCE
AUST-
RIA
GA
SWITZ
ITALY
YUGOSLAVI
PORTUGAL
SPAIN
ALBAN

MOROCCO
TUNISIA
ALGERIA
MAURITANIA
MALI
NIGER
SENEGAL
UPPER
VOLTA
NIGERIA
GUINEA
IVORY
COAST
GHANA
BENIN
LIBERIA
CAMEROON
EG
GABON
CONGO
C
AN
NAMI

The Big Producers
and the Big Consumers

producers of 0.5% or more
of world output 1979

consumers of 0.5% or more
of world output 1979

100 million metric tons
*producers/consumers of
0.5% or more of world total 1979*
4 million metric tons

Growth/decline in oil production

growth

5% and over

under 5%

decline

under 5%

5% and over

Annual average
1974-79

Growth/decline in oil consumption

growth

5% and over

under 5%

decline

under 2%

2% and over

Annual average
1974-79
where data available

Production extreme range:
UK 285.9% growth —
Iran 12.4% decline

Consumption extreme range:
China 8% growth —
UK 2.2% decline

*Source: BP Statistical Review of the World
Oil Industry 1979*

OPEC members

Major oil movements 1979
(over 5 million metric tons)

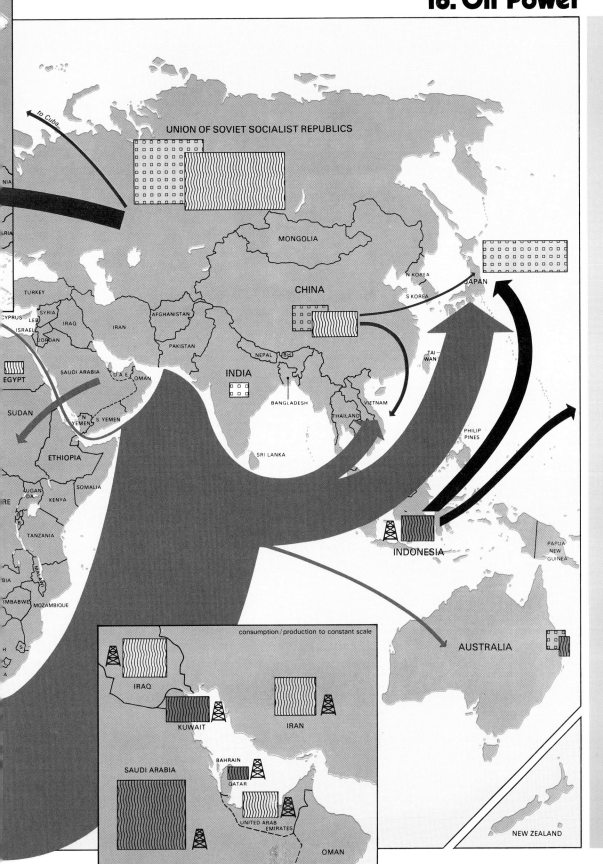

UNION OF SOVIET SOCIALIST REPUBLICS

to Cuba

MONGOLIA

CHINA

N KOREA

S KOREA

JAPAN

TURKEY

CYPRUS
SYRIA
LEB
ISRAEL
JORDAN

IRAQ

IRAN

AFGHANISTAN

PAKISTAN

NEPAL
BH

TAI—
WAN

EGYPT

SAUDI ARABIA

U A E
OMAN

INDIA

BANGLADESH

SUDAN

N
YEMEN
S YEMEN

SRI LANKA

THAILAND

VIETNAM

PHILIP
PINES

ETHIOPIA

UGAN
DA

SOMALIA

KENYA

INDONESIA

PAPUA
NEW
GUINEA

RE

B

TANZANIA

BIA

MALAWI

IMBABWE
MOZAMBIQUE

consumption/production to constant scale

AUSTRALIA

H

S

A

IRAQ

KUWAIT

IRAN

BAHRAIN

SAUDI ARABIA

QATAR

UNITED ARAB
EMIRATES

OMAN

NEW ZEALAND

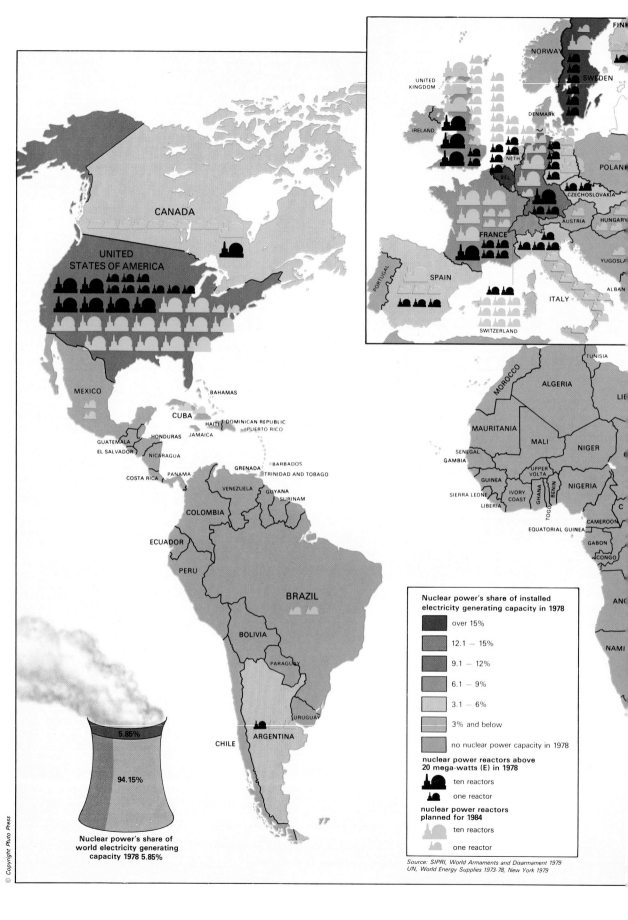

CANADA

UNITED
STATES OF AMERICA

MEXICO

BAHAMAS

CUBA
HAITI — DOMINICAN REPUBLIC
PUERTO RICO
JAMAICA

GUATEMALA
EL SALVADOR
HONDURAS
NICARAGUA
COSTA RICA
PANAMA
GRENADA
BARBADOS
TRINIDAD AND TOBAGO

VENEZUELA
GUYANA
SURINAM
COLOMBIA

ECUADOR

PERU

BRAZIL

BOLIVIA

PARAGUAY

URUGUAY

CHILE
ARGENTINA

NORWAY
SWEDEN
FIN

UNITED
KINGDOM

DENMARK

IRELAND

NETH
POLAN

BEL
CZECHOSLOVAKIA

AUSTRIA
HUNGARY

FRANCE

YUGOSLA

PORTUGAL
SPAIN

ITALY
ALBAN

SWITZERLAND

TUNISIA

MOROCCO
ALGERIA
LIE

MAURITANIA
MALI
NIGER

SENEGAL
GAMBIA
UPPER
VOLTA

GUINEA
NIGERIA

SIERRA LEONE
IVORY
COAST
GHANA
BENIN
TOGO

LIBERIA

CAMEROON
EQUATORIAL GUINEA

GABON
CONGO

ANG

NAMI

5.85%

94.15%

Nuclear power's share of
world electricity generating
capacity 1978 5.85%

Nuclear power's share of installed
electricity generating capacity in 1978

over 15%

12.1 — 15%

9.1 — 12%

6.1 — 9%

3.1 — 6%

3% and below

no nuclear power capacity in 1978

nuclear power reactors above
20 mega-watts (E) in 1978

ten reactors

one reactor

nuclear power reactors
planned for 1984

ten reactors

one reactor

Source: SIPRI, World Armaments and Disarmament 1979
UN, World Energy Supplies 1973-78, New York 1979

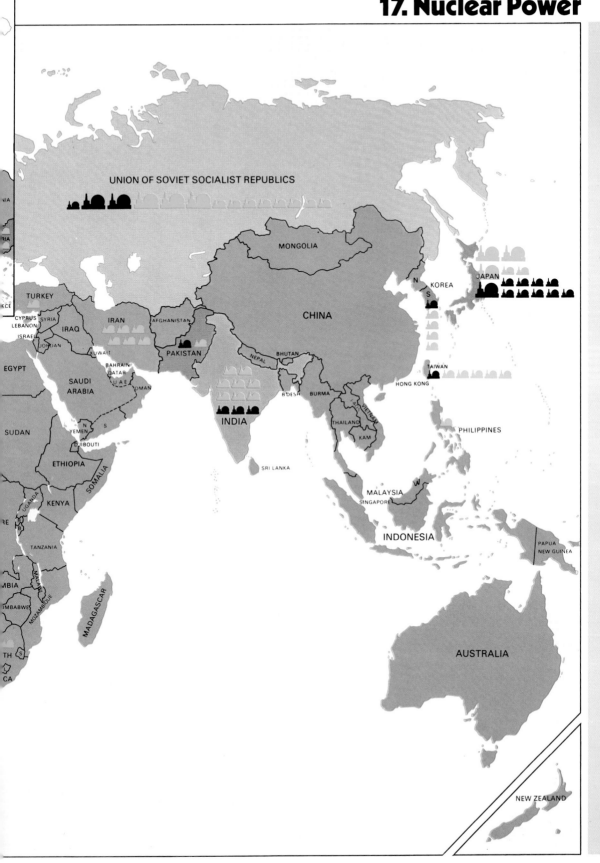

UNION OF SOVIET SOCIALIST REPUBLICS

MONGOLIA

CHINA

N KOREA
S

JAPAN

TURKEY

CYPRUS
LEBANON
ISRAEL
JORDAN

SYRIA
IRAQ
IRAN

AFGHANISTAN

PAKISTAN

NEPAL

BHUTAN

TAIWAN

HONG KONG

EGYPT

SAUDI
ARABIA

KUWAIT
BAHRAIN
QATAR
U.A.E.
OMAN

INDIA

B'DESH

BURMA

THAILAND

VIETNAM

KAM

PHILIPPINES

SUDAN

N
YEMEN
S
DJIBOUTI

ETHIOPIA

SOMALIA

KENYA

SRI LANKA

MALAYSIA

SINGAPORE

TANZANIA

MADAGASCAR

MOZAMBIQUE

ZIMBABWE

MBIA

INDONESIA

PAPUA
NEW GUINEA

TH
CA
S

AUSTRALIA

NEW ZEALAND

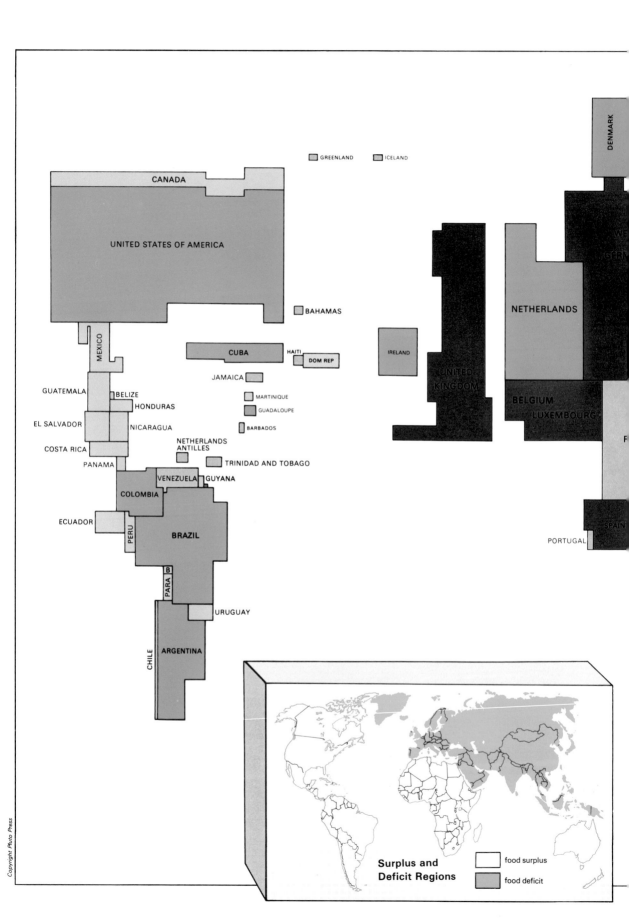

GREENLAND   ICELAND

CANADA

UNITED STATES OF AMERICA

DENMARK

W
GERM

NETHERLANDS

BAHAMAS

IRELAND

CUBA   HAITI
DOM REP

UNITED
KINGDOM

MEXICO

JAMAICA

BELGIUM
LUXEMBOURG

GUATEMALA

BELIZE

MARTINIQUE

HONDURAS

GUADALOUPE

F

EL SALVADOR

NICARAGUA

COSTA RICA

BARBADOS

PANAMA

NETHERLANDS
ANTILLES

TRINIDAD AND TOBAGO

VENEZUELA   GUYANA

COLOMBIA

ECUADOR

PERU

BRAZIL

SPAIN

PORTUGAL

B

PARA

URUGUAY

CHILE

ARGENTINA

Surplus and
Deficit Regions

food surplus

food deficit

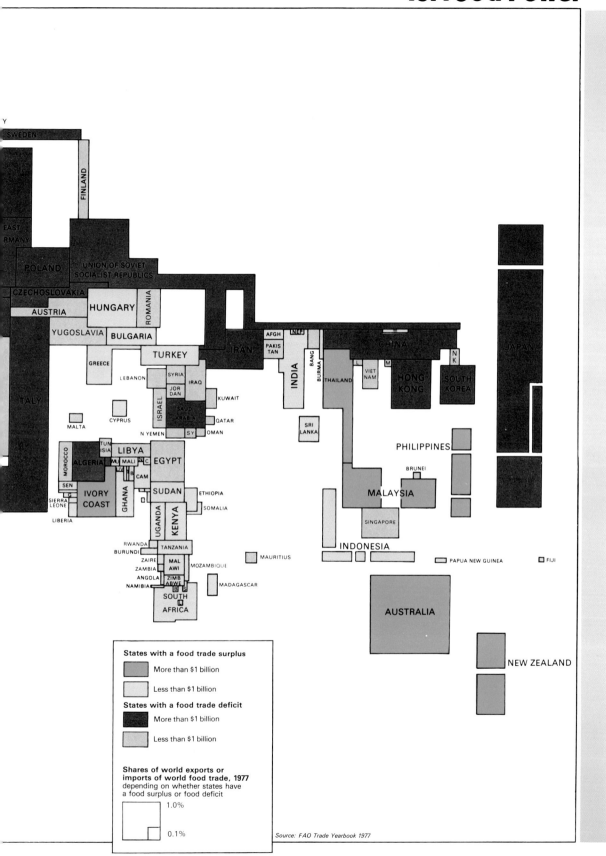

Y

SWEDEN

FINLAND

EAST
RMANY

POLAND

UNION OF SOVIET
SOCIALIST REPUBLICS

CZECHOSLOVAKIA

AUSTRIA

HUNGARY

ROMANIA

YUGOSLAVIA

BULGARIA

TURKEY

GREECE

LEBANON

SYRIA

IRAQ

JOR
DAN

ISRAEL

KUWAIT

SAUDI
ARABIA

QATAR

N YEMEN

S Y

OMAN

MALTA

CYPRUS

ITALY

IRAN

AFGH

PAKI
STAN

NEP

INDIA

BANG

BURMA

CHINA

M

M

L

VIET
NAM

M

THAILAND

HONG
KONG

N K

SOUTH
KOREA

JAPAN

SRI
LANKA

PHILIPPINES

TUN
ISIA

LIBYA

MOROCCO

ALGERIA

MA

MALI

N

C

EGYPT

BRUNEI

MALAYSIA

SEN

G

IVORY
COAST

GHANA

SUDAN

ETHIOPIA

SINGAPORE

SIERRA
LEONE

SOMALIA

LIBERIA

UGANDA

KENYA

INDONESIA

PAPUA NEW GUINEA

FIJI

RWANDA

BURUNDI

TANZANIA

MAURITIUS

ZAIRE

MAL
AWI

ZAMBIA

MOZAMBIQUE

ANGOLA

ZIMB
ABWE

NAMIBIA

B

MADAGASCAR

AUSTRALIA

SOUTH
AFRICA

NEW ZEALAND

States with a food trade surplus

More than $1 billion

Less than $1 billion

States with a food trade deficit

More than $1 billion

Less than $1 billion

**Shares of world exports or
imports of world food trade, 1977**
depending on whether states have
a food surplus or food deficit

1.0%

0.1%

Source: FAO Trade Yearbook 1977

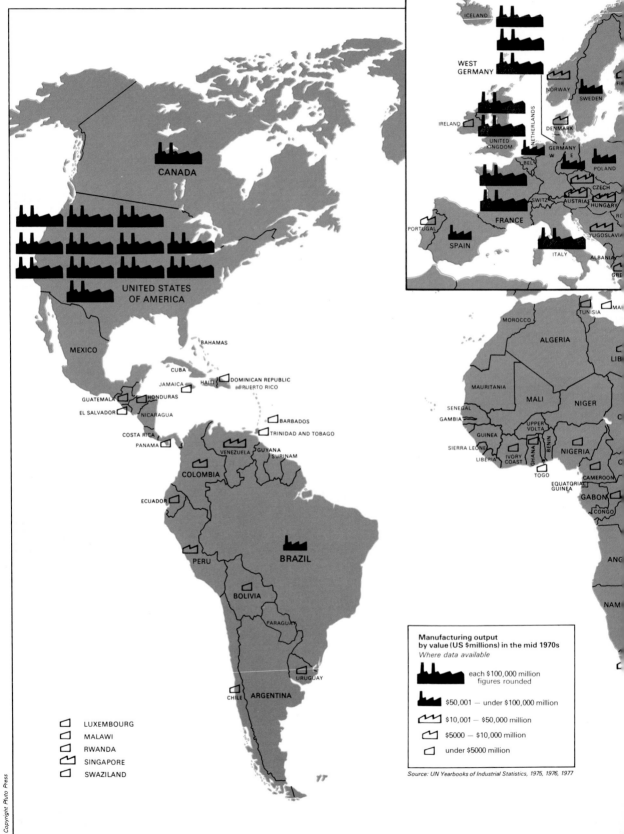

CANADA

UNITED STATES OF AMERICA

MEXICO

BAHAMAS

CUBA

JAMAICA   HAITI   DOMINICAN REPUBLIC
                  PUERTO RICO

GUATEMALA   HONDURAS
EL SALVADOR   NICARAGUA

COSTA RICA
PANAMA

BARBADOS

TRINIDAD AND TOBAGO

VENEZUELA   GUYANA
            SURINAM

COLOMBIA

ECUADOR

PERU

BRAZIL

BOLIVIA

PARAGUAY

URUGUAY

CHILE   ARGENTINA

WEST GERMANY

ICELAND

NORWAY   FINLAND

SWEDEN

IRELAND

NETHERLANDS   DENMARK

UNITED KINGDOM

GERMANY W E

POLAND

BEL

CZECH

PORTUGAL

SWITZ   AUSTRIA   HUNGARY

FRANCE

RO

YUGOSLAVIA

SPAIN

ITALY   ALBANIA

GRE

TUNISIA   MAL

MOROCCO

ALGERIA

LIB

MAURITANIA

MALI   NIGER

SENEGAL

GAMBIA   UPPER VOLTA

GUINEA   BENIN   NIGERIA   C

SIERRA LEONE   IVORY COAST   GHANA

LIBERIA   TOGO   CAMEROON

EQUATORIAL GUINEA   GABON

CONGO

ANG

NAM

LUXEMBOURG
MALAWI
RWANDA
SINGAPORE
SWAZILAND

Manufacturing output
by value (US $millions) in the mid 1970s
Where data available

each $100,000 million
figures rounded

$50,001 — under $100,000 million

$10,001 — $50,000 million

$5000 — $10,000 million

under $5000 million

Source: UN Yearbooks of Industrial Statistics, 1975, 1976, 1977

© Copyright Pluto Press

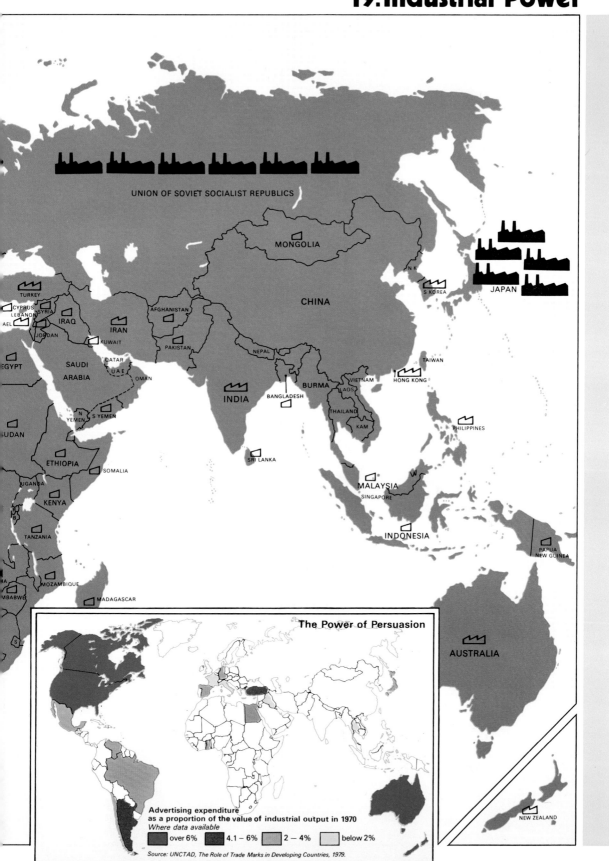

UNION OF SOVIET SOCIALIST REPUBLICS

MONGOLIA

N K

S KOREA

JAPAN

TURKEY

CYPRUS
LEBANON SYRIA
AEL
IRAQ
JORDAN
KUWAIT
IRAN
AFGHANISTAN
PAKISTAN
NEPAL
CHINA

TAIWAN

HONG KONG

EGYPT

SAUDI
ARABIA
QATAR
UAE
OMAN

INDIA
BANGLADESH
BURMA
VIETNAM
LAOS
THAILAND

N
YEMEN S YEMEN

UDAN

ETHIOPIA

SOMALIA

KAM

PHILIPPINES

UGANDA

KENYA

SRI LANKA

MALAYSIA
SINGAPORE
W

TANZANIA

INDONESIA

AUSTRALIA

MOZAMBIQUE

MBABWE

MADAGASCAR

PAPUA
NEW GUINEA

S

The Power of Persuasion

**Advertising expenditure
as a proportion of the value of industrial output in 1970**
Where data available

| over 6% | 4.1 – 6% | 2 – 4% | below 2% |

Source: UNCTAD, The Role of Trade Marks in Developing Countries, 1979.

NEW ZEALAND

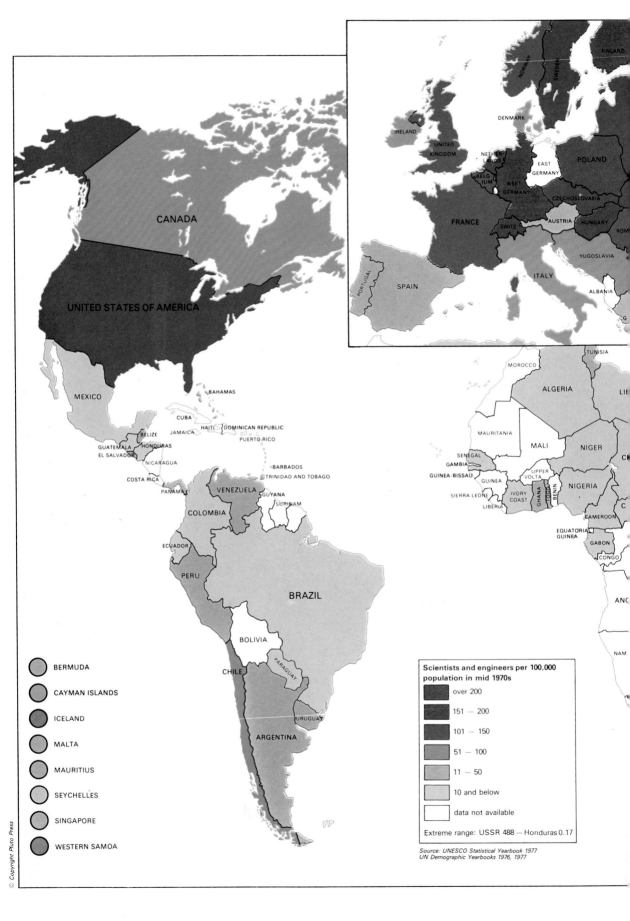

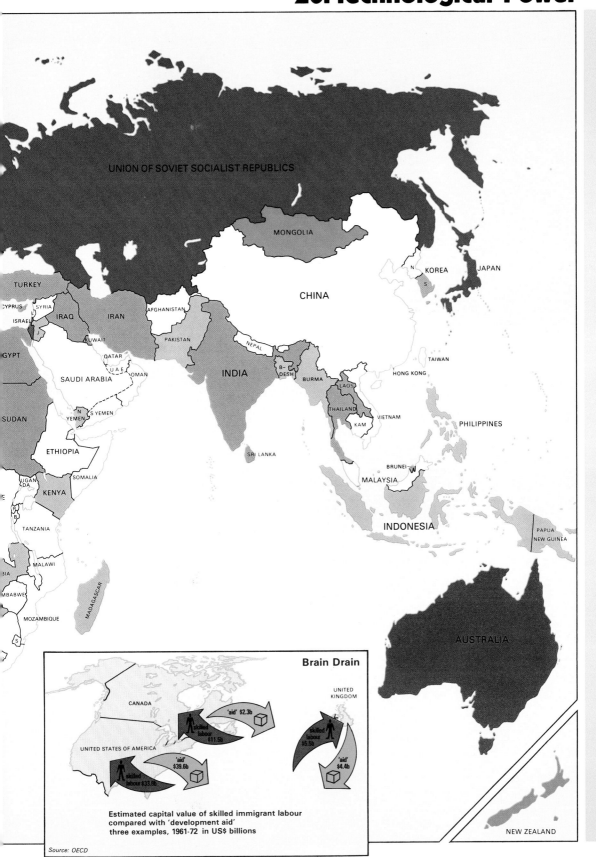

UNION OF SOVIET SOCIALIST REPUBLICS

MONGOLIA

CHINA

N KOREA
S

JAPAN

TURKEY

CYPRUS

SYRIA

L

ISRAEL

J

IRAQ

IRAN

AFGHANISTAN

KUWAIT

QATAR

U.A.E

OMAN

SAUDI ARABIA

PAKISTAN

NEPAL

INDIA

B-
DESH

BURMA

TAIWAN

HONG KONG

GYPT

N S YEMEN
YEMEN

LAOS

THAILAND

VIETNAM

KAM

PHILIPPINES

SUDAN

ETHIOPIA

SOMALIA

UGAN
DA

KENYA

SRI LANKA

BRUNEI

MALAYSIA

TANZANIA

INDONESIA

PAPUA
NEW GUINEA

MALAWI

MADAGASCAR

MBABWE

MOZAMBIQUE

S

AUSTRALIA

Brain Drain

CANADA

UNITED
KINGDOM

'aid' $2.3b

skilled
labour
$11.5b

skilled
labour
$5.5b

'aid'
$4.4b

UNITED STATES OF AMERICA

'aid'
$39.6b

skilled
labour $33.8b

Estimated capital value of skilled immigrant labour
compared with 'development aid'
three examples, 1961-72 in US$ billions

NEW ZEALAND

Source: OECD

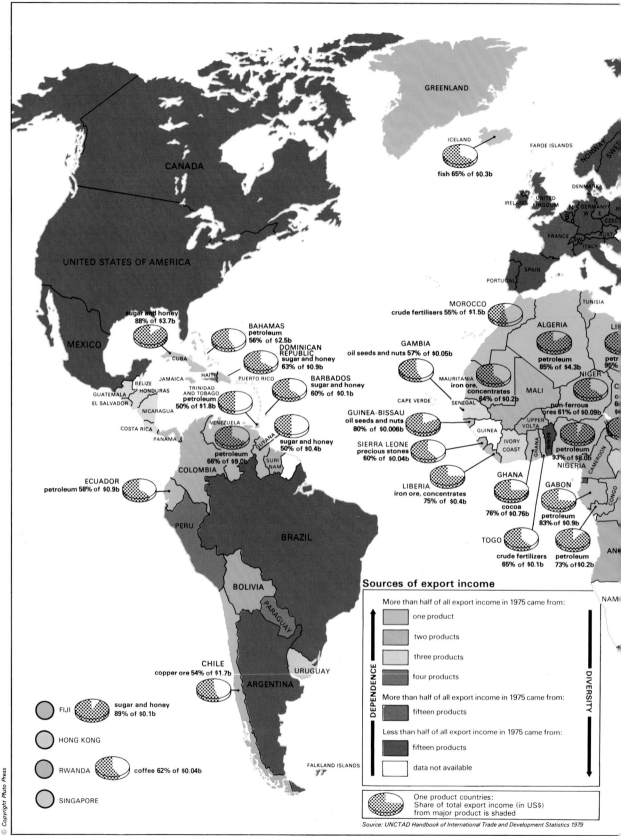

GREENLAND

FAROE ISLANDS

NORWAY SWE...

ICELAND
fish 65% of $0.3b

DENMARK

IRELAND UNITED GERMANY...
KINGDOM N
W E
CZEC...
FRANCE S... AUST...
ITALY

SPAIN

PORTUGAL

CANADA

UNITED STATES OF AMERICA

MEXICO

sugar and honey
88% of $3.7b

CUBA

BAHAMAS
petroleum
56% of $2.5b

JAMAICA HAITI
BELIZE
GUATEMALA HONDURAS PUERTO RICO
EL SALVADOR
NICARAGUA

COSTA RICA
PANAMA

DOMINICAN
REPUBLIC
sugar and honey
63% of $0.9b

BARBADOS
sugar and honey
60% of $0.1b

TRINIDAD
AND TOBAGO
petroleum
50% of $1.8b

VENEZUELA

sugar and honey
50% of $0.4b

GUYANA
SURI
NAM

petroleum
66% of $9.0b

COLOMBIA

ECUADOR
petroleum 58% of $0.9b

PERU

BRAZIL

BOLIVIA

PARAGUAY

CHILE
copper ore 54% of $1.7b

ARGENTINA

URUGUAY

FALKLAND ISLANDS

MOROCCO
crude fertilisers 55% of $1.5b

TUNISIA

ALGERIA

LI...

GAMBIA
oil seeds and nuts 57% of $0.05b

petroleum
85% of $4.3b

petr...
95%...

MAURITANIA
iron ore,
concentrates
54% of $0.2b

MALI

NIGER

non-ferrous
ores 61% of $0.09b

C...
c...
6...
$...

CAPE VERDE

SENEGAL

GUINEA-BISSAU
oil seeds and nuts
80% of $0.006b

GUINEA

UPPER
VOLTA

B
E
N
I
N

petroleum
93% of $8.0b
NIGERIA

CAMEROON

SIERRA LEONE
precious stones
60% of $0.04b

IVORY
COAST

G
H
A
N
A

CONGO

LIBERIA
iron ore, concentrates
75% of $0.4b

GHANA
cocoa
76% of $0.76b

GABON
petroleum
83% of $0.9b

AN...

TOGO
crude fertilizers
65% of $0.1b

petroleum
73% of $0.2b

Sources of export income

NAM...

More than half of all export income in 1975 came from:

one product

two products

three products

four products

More than half of all export income in 1975 came from:

fifteen products

Less than half of all export income in 1975 came from:

fifteen products

data not available

DEPENDENCE

DIVERSITY

FIJI
sugar and honey
89% of $0.1b

HONG KONG

RWANDA
coffee 62% of $0.04b

SINGAPORE

One product countries:
Share of total export income (in US$)
from major product is shaded

Source: UNCTAD Handbook of International Trade and Development Statistics 1979

UNION OF SOVIET SOCIALIST REPUBLICS

MONGOLIA

TURKEY

CYPRUS

SYRIA

IRAQ

IRAN
petroleum
91% of $19.2b

AFGHANISTAN

PAKISTAN

NEPAL

BHUTAN

B-DESH

CHINA

N KOREA
S

JAPAN

KOREA

TAIWAN

HONG KONG

PHILIPPINES

EGYPT

SAUDI ARABIA
petroleum
93% of $29.7b

OMAN
petroleum 100% of $1.4b

INDIA

BURMA

LA

THAILAND

KAM

VIETNAM

KIRIBATI
(GILBERT ISLANDS)

SUDAN

DJIBOUTI

S YEMEN
petroleum
and products
74% of $0.1b

N YEMEN
cotton 54%
of $0.16b

SRI LANKA

BRUNEI

MALAYSIA

SINGAPORE

PAPUA
NEW GUINEA
non-ferrous ores
56% of $0.1b

ETHIOPIA

animals 69% of $0.09b
SOMALIA

KENYA

UGANDA
coffee 76% of $0.3b

er
of
b

BURUNDI
coffee 88% of $0.03b

INDONESIA
petroleum 69% of $7.1b

TANZANIA

COMOROS

MOZAMBIQUE

MALAWI

BIA

MBABWE

MADAGASCAR

MAURITIUS
sugar and honey 86% of $0.3b

AUSTRALIA

copper
90% of $0.8b

S AFRICA

S

NEW ZEALAND

inset

ISRAEL

LEBANON

SYRIA

petroleum
69% of $0.9b

IRAQ
petroleum 99% of $8.4b

IRAN

JORDAN

KUWAIT
petroleum 81% of $9.2b

UNITED
ARAB
EMIRATES
petroleum
98% of $6.7b

SAUDI
ARABIA

BAHRAIN
petroleum 74% of $1.1b

QATAR
petroleum 97% of $1.8b

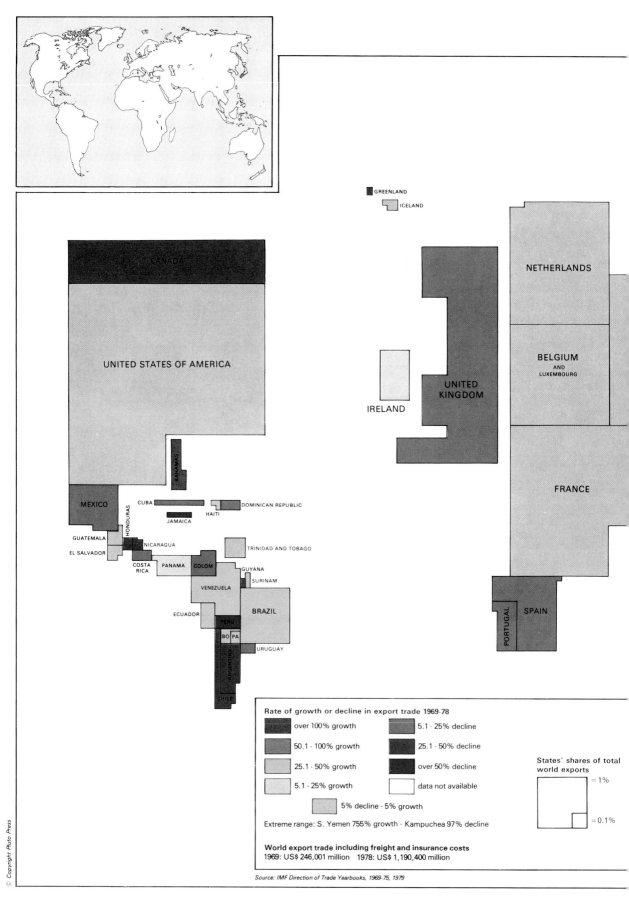

GREENLAND

ICELAND

CANADA

UNITED STATES OF AMERICA

NETHERLANDS

BELGIUM
AND
LUXEMBOURG

UNITED
KINGDOM

IRELAND

FRANCE

BAHAMAS

MEXICO

CUBA

DOMINICAN REPUBLIC

HAITI

JAMAICA

HONDURAS

GUATEMALA

NICARAGUA

TRINIDAD AND TOBAGO

EL SALVADOR

COSTA
RICA

PANAMA

COLOM

GUYANA

VENEZUELA

SURINAM

ECUADOR

BRAZIL

PERU

PORTUGAL

SPAIN

BO PA

URUGUAY

ARGENTINA

CHILE

Rate of growth or decline in export trade 1969-78

over 100% growth

5.1 - 25% decline

50.1 - 100% growth

25.1 - 50% decline

25.1 - 50% growth

over 50% decline

5.1 - 25% growth

data not available

5% decline - 5% growth

States' shares of total
world exports

= 1%

= 0.1%

Extreme range: S. Yemen 755% growth - Kampuchea 97% decline

World export trade including freight and insurance costs
1969: US$ 246,001 million   1978: US$ 1,190,400 million

Source: IMF Direction of Trade Yearbooks, 1969-75, 1979

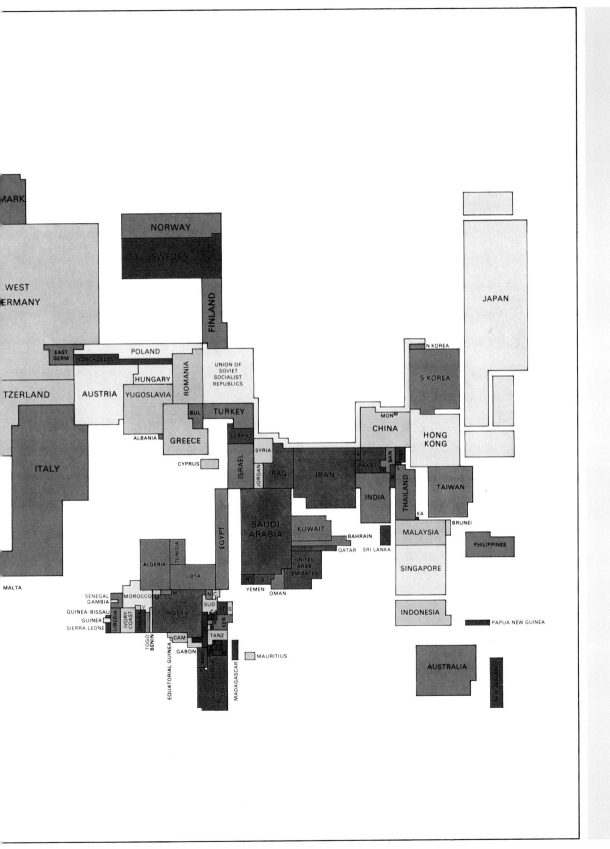

MARK

NORWAY

SWEDEN

WEST
ERMANY

FINLAND

JAPAN

EAST
GERM

POLAND

N KOREA

CZECHOSLOV

TZERLAND

AUSTRIA

HUNGARY

YUGOSLAVIA

ROMANIA

UNION OF
SOVIET
SOCIALIST
REPUBLICS

S KOREA

BUL

TURKEY

MON

ALBANIA

GREECE

LEBAN

CHINA

HONG
KONG

ITALY

CYPRUS

ISRAEL

SYRIA

JORDAN

IRAQ

IRAN

A

PAKIST

BAN

L

VIET

NI

THAILAND

TAIWAN

INDIA

MALTA

EGYPT

SAUDI
ARABIA

KUWAIT

BAHRAIN

KA

BRUNEI

MALAYSIA

PHILIPPINES

TUNISIA

QATAR

SRI LANKA

ALGERIA

LIBYA

UNITED
ARAB
EMIRATES

SINGAPORE

SENEGAL
GAMBIA

MOROCCO

M

M

NC

N

S

YEMEN

OMAN

INDONESIA

PAPUA NEW GUINEA

GUINEA-BISSAU

GUINEA

IVORY
COAST

TV

NIGERIA

SUD

C

E

S

SIERRA LEONE

LIBERIA

GHANA

KEN

TOGO
BENIN

CAM

TANZ

MAURITIUS

GABON

M

AUSTRALIA

NEW ZEALAND

EQUATORIAL GUINEA

ANG

Z

B

D

SOUTH AFRICA

MADAGASCAR

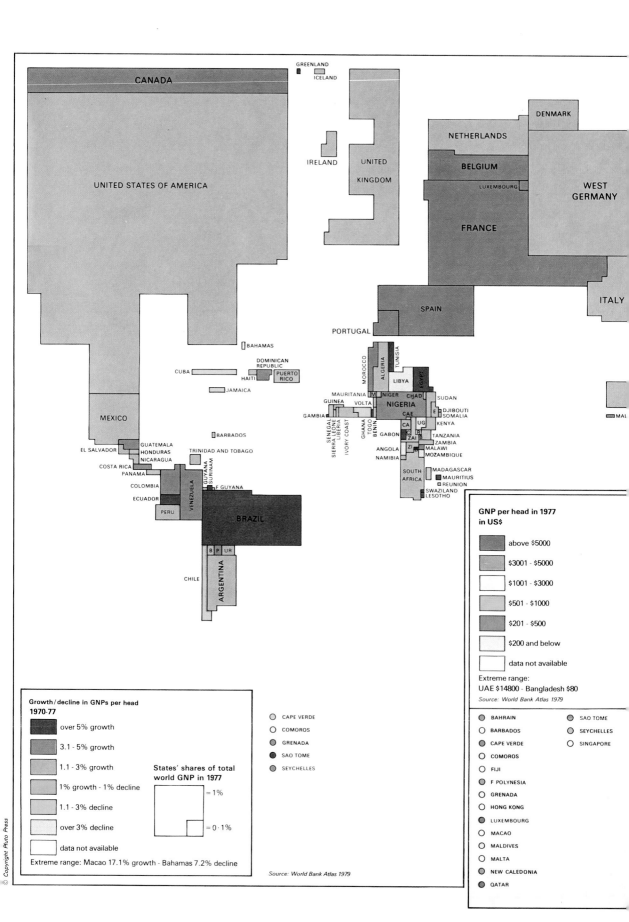

GNP per head in 1977 in US$

- above $5000
- $3001 - $5000
- $1001 - $3000
- $501 - $1000
- $201 - $500
- $200 and below
- data not available

Extreme range: UAE $14800 - Bangladesh $80

Source: World Bank Atlas 1979

Growth/decline in GNPs per head 1970-77

- over 5% growth
- 3.1 - 5% growth
- 1.1 - 3% growth
- 1% growth - 1% decline
- 1.1 - 3% decline
- over 3% decline
- data not available

Extreme range: Macao 17.1% growth - Bahamas 7.2% decline

States' shares of total world GNP in 1977

= 1%
= 0·1%

Source: World Bank Atlas 1979

CAPE VERDE
COMOROS
GRENADA
SAO TOME
SEYCHELLES

BAHRAIN
BARBADOS
CAPE VERDE
COMOROS
FIJI
F POLYNESIA
GRENADA
HONG KONG
LUXEMBOURG
MACAO
MALDIVES
MALTA
NEW CALEDONIA
QATAR
SAO TOME
SEYCHELLES
SINGAPORE

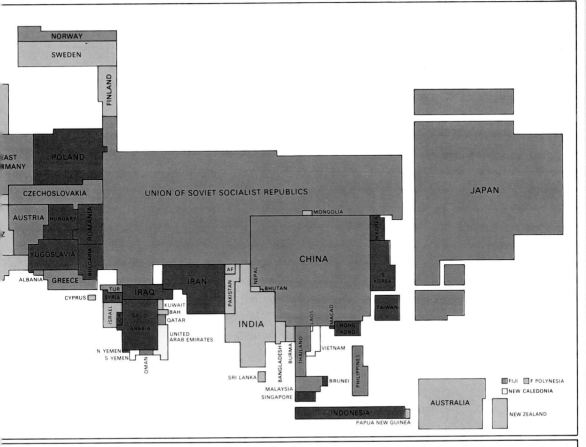

NORWAY
SWEDEN
FINLAND
EAST GERMANY
POLAND
CZECHOSLOVAKIA
AUSTRIA
HUNGARY
ROMANIA
YUGOSLAVIA
BULGARIA
ALBANIA
GREECE
CYPRUS
UNION OF SOVIET SOCIALIST REPUBLICS
MONGOLIA
N. KOREA
CHINA
S KOREA
TAIWAN
JAPAN
TUR
SYRIA
IRAQ
ISRAEL
JOR
SAUDI ARABIA
KUWAIT
BAH
QATAR
UNITED ARAB EMIRATES
IRAN
AF
PAKISTAN
NEPAL
BHUTAN
INDIA
LAOS
MACAO
HONG KONG
BURMA
THAILAND
VIETNAM
N YEMEN
S YEMEN
OMAN
SRI LANKA
BANGLADESH
MALAYSIA
SINGAPORE
BRUNEI
PHILIPPINES
INDONESIA
PAPUA NEW GUINEA
AUSTRALIA
FIJI
F POLYNESIA
NEW CALEDONIA
NEW ZEALAND

People and Purses

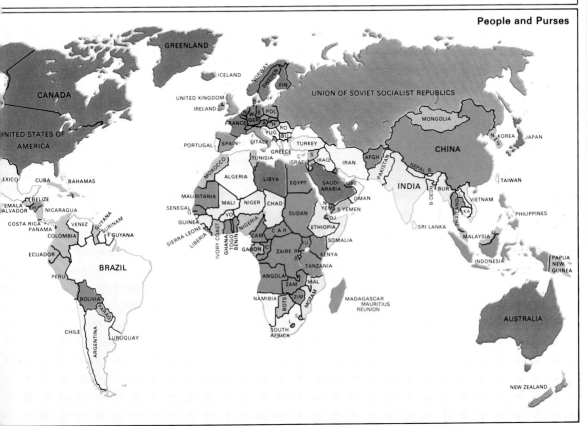

GREENLAND
ICELAND
NORWAY
SWEDEN
FIN
CANADA
UNITED KINGDOM
IRELAND
UNION OF SOVIET SOCIALIST REPUBLICS
MONGOLIA
N. KOREA
S
JAPAN
UNITED STATES OF AMERICA
FRANCE
GER
POL
RO
BU
YUG
PORTUGAL
SPAIN
ITALY
GREECE
TURKEY
CHINA
TAIWAN
MEXICO
CUBA
BAHAMAS
MOROCCO
TUNISIA
ISRAEL
IRAQ
IRAN
AFGH
PAKISTAN
NEPAL
B
GUATEMALA
BELIZE
SALVADOR
NICARAGUA
ALGERIA
LIBYA
EGYPT
SAUDI ARABIA
INDIA
BUR
VIETNAM
COSTA RICA
PANAMA
VENEZ
GUYANA
SURINAM
F GUYANA
MAURITANIA
OMAN
B DESH
KA
PHILIPPINES
COLOMBIA
SENEGAL
MALI
NIGER
CHAD
SUDAN
N YEMEN
S YEMEN
DJ
SRI LANKA
THAILAND
MALAYSIA
ECUADOR
GUINEA
SIERRA LEONE
LIBERIA
IVORY COAST
GHANA
TOGO
BENIN
NIGERIA
CAM
CAR
ETHIOPIA
SOMALIA
INDONESIA
PAPUA NEW GUINEA
PERU
BRAZIL
GABON
ZAIRE
U
KENYA
TANZANIA
BOLIVIA
PARAG
ANGOLA
ZAM
MAL
NAMIBIA
BOTS
ZIM
MOZAM
MADAGASCAR
MAURITIUS
REUNION
AUSTRALIA
CHILE
ARGENTINA
URUGUAY
SOUTH AFRICA
L
S
NEW ZEALAND

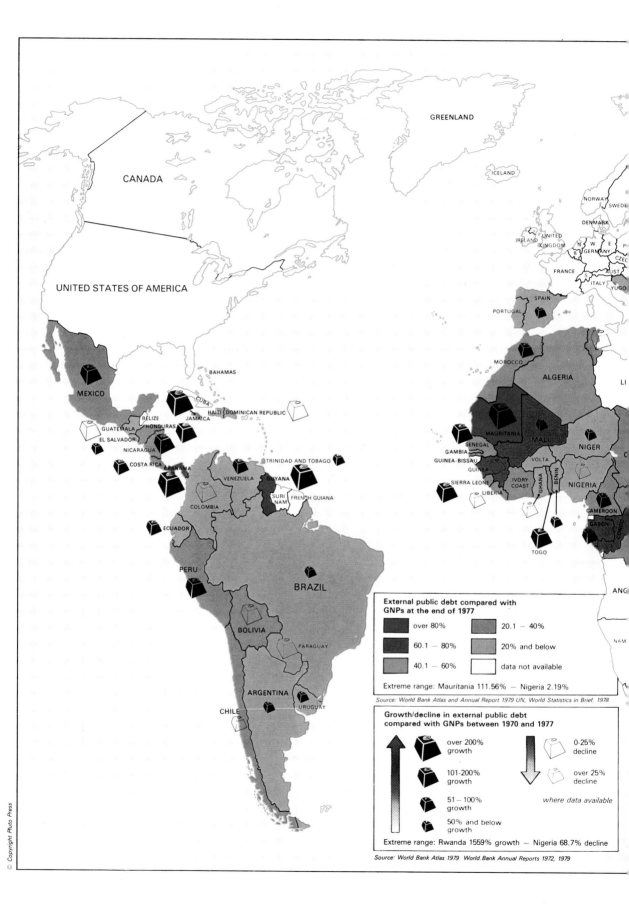

GREENLAND

CANADA

ICELAND

NORWAY

SWEDE

DENMARK

IRELAND | UNITED KINGDOM

N W E
GERMANY
CZEC

FRANCE

S
ITALY

AUST

YUGO

UNITED STATES OF AMERICA

SPAIN

PORTUGAL

MOROCCO

ALGERIA

LI

MEXICO

BAHAMAS

CUBA
HAITI | DOMINICAN REPUBLIC
JAMAICA

BELIZE
HONDURAS
GUATEMALA
EL SALVADOR
NICARAGUA
COSTA RICA | PANAMA

TRINIDAD AND TOBAGO

VENEZUELA
GUYANA
SURI
NAM
FRENCH GUIANA

COLOMBIA

ECUADOR

MAURITANIA

MALI

NIGER

SENEGAL
GAMBIA
GUINEA-BISSAU
GUINEA

VOLTA

SIERRA LEONE
LIBERIA

IVORY
COAST
GHANA
BENIN

NIGERIA

CAMEROON
GABON
CONGO

TOGO

PERU

BRAZIL

ANG

External public debt compared with GNPs at the end of 1977

over 80%	20.1 — 40%
60.1 — 80%	20% and below
40.1 — 60%	data not available

Extreme range: Mauritania 111.56% — Nigeria 2.19%

Source: World Bank Atlas and Annual Report 1979 UN, World Statistics in Brief, 1978

BOLIVIA

PARAGUAY

NAM

Growth/decline in external public debt compared with GNPs between 1970 and 1977

over 200% growth

101-200% growth

51 — 100% growth

50% and below growth

0-25% decline

over 25% decline

where data available

ARGENTINA

URUGUAY

CHILE

Extreme range: Rwanda 1559% growth — Nigeria 68.7% decline

Source: World Bank Atlas 1979 World Bank Annual Reports 1972, 1979

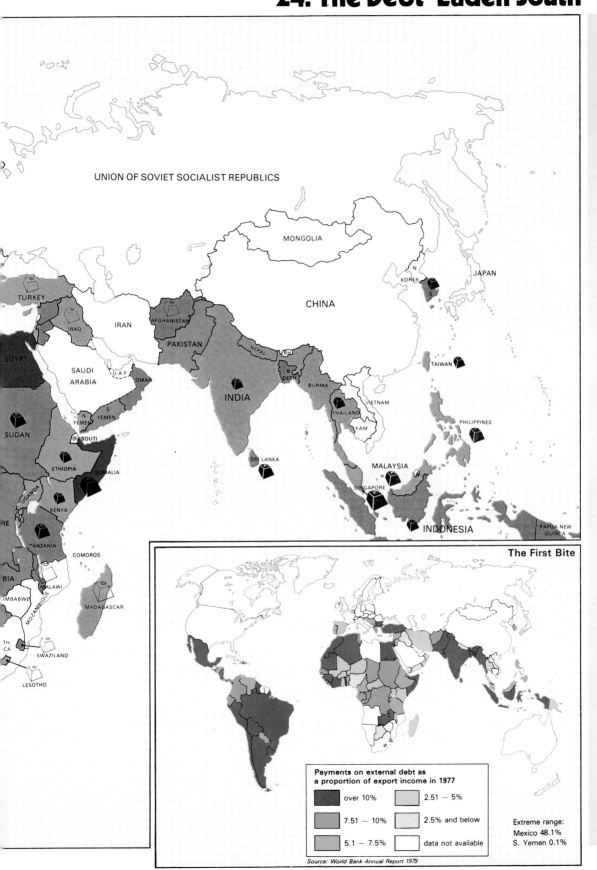

UNION OF SOVIET SOCIALIST REPUBLICS

MONGOLIA

CHINA

TURKEY

IRAN

AFGHANISTAN

IRAQ

PAKISTAN

NEPAL

B H

JAPAN

N KOREA

S

TAIWAN

EGYPT

SAUDI ARABIA

U A E

OMAN

INDIA

B DESH

BURMA

VIETNAM

N YEMEN

S YEMEN

DJIBOUTI

THAILAND

KAM

PHILIPPINES

SUDAN

ETHIOPIA

SOMALIA

SRI LANKA

MALAYSIA

N

UGANDA

KENYA

SINGAPORE

RE

B

INDONESIA

PAPUA NEW GUINEA

TANZANIA

COMOROS

BIA

MALAWI

IMBABWE

MOZAMBIQUE

MADAGASCAR

TH CA

SWAZILAND

LESOTHO

The First Bite

Payments on external debt as a proportion of export income in 1977

over 10%		2.51 — 5%
7.51 — 10%		2.5% and below
5.1 — 7.5%		data not available

Extreme range:
Mexico 48.1%
S. Yemen 0.1%

Source: World Bank Annual Report 1979

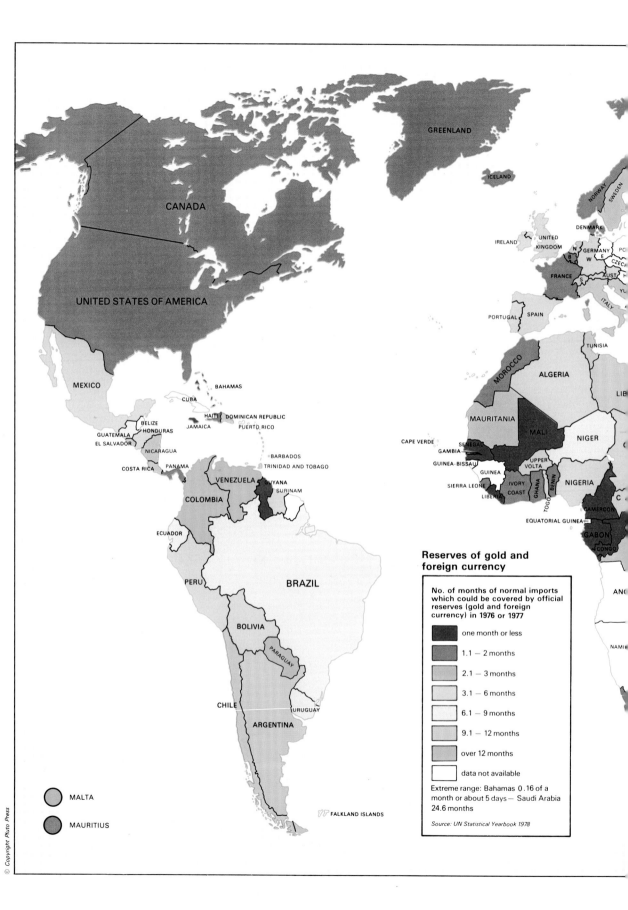

CANADA

GREENLAND

ICELAND

NORWAY SWEDEN

DENMARK

IRELAND UNITED
         KINGDOM
N GERMANY PC
B
W   CZEC
FRANCE   AUST H
              YU

UNITED STATES OF AMERICA

PORTUGAL SPAIN   ITALY

MEXICO

BAHAMAS

CUBA

HAITI DOMINICAN REPUBLIC

JAMAICA   PUERTO RICO

BELIZE
HONDURAS

GUATEMALA
EL SALVADOR

NICARAGUA

COSTA RICA PANAMA

BARBADOS

TRINIDAD AND TOBAGO

VENEZUELA GUYANA
           SURINAM

COLOMBIA

ECUADOR

PERU

BRAZIL

BOLIVIA

PARAGUAY

CHILE   URUGUAY

ARGENTINA

FALKLAND ISLANDS

TUNISIA

MOROCCO ALGERIA   LIB

MAURITANIA MALI NIGER

CAPE VERDE
           SENEGAL
GAMBIA
GUINEA-BISSAU   UPPER
        GUINEA   VOLTA
SIERRA LEONE   IVORY   NIGERIA
        LIBERIA COAST GHANA BENIN
                          TOGO
                    CAMEROON
EQUATORIAL GUINEA
                          GABON
                          CONGO

ANG

NAMI

Reserves of gold and foreign currency

No. of months of normal imports
which could be covered by official
reserves (gold and foreign
currency) in 1976 or 1977

	one month or less
	1.1 — 2 months
	2.1 — 3 months
	3.1 — 6 months
	6.1 — 9 months
	9.1 — 12 months
	over 12 months
	data not available

Extreme range: Bahamas 0.16 of a
month or about 5 days — Saudi Arabia
24.6 months

Source: UN Statistical Yearbook 1978

MALTA

MAURITIUS

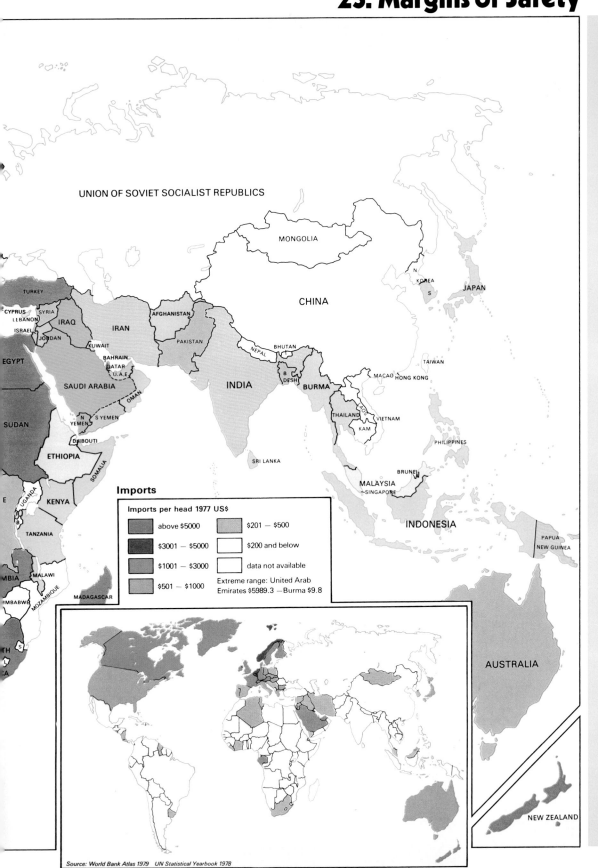

UNION OF SOVIET SOCIALIST REPUBLICS

MONGOLIA

CHINA

TURKEY
CYPRUS
LEBANON
SYRIA
IRAQ
ISRAEL
JORDAN
KUWAIT
IRAN
AFGHANISTAN
PAKISTAN
NEPAL
BHUTAN
N KOREA
S
JAPAN
TAIWAN
MACAO
HONG KONG
BAHRAIN
QATAR
U.A.E.
EGYPT
SAUDI ARABIA
OMAN
INDIA
B DESH
BURMA
SUDAN
N YEMEN
S YEMEN
DJIBOUTI
ETHIOPIA
SOMALIA
SRI LANKA
THAILAND
LAOS
VIETNAM
KAM
PHILIPPINES
UGANDA
KENYA
B
TANZANIA
BRUNEI
MALAYSIA
SINGAPORE
INDONESIA
MBIA
MALAWI
MOZAMBIQUE
MADAGASCAR
IMBABWE
PAPUA NEW GUINEA
TH
S
A
AUSTRALIA

Imports

Imports per head 1977 US$

above $5000	$201 — $500
$3001 — $5000	$200 and below
$1001 — $3000	data not available
$501 — $1000	

Extreme range: United Arab
Emirates $5989.3 — Burma $9.8

NEW ZEALAND

Source: World Bank Atlas 1979   UN Statistical Yearbook 1978

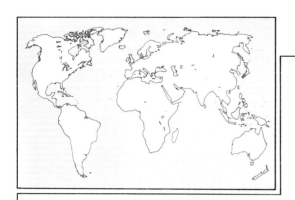

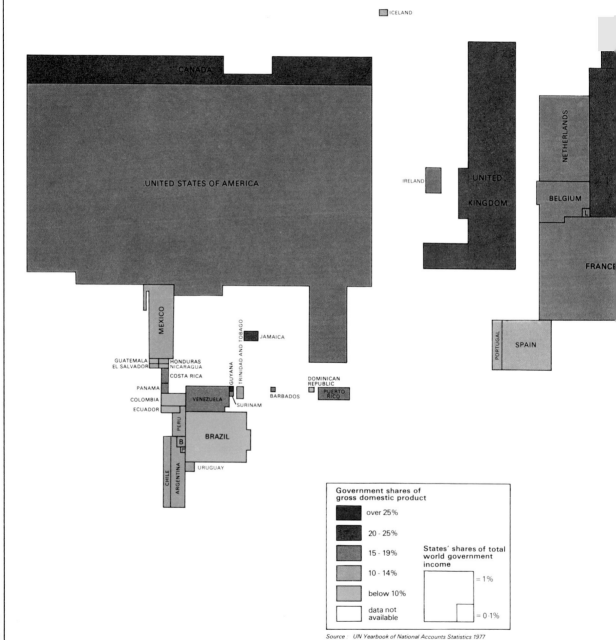

ICELAND

CANADA

UNITED STATES OF AMERICA

IRELAND

UNITED
KINGDOM

NETHERLANDS

BELGIUM

L

FRANCE

MEXICO

TRINIDAD AND TOBAGO

JAMAICA

PORTUGAL

SPAIN

GUATEMALA
EL SALVADOR

HONDURAS
NICARAGUA

COSTA RICA

PANAMA

GUYANA

DOMINICAN
REPUBLIC

BARBADOS

PUERTO
RICO

COLOMBIA

VENEZUELA

ECUADOR

SURINAM

PERU

BRAZIL

B

CHILE

ARGENTINA

URUGUAY

**Government shares of
gross domestic product**

over 25%

20 - 25%

15 - 19%

10 - 14%

below 10%

data not
available

**States' shares of total
world government
income**

= 1%

= 0·1%

Source : UN Yearbook of National Accounts Statistics 1977
US Congress Joint Economic Committee, East European
Economies Post-Helsinki 1977 and Soviet Economy in
a New Perspective 1976

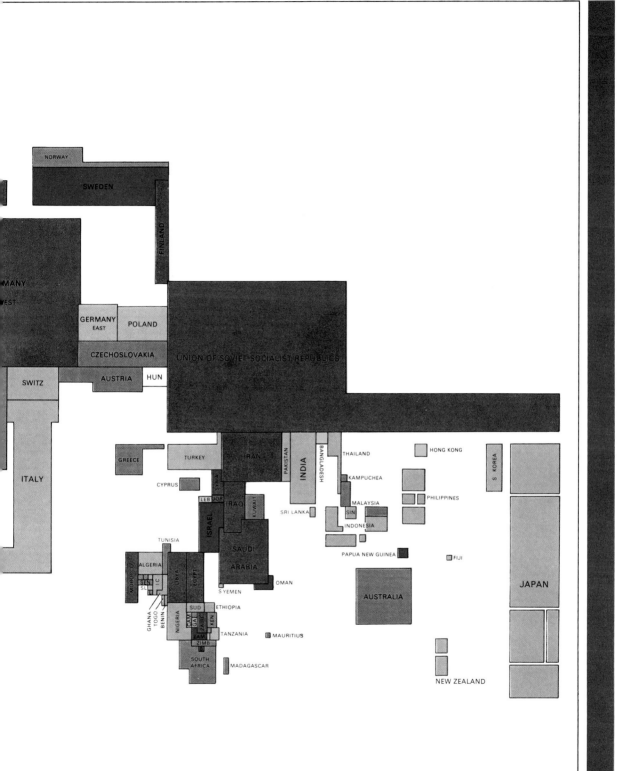

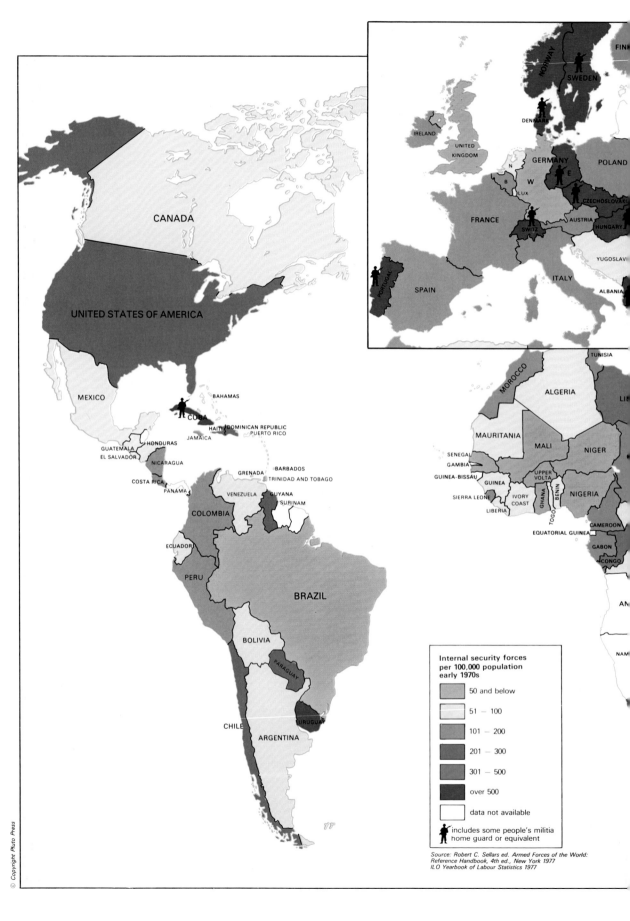

CANADA

UNITED STATES OF AMERICA

MEXICO

BAHAMAS

CUBA

HAITI | DOMINICAN REPUBLIC
PUERTO RICO

JAMAICA

GUATEMALA | HONDURAS

EL SALVADOR

NICARAGUA

COSTA RICA

PANAMA

GRENADA

BARBADOS

TRINIDAD AND TOBAGO

VENEZUELA | GUYANA

SURINAM

COLOMBIA

ECUADOR

PERU

BRAZIL

BOLIVIA

PARAGUAY

CHILE

URUGUAY

ARGENTINA

NORWAY

SWEDEN

FINL

DENMARK

IRELAND

UNITED KINGDOM

GERMANY

POLAND

N

B

W

LUX

E

CZECHOSLOVAK

FRANCE

AUSTRIA

HUNGARY

SWITZ

YUGOSLAV

PORTUGAL

SPAIN

ITALY

ALBANIA

TUNISIA

MOROCCO

ALGERIA

LIB

MAURITANIA

MALI

NIGER

SENEGAL

GAMBIA

GUINEA-BISSAU

GUINEA

UPPER VOLTA

SIERRA LEONE

IVORY COAST

GHANA

TOGO

BENIN

NIGERIA

LIBERIA

EQUATORIAL GUINEA

CAMEROON

GABON

CONGO

AN

NAM

Internal security forces per 100,000 population early 1970s

- 50 and below
- 51 – 100
- 101 – 200
- 201 – 300
- 301 – 500
- over 500
- data not available

includes some people's militia home guard or equivalent

Source: Robert C. Sellars ed. Armed Forces of the World:
Reference Handbook, 4th ed., New York 1977
ILO Yearbook of Labour Statistics 1977

UNION OF SOVIET SOCIALIST REPUBLICS

MONGOLIA

JAPAN

TURKEY

N
KOREA
S

CYPRUS SYRIA
LEBANON
ISRAEL

IRAQ

AFGHANISTAN

CHINA

IRAN

KUWAIT
BAHRAIN
QATAR
U.A.E.

EGYPT

SAUDI
ARABIA

OMAN

PAKISTAN

NEPAL

BHUTAN

B
DESH

TAIWAN

HONG KONG

INDIA

BURMA

LAOS

SUDAN

N
YEMEN
S. YEMEN

THAILAND

KAM

VIETNAM

PHILIPPINES

ETHIOPIA

SOMALIA

SRI LANKA

...E
UGANDA

KENYA

W

B...

TANZANIA

MALAYSIA
SINGAPORE

INDONESIA

...BIA

MALAWI

...MBABWE

MOZAMBIQUE

S

Workers in public administration (excluding
teachers and soldiers) as a proportion of
economically active population in the late 1970s

3 – 4%	above 6%
4.1 – 5%	data not available
5.1 – 6%	

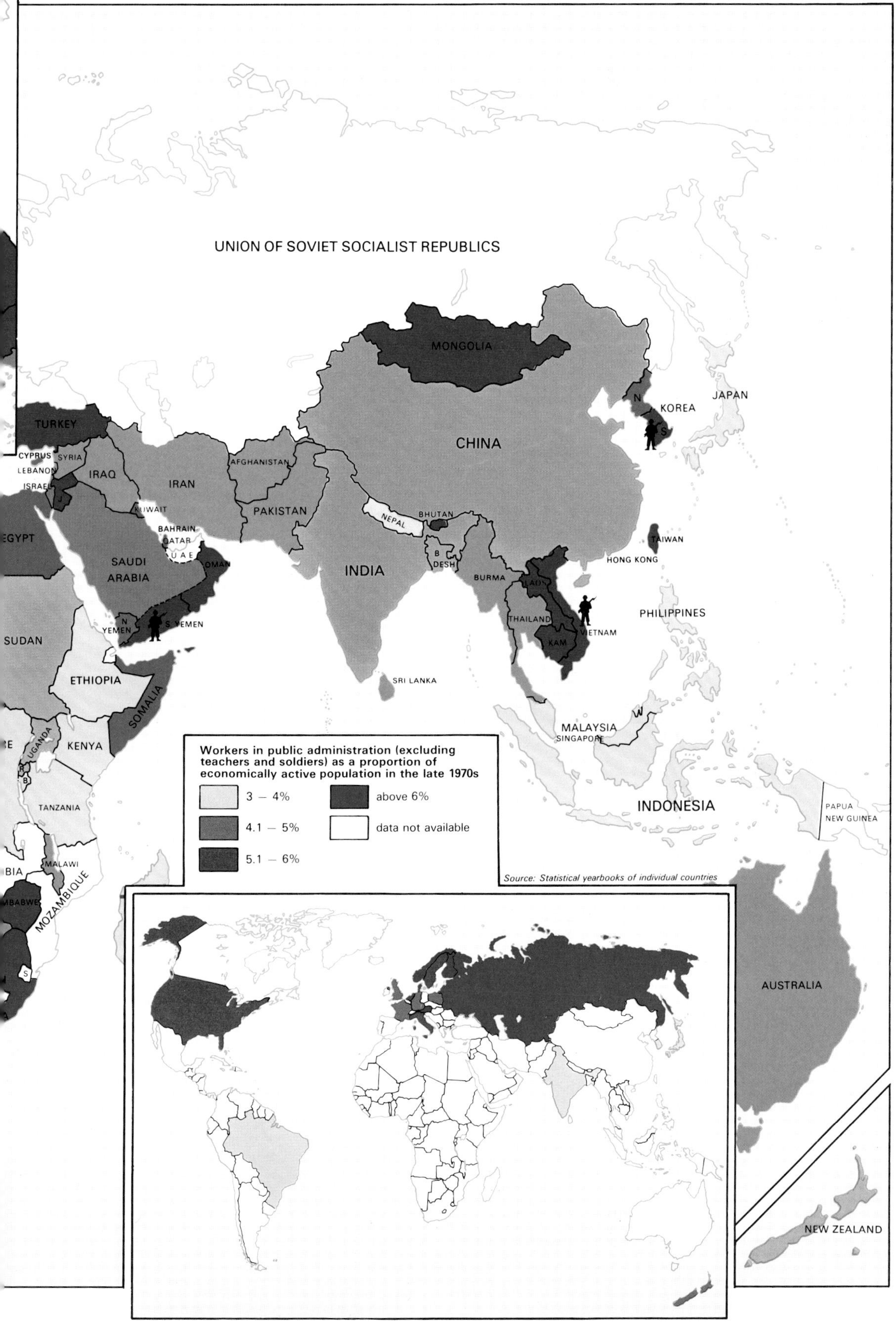

Source: Statistical yearbooks of individual countries

AUSTRALIA

PAPUA
NEW GUINEA

NEW ZEALAND

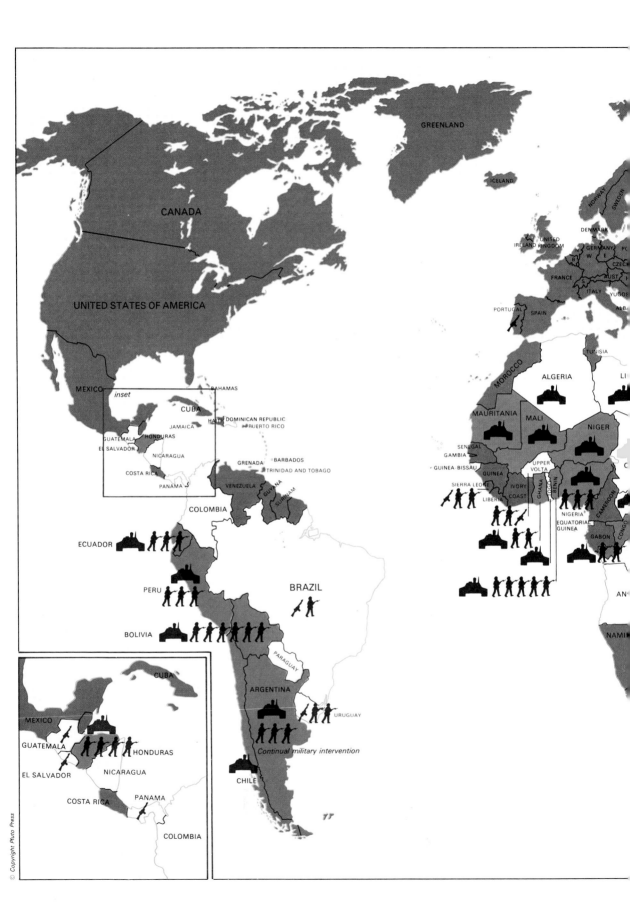

GREENLAND

ICELAND

CANADA

UNITED STATES OF AMERICA

NORWAY

SWEDEN

DENMARK

IRELAND UNITED KINGDOM

N GERMANY PO

B W E CZECH

S AUST H

FRANCE

ITALY YUGOS

PORTUGAL SPAIN

ALB

TUNISIA

MOROCCO

ALGERIA

LI

MEXICO

inset

BAHAMAS

CUBA

JAMAICA

HAITI DOMINICAN REPUBLIC

PUERTO RICO

MAURITANIA

MALI

NIGER

GUATEMALA

HONDURAS

EL SALVADOR

NICARAGUA

GRENADA

BARBADOS

TRINIDAD AND TOBAGO

SENEGAL

GAMBIA

GUINEA-BISSAU

UPPER VOLTA

COSTA RICA

PANAMA

VENEZUELA

GUYANA

SURINAM

SIERRA LEONE

GUINEA

IVORY COAST

GHANA

TOGO

BENIN

C

LIBERIA

COLOMBIA

NIGERIA

CAMEROON

EQUATORIAL GUINEA

GABON

CONGO

ECUADOR

PERU

AN

BRAZIL

NAMI

BOLIVIA

PARAGUAY

ARGENTINA

URUGUAY

Continual military intervention

CHILE

17

CUBA

MEXICO

GUATEMALA

HONDURAS

EL SALVADOR

NICARAGUA

COSTA RICA

PANAMA

COLOMBIA

© Copyright Pluto Press

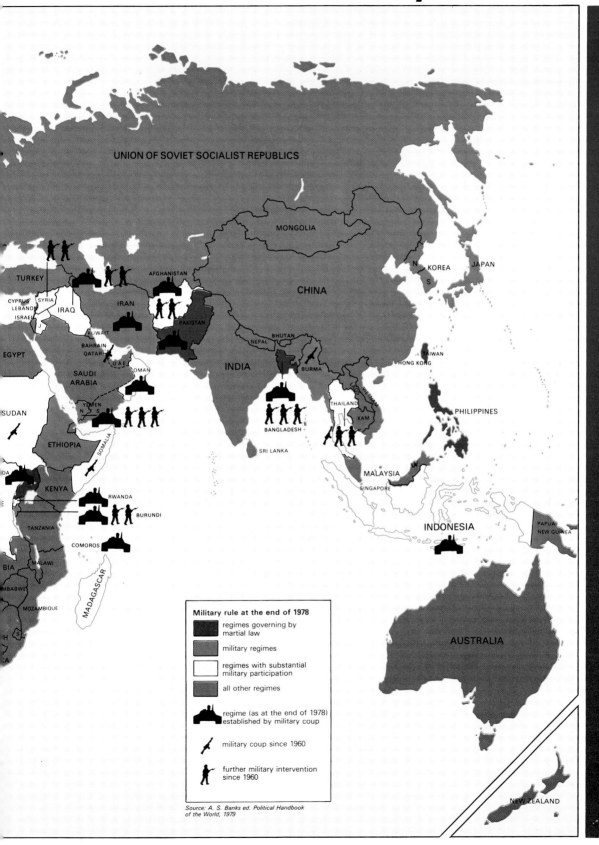

UNION OF SOVIET SOCIALIST REPUBLICS

MONGOLIA

CHINA

TURKEY

CYPRUS
LEBANON
ISRAEL

SYRIA

IRAQ

IRAN

AFGHANISTAN

N KOREA
S

JAPAN

KUWAIT

BAHRAIN
QATAR

U.A.E.

OMAN

EGYPT

SAUDI
ARABIA

YEMEN
N S

SUDAN

ETHIOPIA

SOMALIA

KENYA

RWANDA

BURUNDI

TANZANIA

COMOROS

MALAWI

BIA

MBABWE

MOZAMBIQUE

MADAGASCAR

PAKISTAN

NEPAL

BHUTAN

INDIA

BURMA

SRI LANKA

BANGLADESH

THAILAND

KAM

VIETNAM

TAIWAN

HONG KONG

PHILIPPINES

MALAYSIA

SINGAPORE

INDONESIA

PAPUA
NEW GUINEA

AUSTRALIA

NEW ZEALAND

Military rule at the end of 1978

- regimes governing by martial law
- military regimes
- regimes with substantial military participation
- all other regimes

- regime (as at the end of 1978) established by military coup

- military coup since 1960

- further military intervention since 1960

Source: A. S. Banks ed. Political Handbook of the World, 1979

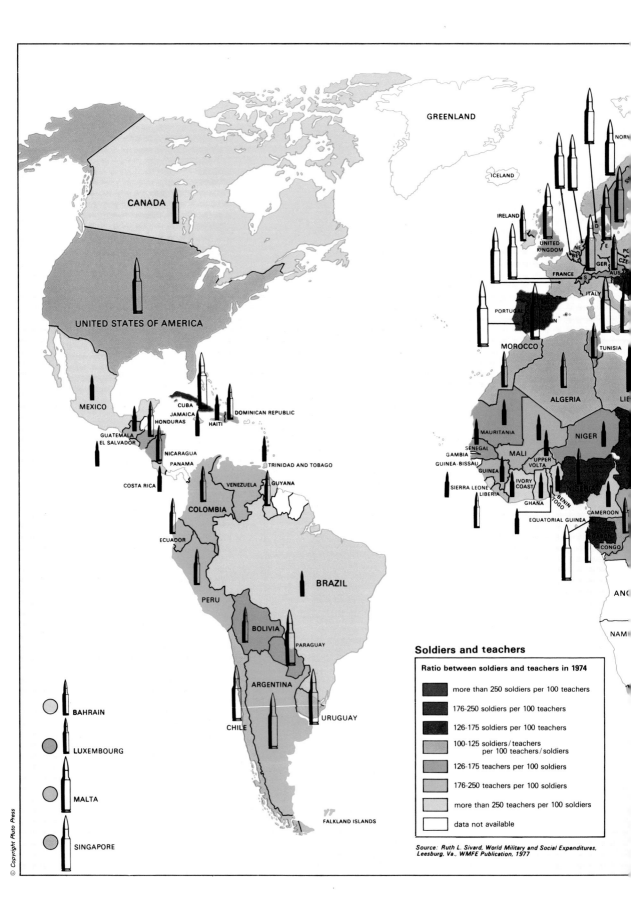

GREENLAND

ICELAND

NORW

IRELAND

UNITED
KINGDOM

FRANCE

ITALY

PORTUGAL

MOROCCO

TUNISIA

ALGERIA

LI

CANADA

UNITED STATES OF AMERICA

MEXICO

CUBA
JAMAICA
HONDURAS
HAITI
DOMINICAN REPUBLIC

GUATEMALA
EL SALVADOR
NICARAGUA
PANAMA

COSTA RICA

TRINIDAD AND TOBAGO

VENEZUELA
GUYANA

COLOMBIA

ECUADOR

PERU

BRAZIL

BOLIVIA

PARAGUAY

ARGENTINA

CHILE

URUGUAY

FALKLAND ISLANDS

MAURITANIA

SENEGAL

GAMBIA

GUINEA-BISSAU

GUINEA

SIERRA LEONE

LIBERIA

MALI

IVORY
COAST

GHANA

UPPER
VOLTA

NIGER

TOGO

BENIN

CAMEROON

EQUATORIAL GUINEA

CONGO

ANG

NAM

Soldiers and teachers

Ratio between soldiers and teachers in 1974

	more than 250 soldiers per 100 teachers
	176-250 soldiers per 100 teachers
	126-175 soldiers per 100 teachers
	100-125 soldiers / teachers per 100 teachers / soldiers
	126-175 teachers per 100 soldiers
	176-250 teachers per 100 soldiers
	more than 250 teachers per 100 soldiers
	data not available

BAHRAIN

LUXEMBOURG

MALTA

SINGAPORE

Source: Ruth L. Sivard, World Military and Social Expenditures,
Leesburg, Va., WMFE Publication, 1977

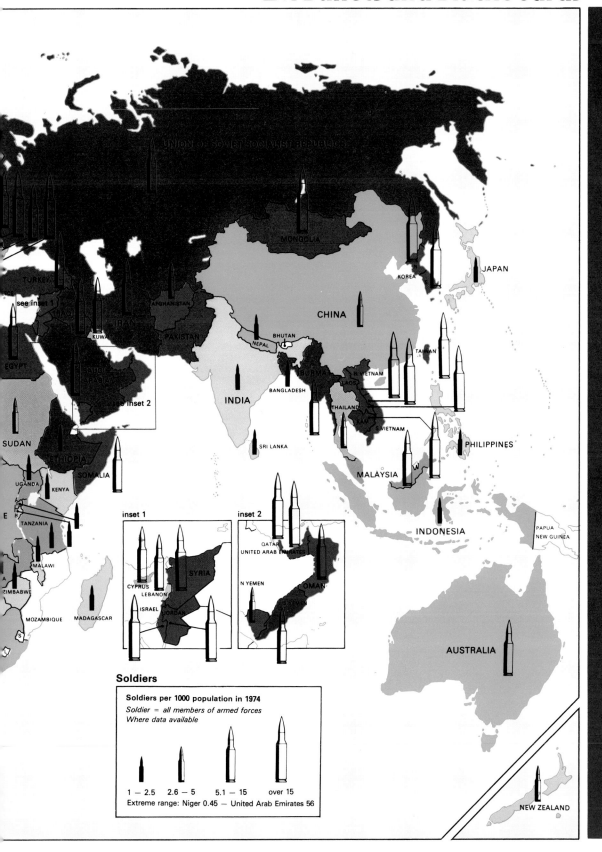

UNION OF SOVIET SOCIALIST REPUBLICS

MONGOLIA

KOREA

JAPAN

TURKEY

see inset 1

AFGHANISTAN

IRAN

CHINA

TAIWAN

KUWAIT

PAKISTAN

NEPAL

BHUTAN

EGYPT

SAUDI ARABIA

see inset 2

INDIA

BANGLADESH

BURMA

N VIETNAM

LAOS

THAILAND

KAM

S VIETNAM

SUDAN

ETHIOPIA

SOMALIA

SRI LANKA

MALAYSIA

PHILIPPINES

UGANDA

KENYA

TANZANIA

MALAWI

ZIMBABWE

INDONESIA

PAPUA NEW GUINEA

MOZAMBIQUE

MADAGASCAR

inset 1

CYPRUS

LEBANON

SYRIA

ISRAEL

JORDAN

inset 2

QATAR

UNITED ARAB EMIRATES

N YEMEN

OMAN

S YEMEN

AUSTRALIA

Soldiers

Soldiers per 1000 population in 1974

Soldier = all members of armed forces
Where data available

1 — 2.5   2.6 — 5   5.1 — 15   over 15

Extreme range: Niger 0.45 — United Arab Emirates 56

NEW ZEALAND

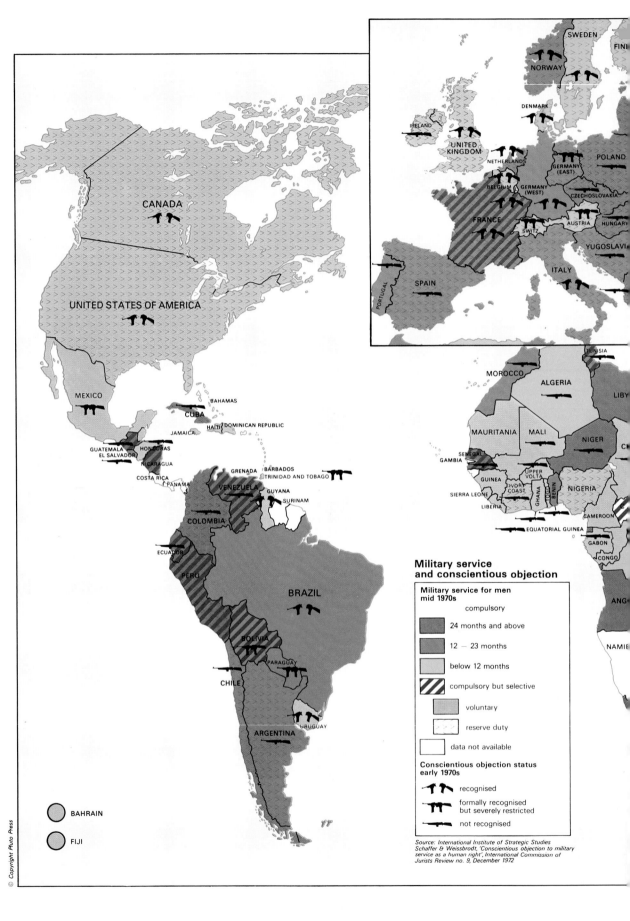

Military service and conscientious objection

Military service for men mid 1970s

compulsory

- 24 months and above
- 12 — 23 months
- below 12 months
- compulsory but selective
- voluntary
- reserve duty
- data not available

Conscientious objection status early 1970s

- recognised
- formally recognised but severely restricted
- not recognised

Source: International Institute of Strategic Studies
Schaffer & Weissbrodt, 'Conscientious objection to military
service as a human right', International Commission of
Jurists Review no. 9, December 1972

© Copyright Pluto Press

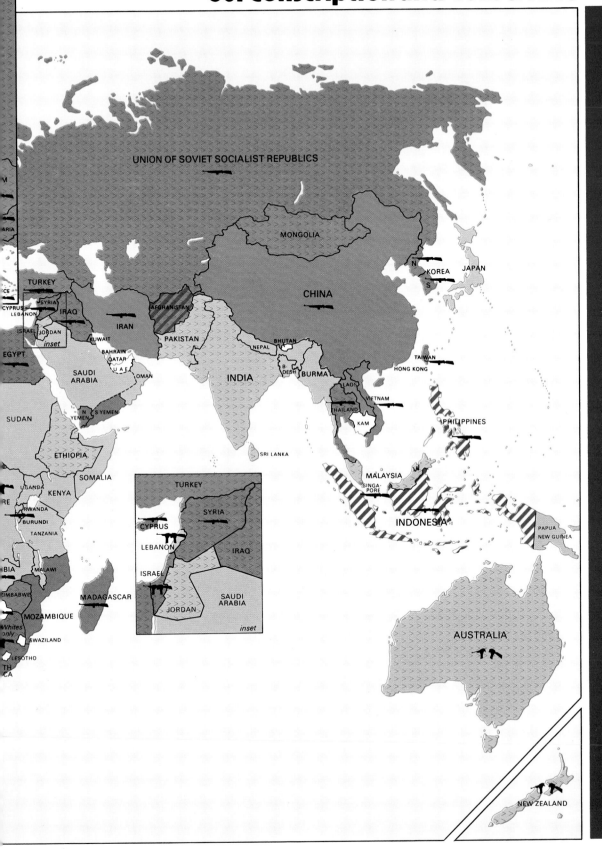

UNION OF SOVIET SOCIALIST REPUBLICS

MONGOLIA

CHINA

N
KOREA
S

JAPAN

TURKEY
SYRIA
IRAQ
CYPRUS
LEBANON
ISRAEL JORDAN
inset
KUWAIT
BAHRAIN
QATAR
U.A.E.
OMAN
SAUDI ARABIA

AFGHANISTAN

IRAN

PAKISTAN

NEPAL
BHUTAN
B-DESH
BURMA
LAOS
VIETNAM
THAILAND
KAM

INDIA

TAIWAN
HONG KONG

PHILIPPINES

EGYPT

SUDAN

N YEMEN S YEMEN

ETHIOPIA

SOMALIA

UGANDA KENYA
RWANDA
BURUNDI
TANZANIA

MALAWI

MADAGASCAR

MOZAMBIQUE

ZIMBABWE

Whites only
SWAZILAND
LESOTHO

SRI LANKA

MALAYSIA
SINGA-PORE

INDONESIA

PAPUA NEW GUINEA

AUSTRALIA

NEW ZEALAND

inset

TURKEY

SYRIA

CYPRUS

LEBANON

IRAQ

ISRAEL

JORDAN

SAUDI ARABIA

inset

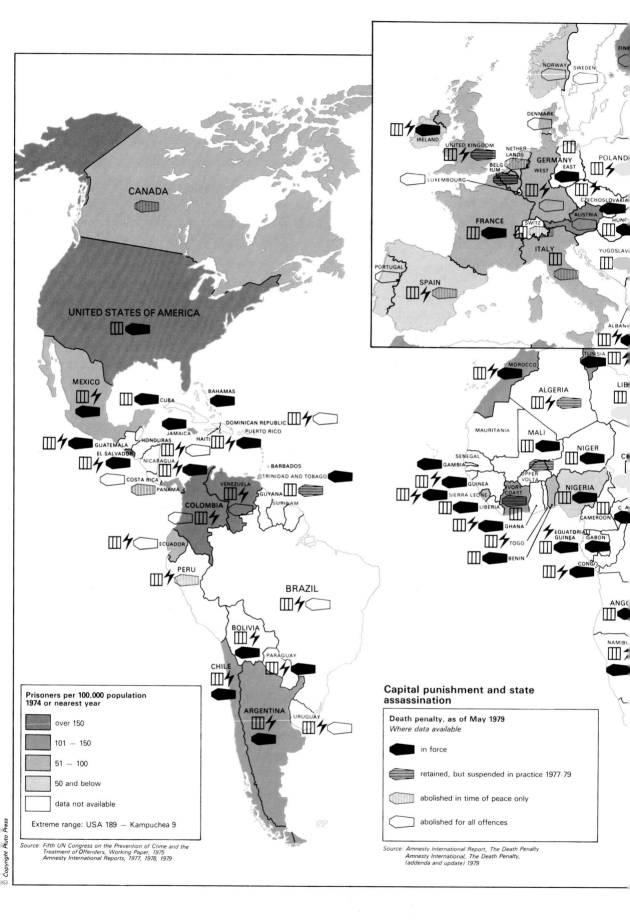

Prisoners per 100,000 population
1974 or nearest year

- over 150
- 101 — 150
- 51 — 100
- 50 and below
- data not available

Extreme range: USA 189 — Kampuchea 9

Source: Fifth UN Congress on the Prevention of Crime and the
Treatment of Offenders, Working Paper, 1975
Amnesty International Reports, 1977, 1978, 1979

Capital punishment and state assassination

Death penalty, as of May 1979
Where data available

- in force
- retained, but suspended in practice 1977-79
- abolished in time of peace only
- abolished for all offences

Source: Amnesty International Report, The Death Penalty
Amnesty International, The Death Penalty,
(addenda and update) 1979

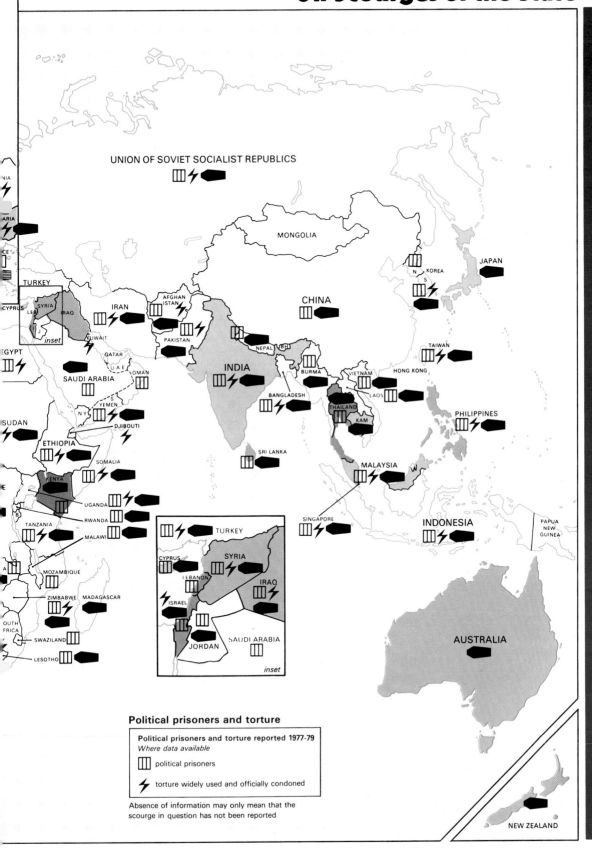

UNION OF SOVIET SOCIALIST REPUBLICS

MONGOLIA

JAPAN

N KOREA
S

CHINA

TAIWAN

TURKEY
CYPRUS SYRIA
LEB
J IRAQ
inset

IRAN

AFGHAN
ISTAN

PAKISTAN

NEPAL BH

HONG KONG

KUWAIT

QATAR
U.A.E
OMAN

SAUDI ARABIA

INDIA

BURMA
VIETNAM
LAOS

PHILIPPINES

EGYPT

N Y
YEMEN

BANGLADESH

THAILAND
KAM

SUDAN

DJIBOUTI

ETHIOPIA

SOMALIA

SRI LANKA

MALAYSIA

KENYA

UGANDA

SINGAPORE

INDONESIA

PAPUA
NEW
GUINEA

RWANDA

TANZANIA

MALAWI

TURKEY

MOZAMBIQUE

CYPRUS

SYRIA

ZIMBABWE MADAGASCAR

LEBANON

IRAQ

OUTH
FRICA

ISRAEL

AUSTRALIA

SWAZILAND

LESOTHO

JORDAN

SAUDI ARABIA

inset

Political prisoners and torture

Political prisoners and torture reported 1977-79
Where data available

political prisoners

torture widely used and officially condoned

Absence of information may only mean that the
scourge in question has not been reported

NEW ZEALAND

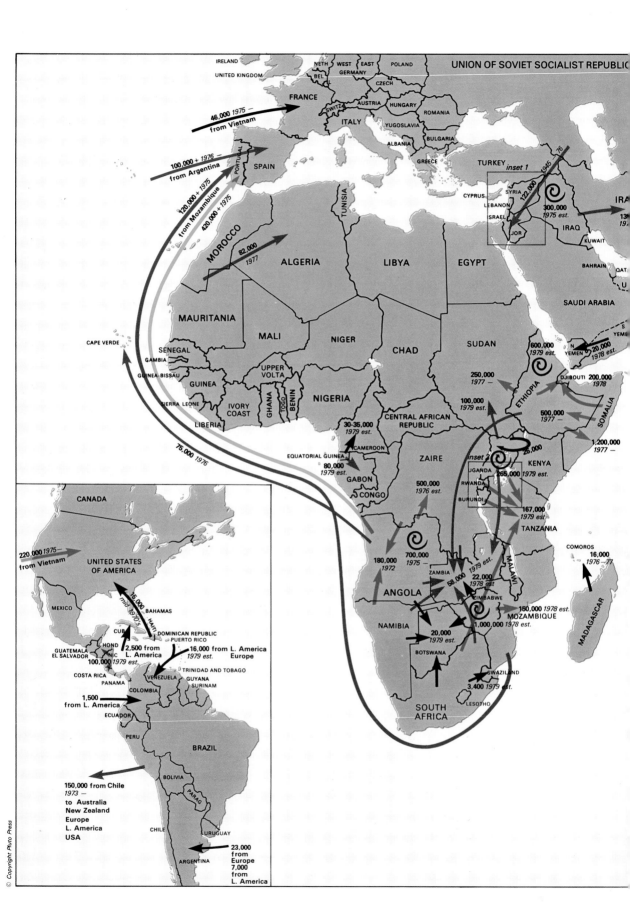

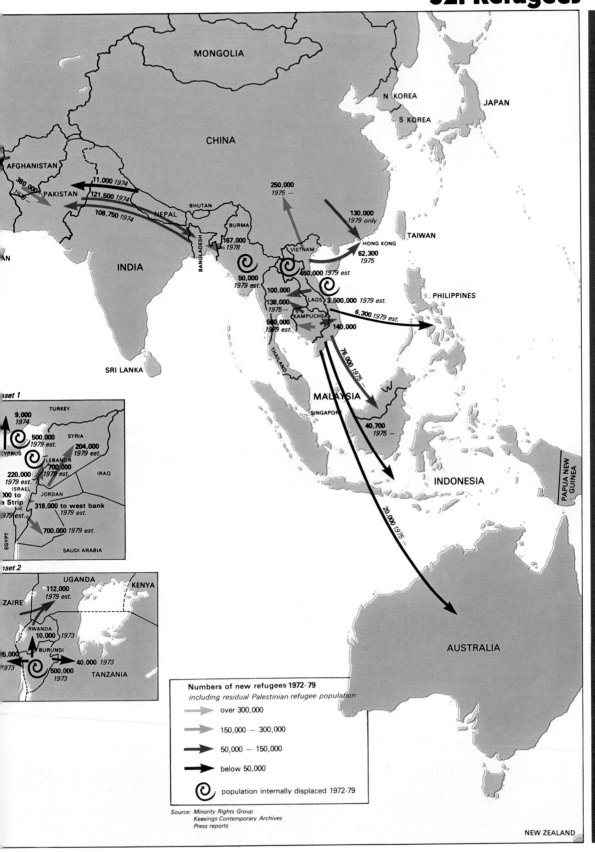

MONGOLIA

N KOREA

JAPAN

S KOREA

CHINA

AFGHANISTAN

380,000
1978

PAKISTAN

11,000 1974

121,500 1974

108,750 1974

NEPAL

BHUTAN

250,000
1975 —

130,000
1979 only

TAIWAN

BURMA

167,000
1978

HONG KONG

62,300
1975

INDIA

BANGLADESH

50,000
1979 est.

VIETNAM

450,000 1979 est

100,000

138,000
1975 —

LAOS 3,500,000 1979 est.

6,300 1979 est.

SRI LANKA

KAMPUCHEA

140,000

PHILIPPINES

THAILAND

580,000
1979 est.

76,000 1975

MALAYSIA

SINGAPORE

40,700
1975 —

PAPUA NEW GUINEA

20,000 1975 —

INDONESIA

AUSTRALIA

Inset 1

TURKEY

9,000
1974

SYRIA

CYPRUS

500,000
1979 est.

204,000
1979 est.

LEBANON

700,000
1979 est.

IRAQ

220,000
1979 est.

ISRAEL

JORDAN

000 to
a Strip

979 est.

318,000 to west bank
1979 est.

700,000 1979 est.

EGYPT

SAUDI ARABIA

Inset 2

UGANDA

KENYA

112,000
1979 est.

ZAIRE

RWANDA

10,000 1973

BURUNDI

5,000
1973

40,000 1973

500,000
1973

TANZANIA

Numbers of new refugees 1972-79
including residual Palestinian refugee population

over 300,000

150,000 — 300,000

50,000 — 150,000

below 50,000

population internally displaced 1972-79

Source: Minority Rights Group
Keesings Contemporary Archives
Press reports

NEW ZEALAND

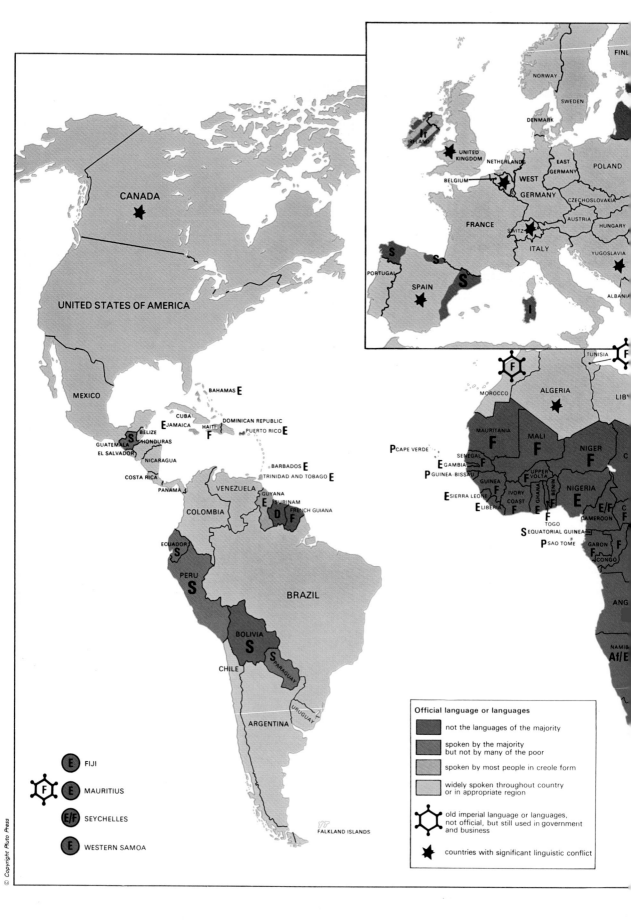

Official language or languages

- not the languages of the majority
- spoken by the majority but not by many of the poor
- spoken by most people in creole form
- widely spoken throughout country or in appropriate region

- old imperial language or languages, not official, but still used in government and business
- countries with significant linguistic conflict

E FIJI

E MAURITIUS

E/F SEYCHELLES

E WESTERN SAMOA

CANADA

UNITED STATES OF AMERICA

MEXICO

BAHAMAS **E**

CUBA **E** JAMAICA

DOMINICAN REPUBLIC

HAITI **F**

PUERTO RICO **E**

BELIZE

GUATEMALA **S** HONDURAS

EL SALVADOR

NICARAGUA

COSTA RICA

PANAMA **S**

BARBADOS **E**

TRINIDAD AND TOBAGO **E**

VENEZUELA

GUYANA **E** SURINAM **D** FRENCH GUIANA **F**

COLOMBIA

ECUADOR **S**

PERU **S**

BRAZIL

BOLIVIA **S** PARAGUAY **S**

CHILE

URUGUAY

ARGENTINA

FALKLAND ISLANDS

NORWAY

SWEDEN

FINL

DENMARK

IRELAND **It**

UNITED KINGDOM

NETHERLANDS

BELGIUM

EAST GERMANY

WEST GERMANY

POLAND

CZECHOSLOVAKIA

AUSTRIA

HUNGARY

FRANCE

S/VITZ

ITALY

YUGOSLAVIA

PORTUGAL **S**

SPAIN **S**

S

I

ALBANIA

TUNISIA **F**

MOROCCO

ALGERIA

LIB

F

P CAPE VERDE

MAURITANIA

MALI **F**

NIGER **F**

SENEGAL **E** GAMBIA

P GUINEA-BISSAU

GUINEA **F**

UPPER VOLTA **F**

E SIERRA LEONE

IVORY COAST **F**

GHANA

BENIN

NIGERIA **E**

C

E/F CAMEROON

E LIBERIA

TOGO **F**

S EQUATORIAL GUINEA

P SAO TOME

GABON **F**

CONGO

C

ANG

NAMIB **Af/E**

© Copyright Pluto Press

A language of rule is one which is used by the governing classes, and which helps to secure their dominance

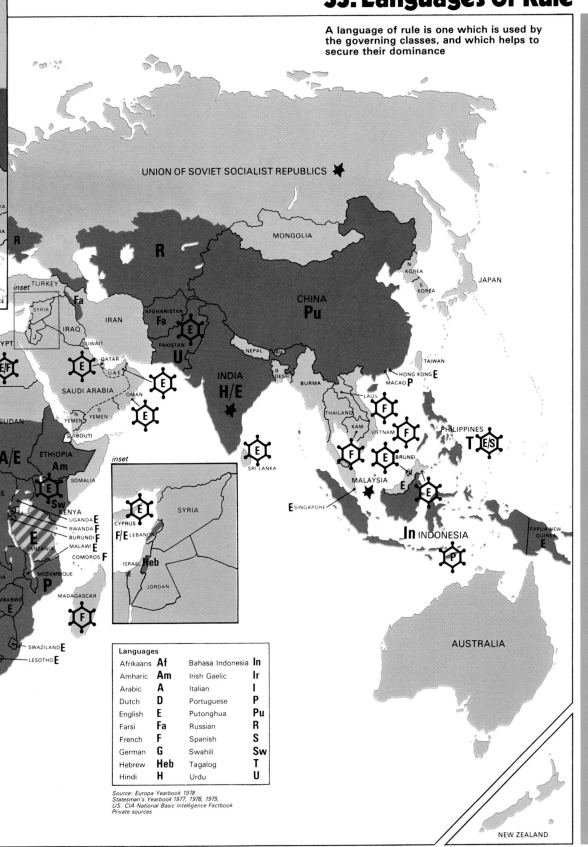

UNION OF SOVIET SOCIALIST REPUBLICS

MONGOLIA

R

R

CHINA
Pu

N KOREA

S KOREA

JAPAN

TURKEY

SYRIA

J

IRAQ

Fa

IRAN

AFGHANISTAN
Fa

PAKISTAN
U

KUWAIT

QATAR

U.A.E.

SAUDI ARABIA

OMAN

N YEMEN

S YEMEN

DJIBOUTI

EGYPT

SUDAN

E/F

A/E

ETHIOPIA
Am

SOMALIA

Sw KENYA

UGANDA **E**

RWANDA **F**

BURUNDI **F**

MALAWI **E**

COMOROS **F**

TANZANIA

E

MOZAMBIQUE
P

MBABWE

MADAGASCAR

F

SWAZILAND **E**

LESOTHO **E**

NEPAL

B DESH

BH

INDIA
H/E

BURMA

SRI LANKA

E

LAOS

THAILAND

KAM

VIETNAM

HONG KONG **E**

MACAO **P**

TAIWAN

PHILIPPINES

T **E/S**

F

F

F

E BRUNEI

MALAYSIA

E

E

E

E SINGAPORE

PAPUA NEW GUINEA **E**

In INDONESIA

P

AUSTRALIA

NEW ZEALAND

inset

CYPRUS
E

F/E LEBANON

SYRIA

ISRAEL
Heb

JORDAN

Languages

Afrikaans	**Af**	Bahasa Indonesia	**In**
Amharic	**Am**	Irish Gaelic	**Ir**
Arabic	**A**	Italian	**I**
Dutch	**D**	Portuguese	**P**
English	**E**	Putonghua	**Pu**
Farsi	**Fa**	Russian	**R**
French	**F**	Spanish	**S**
German	**G**	Swahili	**Sw**
Hebrew	**Heb**	Tagalog	**T**
Hindi	**H**	Urdu	**U**

Source: Europa Yearbook 1978
Statesman's Yearbook 1977, 1978, 1979,
US. CIA National Basic Intelligence Factbook
Private sources

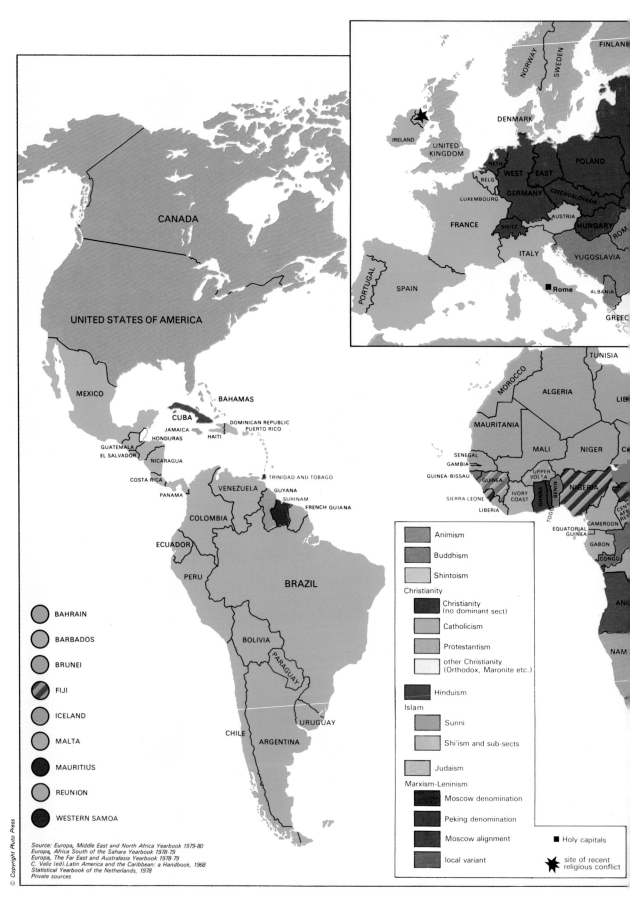

A religion of rule is one which is professed by the governing classes and which sustains their solidarity

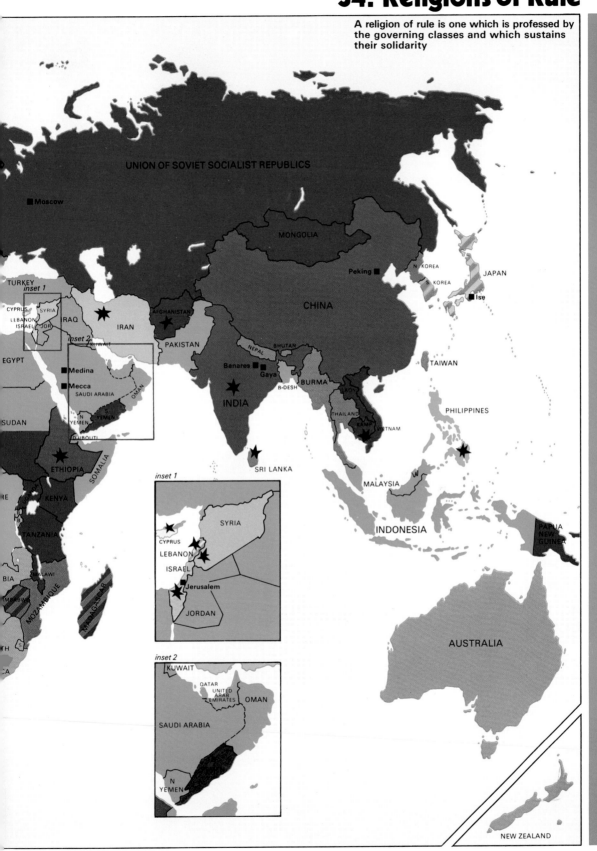

Big money

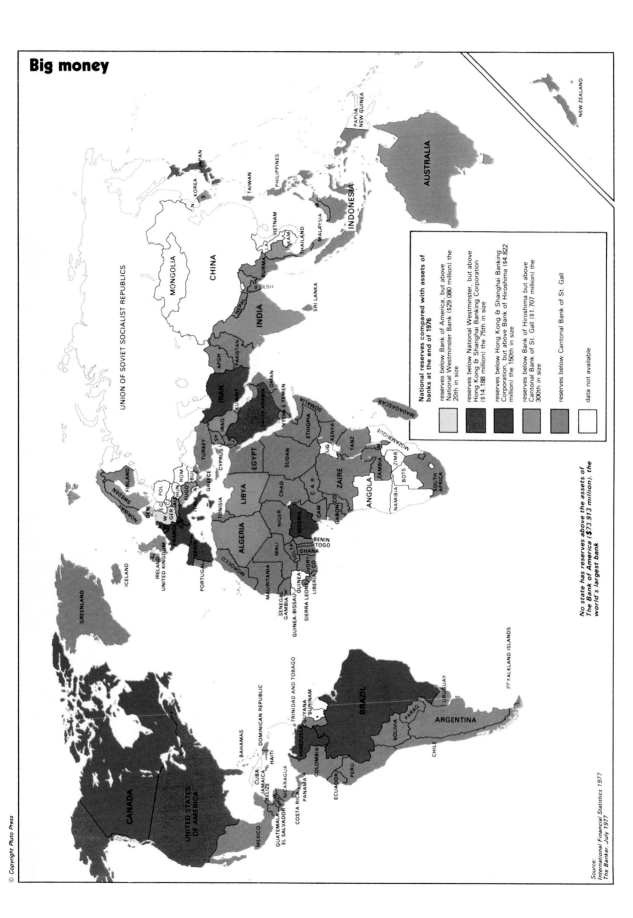

National reserves compared with assets of banks at the end of 1976

reserves below Bank of America, but above National Westminster Bank ($29,080 million) the 20th in size

reserves below National Westminster, but above Hong Kong & Shanghai Banking Corporation ($14,188 million) the 75th in size

reserves below Hong Kong & Shanghai Banking Corporation, but above Bank of Hiroshima ($4,822 million) the 150th in size

reserves below Bank of Hiroshima but above Cantonal Bank of St. Gall ($1,707 million) the 300th in size

reserves below Cantonal Bank of St. Gall

data not available

No state has reserves above the assets of The Bank of America ($73,913 million), the world's largest bank.

Source:
International Financial Statistics 1977
The Banker, July 1977

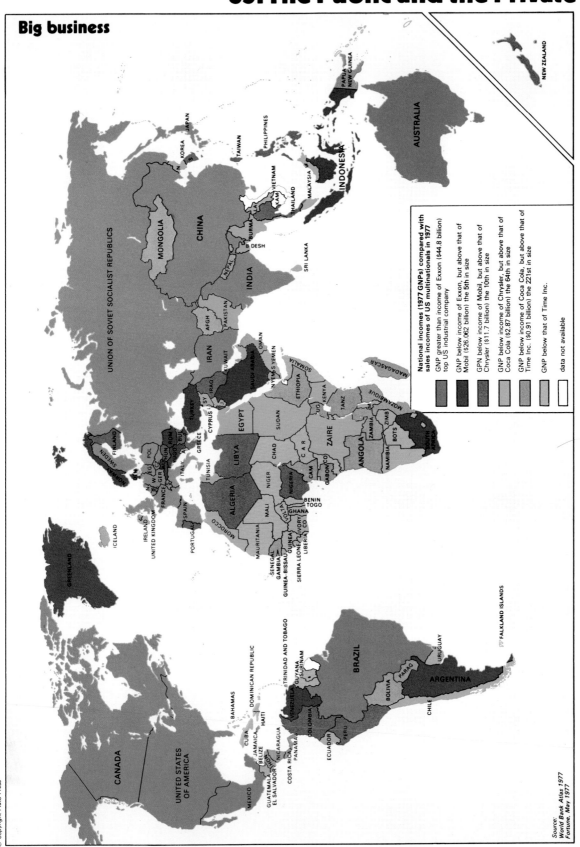

Big business

NEW ZEALAND

PAPUA NEW GUINEA

AUSTRALIA

JAPAN

N KOREA
S KOREA
TAIWAN
PHILIPPINES
VIETNAM
KAM
THAILAND
MALAYSIA
INDONESIA

CHINA
BURMA
MONGOLIA

B DESH
NEPAL
INDIA
PAKISTAN

UNION OF SOVIET SOCIALIST REPUBLICS

SRI LANKA

AFGH

IRAN
KUWAIT
SAUDI ARABIA
OMAN
N YEM
S YEMEN
IRAQ
TURKEY
CYPRUS
SY
L

MADAGASCAR

SOMALIA
ETHIOPIA
KENYA
UG
TANZ
MOZAMBIQUE

EGYPT
SUDAN
C A R
ZAIRE
ZAMBIA
ZIMB
BOTS
SOUTH AFRICA
NAMIBIA
ANGOLA
GABON
CO

FINLAND
NORWAY
SWEDEN
POL
E GER
W GER
FRANCE
ITALY
GREECE
ROM
HUN
YUGO
BUL
AUS

LIBYA
CHAD
NIGER
CAM
NIGERIA
BENIN
TOGO
GHANA
IVORY CO
LIBERIA
SIERRA LEONE
GUINEA
GUINEA-BISSAU
GAMBIA
SENEGAL
MAURITANIA
MALI
VOLTA
TUNISIA
ALGERIA
MOROCCO
SPAIN
PORTUGAL
IRELAND
UNITED KINGDOM
ICELAND

GREENLAND

National incomes (1977 GNPs) compared with sales incomes of US multinationals in 1977

GNP greater than income of Exxon ($44.8 billion) top US industrial company

GNP below income of Exxon, but above that of Mobil ($26.062 billion) the 5th in size

GPN below income of Mobil, but above that of Chrysler ($11.7 billion) the 10th in size

GNP below income of Chrysler, but above that of Coca Cola ($2.87 billion) the 64th in size

GNP below income of Coca Cola, but above that of Time Inc. ($0.91 billion) the 221st in size

GNP below that of Time Inc.

data not available

CANADA

UNITED STATES OF AMERICA

MEXICO
GUATEMALA
EL SALVADOR
HON
BELIZE
JAMAICA
CUBA
BAHAMAS
HAITI
DOMINICAN REPUBLIC
NICARAGUA
COSTA RICA
PANAMA
TRINIDAD AND TOBAGO

FALKLAND ISLANDS

BRAZIL

VENEZUELA
COLOMBIA
ECUADOR
PERU
BOLIVIA
GUYANA
SURINAM
PARAG
URUGUAY
ARGENTINA
CHILE

Source:
World Bank Atlas 1977
Fortune, May 1977

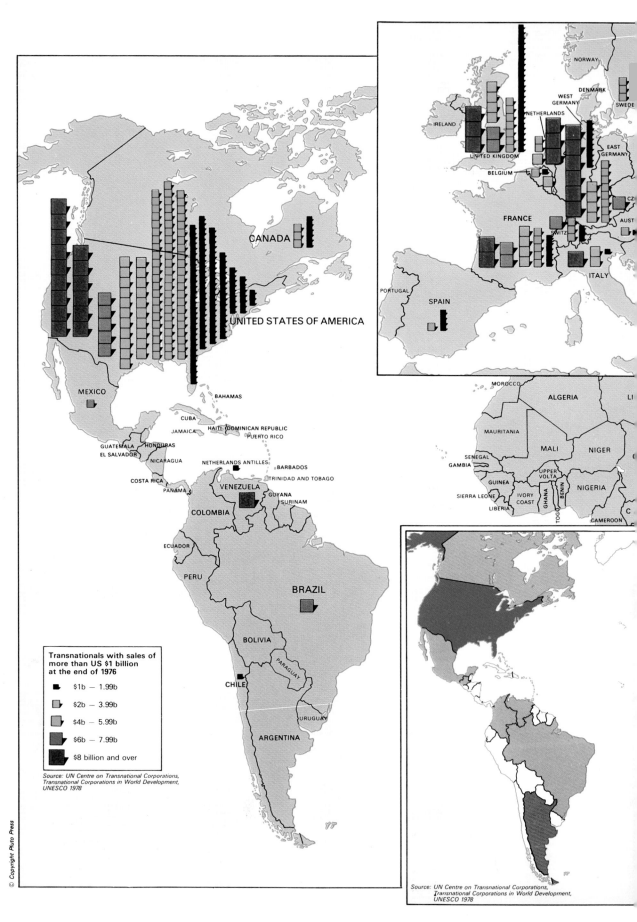

CANADA

UNITED STATES OF AMERICA

MEXICO

BAHAMAS

CUBA

JAMAICA HAITI DOMINICAN REPUBLIC
PUERTO RICO

GUATEMALA HONDURAS
EL SALVADOR
NICARAGUA
COSTA RICA
PANAMA

NETHERLANDS ANTILLES
BARBADOS
TRINIDAD AND TOBAGO

VENEZUELA
GUYANA
SURINAM

COLOMBIA

ECUADOR

PERU

BRAZIL

BOLIVIA

PARAGUAY

CHILE

URUGUAY

ARGENTINA

NORWAY

IRELAND

UNITED KINGDOM

NETHERLANDS

DENMARK

SWEDE

WEST
GERMANY

EAST
GERMANY

BELGIUM

FRANCE

SWITZ.

CZE

AUST

ITALY

PORTUGAL

SPAIN

MOROCCO

ALGERIA

LI

MAURITANIA

MALI

NIGER

SENEGAL

GAMBIA

GUINEA

UPPER
VOLTA

SIERRA LEONE

IVORY
COAST

GHANA

TOGO

BENIN

NIGERIA

LIBERIA

CAMEROON

C

**Transnationals with sales of
more than US $1 billion
at the end of 1976**

- $1b — 1.99b
- $2b — 3.99b
- $4b — 5.99b
- $6b — 7.99b
- $8 billion and over

Source: UN Centre on Transnational Corporations,
Transnational Corporations in World Development,
UNESCO 1978

Source: UN Centre on Transnational Corporations,
Transnational Corporations in World Development,
UNESCO 1978

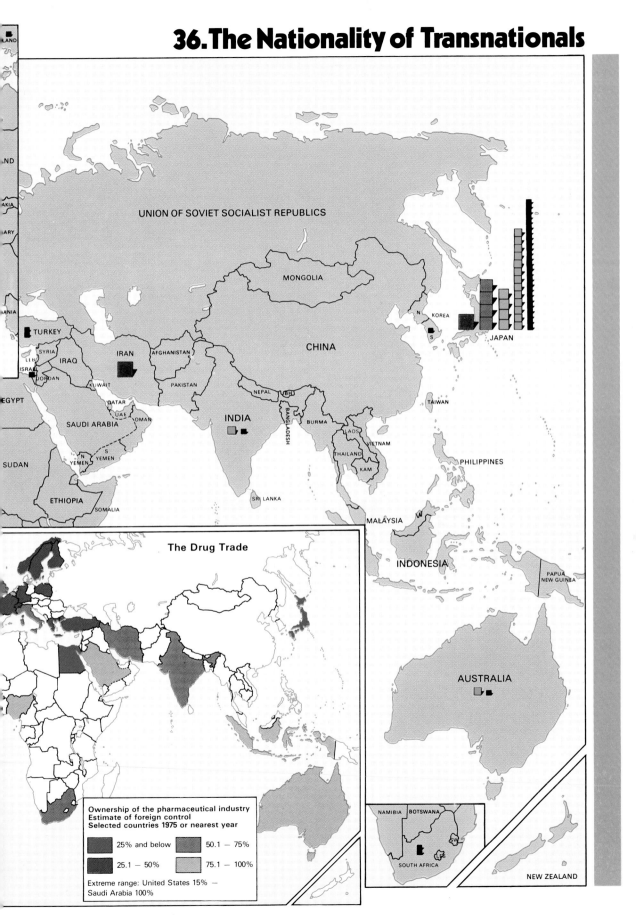

UNION OF SOVIET SOCIALIST REPUBLICS

MONGOLIA

CHINA

N
KOREA
S

JAPAN

TURKEY

SYRIA
LEB
ISRAEL
JORDAN
IRAQ
IRAN
AFGHANISTAN
KUWAIT
PAKISTAN
QATAR
UAE
OMAN
SAUDI ARABIA

EGYPT

SUDAN

N
YEMEN
S
YEMEN

ETHIOPIA

SOMALIA

NEPAL
BH
INDIA
BANGLADESH
BURMA
LAOS
THAILAND
VIETNAM
KAM

SRI LANKA

TAIWAN

PHILIPPINES

MALAYSIA

INDONESIA

PAPUA
NEW GUINEA

AUSTRALIA

NAMIBIA
BOTSWANA
SW

SOUTH AFRICA

NEW ZEALAND

The Drug Trade

Ownership of the pharmaceutical industry
Estimate of foreign control
Selected countries 1975 or nearest year

- 25% and below
- 25.1 — 50%
- 50.1 — 75%
- 75.1 — 100%

Extreme range: United States 15% —
Saudi Arabia 100%

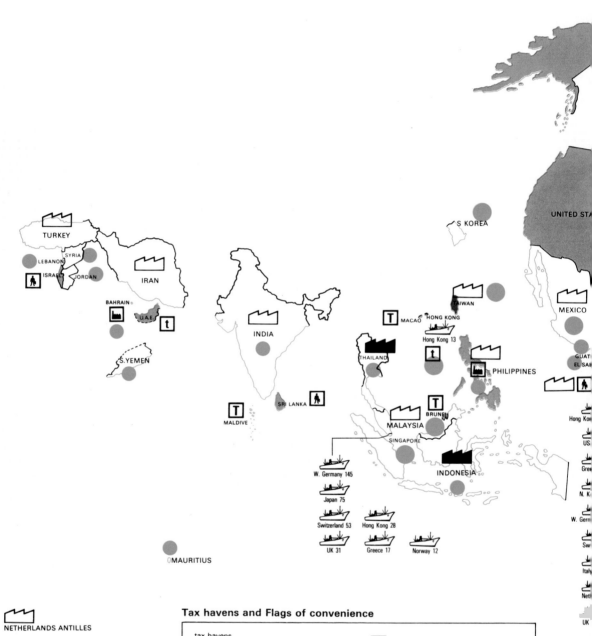

TURKEY

LEBANON SYRIA
ISRAEL JORDAN

IRAN

BAHRAIN

U.A.E. t

S.YEMEN

INDIA

SRI LANKA

MALDIVE

S KOREA

MACAO HONG KONG

Hong Kong 13

TAIWAN

THAILAND

PHILIPPINES

MALAYSIA

SINGAPORE

BRUNEI

INDONESIA

UNITED STA

MEXICO

GUAT
EL SAL

MAURITIUS

W. Germany 145

Japan 75

Switzerland 53   Hong Kong 28

UK 31   Greece 17   Norway 12

Hong Kon

US

Gree

N. K

W. Germ

Sw

Italy

Netl

UK

NETHERLANDS ANTILLES

NICARAGUA

JAMAICA

HAITI

PUERTO RICO

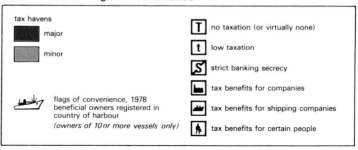

Tax havens and Flags of convenience

tax havens

▮ major

▨ minor

flags of convenience, 1978
beneficial owners registered in
country of harbour

(owners of 10 or more vessels only)

T no taxation (or virtually none)

t low taxation

S strict banking secrecy

tax benefits for companies

tax benefits for shipping companies

tax benefits for certain people

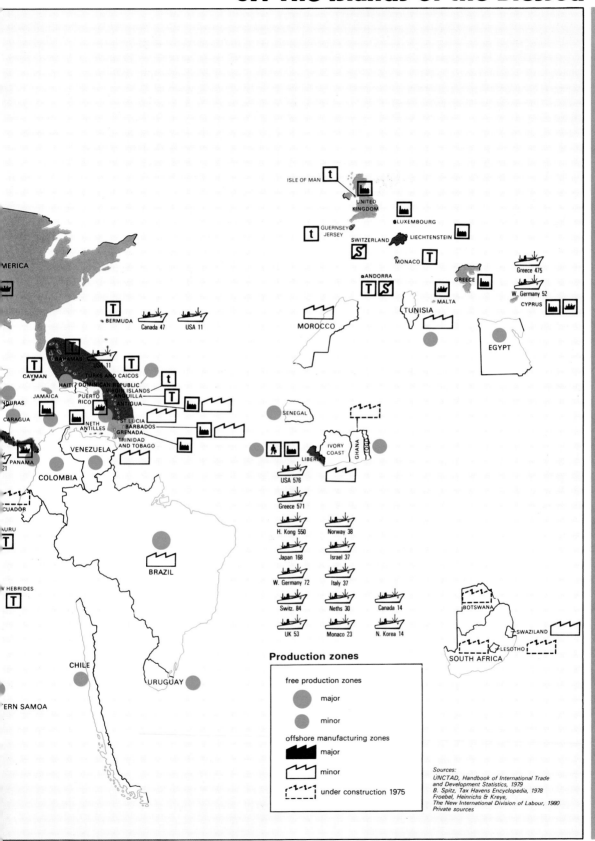

ISLE OF MAN

UNITED
KINGDOM

GUERNSEY
JERSEY

LUXEMBOURG

SWITZERLAND   LIECHTENSTEIN

MONACO

ANDORRA

GREECE

Greece 475

W. Germany 52

MALTA

CYPRUS

TUNISIA

MOROCCO

EGYPT

AMERICA

BERMUDA

Canada 47   USA 11

CAYMAN

BAHAMAS

USA 11

TURKS AND CAICOS

HAITI   DOMINICAN REPUBLIC

VIRGIN ISLANDS

ANGUILLA

ANTIGUA

ST. LUCIA

BARBADOS

GRENADA

TRINIDAD
AND TOBAGO

HONDURAS

JAMAICA

PUERTO
RICO

NETH.
ANTILLES

CARAGUA

RICA

PANAMA
21

VENEZUELA

COLOMBIA

SENEGAL

IVORY
COAST

GHANA   TOGO

LIBERIA

USA 576

Greece 571

H. Kong 550   Norway 38

Japan 168   Israel 37

W. Germany 72   Italy 37

Switz. 84   Neths 30   Canada 14

UK 53   Monaco 23   N. Korea 14

ECUADOR

AURU

NEW HEBRIDES

BRAZIL

CHILE

URUGUAY

ERN SAMOA

BOTSWANA

SWAZILAND

LESOTHO

SOUTH AFRICA

Production zones

free production zones

● major

● minor

offshore manufacturing zones

◤ major

⌐ minor

⌐ under construction 1975

Sources:
UNCTAD, Handbook of International Trade
and Development Statistics, 1979
B. Spitz, Tax Havens Encyclopedia, 1978
Froebel, Heinrichs & Kreye,
The New International Division of Labour, 1980
Private sources

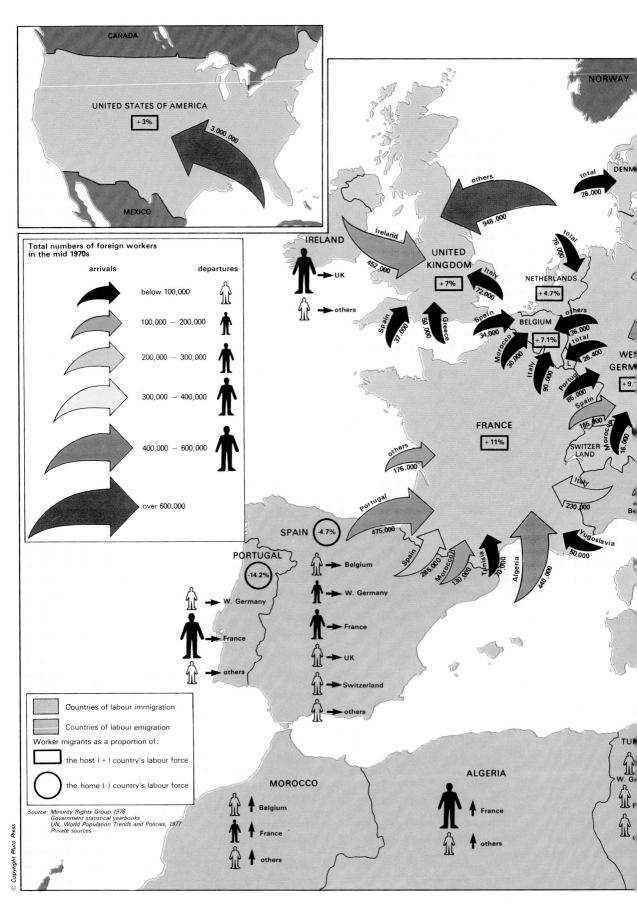

CANADA

UNITED STATES OF AMERICA

+3%

3,000,000

MEXICO

NORWAY

others
948,000

total
28,000

DENM

IRELAND

Ireland
452,000

total
76,000

UNITED
KINGDOM
+7%

Italy
72,000

NETHERLANDS
+4.7%

Spain
37,000

50,000

Greece

Spain
34,000

BELGIUM
+7.1%

others
136,000

total

Morocco
30,000

L

26,400

Italy
90,000

Portugal
85,000

WES
GERM
+9.

Spain
155,000

Morocco
16,000

Total numbers of foreign workers
in the mid 1970s

arrivals   departures

below 100,000

100,000 — 200,000

200,000 — 300,000

300,000 — 400,000

400,000 — 600,000

over 600,000

FRANCE
+11%

SWITZER-
LAND

others
176,000

Italy
230,000

Be

Portugal
475,000

Yugoslavia
50,000

SPAIN   -4.7%

Spain
265,000

Morocco
130,000

Tunisia
70,000

Algeria
440,000

PORTUGAL
-14.2%

Belgium

W. Germany

France

UK

Switzerland

others

Countries of labour immigration

Countries of labour emigration

Worker migrants as a proportion of:

the host (+) country's labour force

the home (-) country's labour force

TU

W. Germany

France

others

MOROCCO

Belgium

France

others

ALGERIA

France

others

Source: Minority Rights Group 1978
Government statistical yearbooks
UN, World Population Trends and Policies, 1977
Private sources

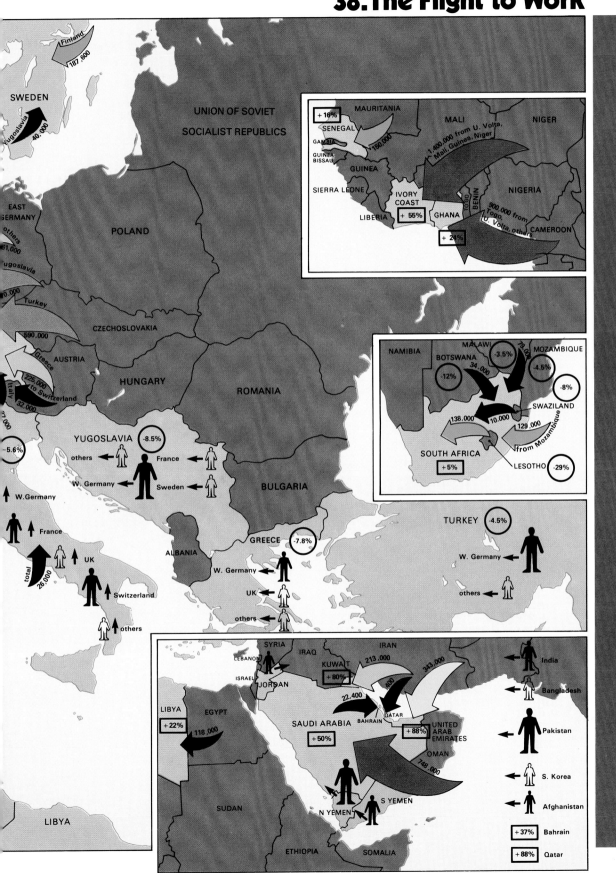

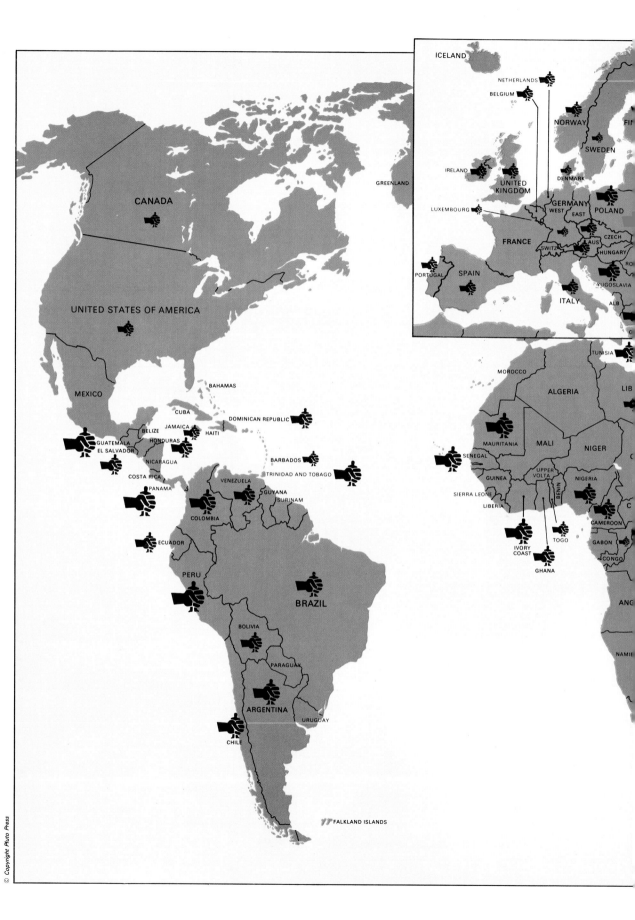

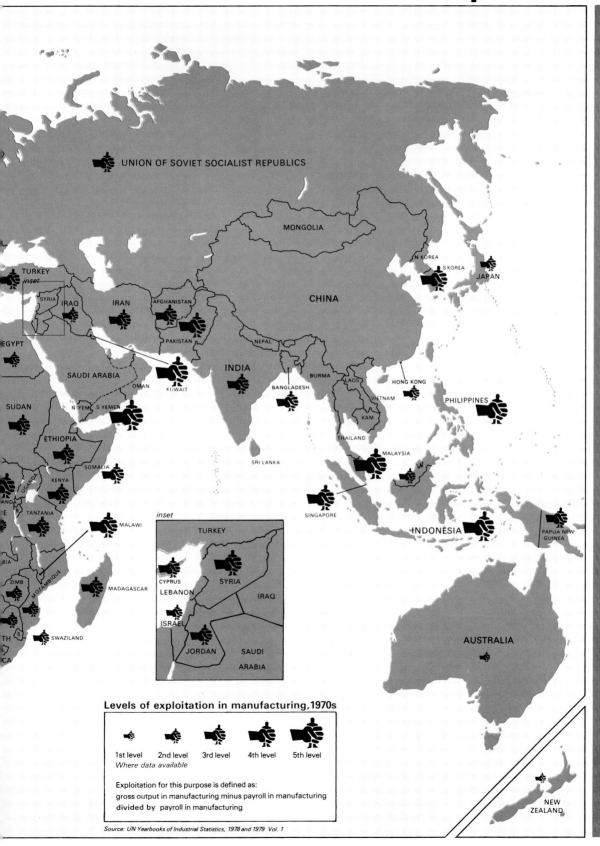

UNION OF SOVIET SOCIALIST REPUBLICS

MONGOLIA

N KOREA

S KOREA

JAPAN

CHINA

TURKEY
inset

SYRIA

IRAQ

IRAN

AFGHANISTAN

PAKISTAN

NEPAL

INDIA

BURMA

LAOS

HONG KONG

VIETNAM

PHILIPPINES

EGYPT

SAUDI ARABIA

OMAN

KUWAIT

BANGLADESH

KAM

THAILAND

SUDAN

N YEM S YEMEN

MALAYSIA

ETHIOPIA

SOMALIA

SRI LANKA

KENYA

SINGAPORE

INDONESIA

PAPUA NEW GUINEA

UGANDA

TANZANIA

MALAWI

inset

TURKEY

MADAGASCAR

ZIMB

MOZAMBIQUE

CYPRUS

LEBANON

SYRIA

IRAQ

ISRAEL

JORDAN

SAUDI ARABIA

SWAZILAND

AUSTRALIA

Levels of exploitation in manufacturing, 1970s

1st level   2nd level   3rd level   4th level   5th level
Where data available

Exploitation for this purpose is defined as:
gross output in manufacturing minus payroll in manufacturing
divided by payroll in manufacturing

NEW ZEALAND

Source: UN Yearbooks of Industrial Statistics, 1978 and 1979 Vol. 1

Workers on the land

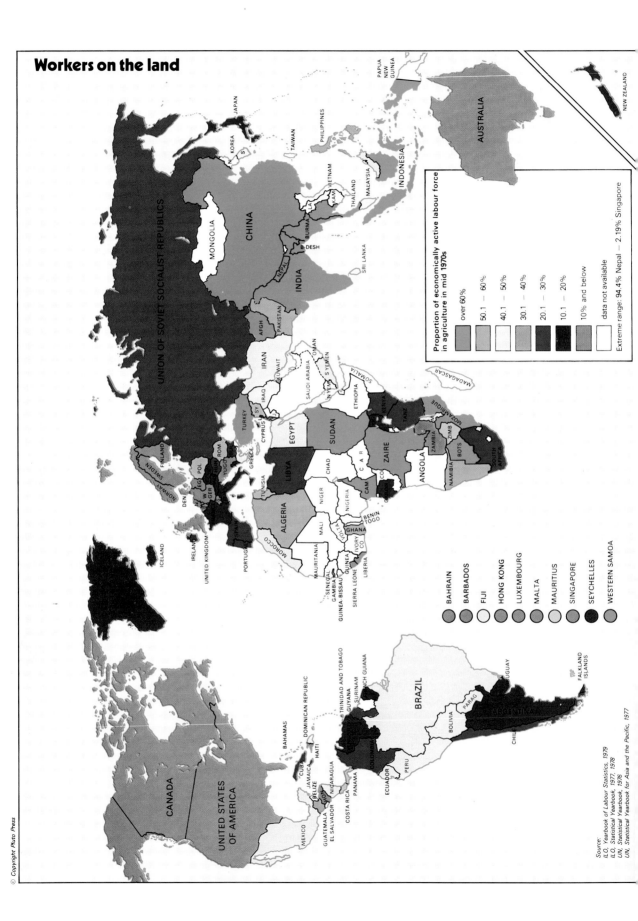

Proportion of economically active labour force in agriculture in mid 1970s

- over 60%
- 50.1 – 60%
- 40.1 – 50%
- 30.1 – 40%
- 20.1 – 30%
- 10.1 – 20%
- 10% and below
- data not available

Extreme range: **94.4%** Nepal – **2.19%** Singapore

- BAHRAIN
- BARBADOS
- FIJI
- HONG KONG
- LUXEMBOURG
- MALTA
- MAURITIUS
- SINGAPORE
- SEYCHELLES
- WESTERN SAMOA

Source:
I.L.O. Yearbook of Labour Statistics, 1979
I.L.O. Statistical Yearbook, 1977, 1978
UN. Statistical Yearbook, 1976
UN. Statistical Yearbook for Asia and the Pacific, 1977

Workers in industry

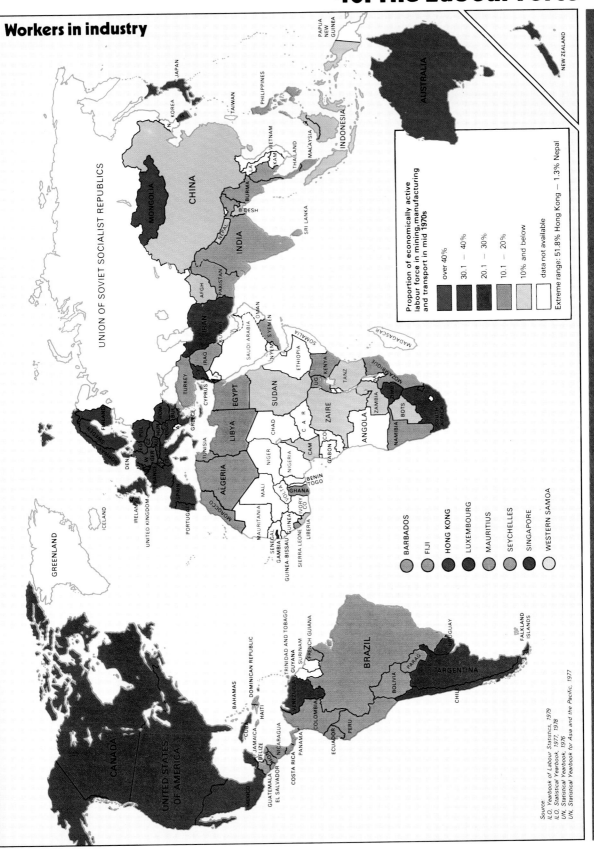

PAPUA NEW GUINEA

NEW ZEALAND

AUSTRALIA

JAPAN

N. KOREA

TAIWAN

PHILIPPINES

VIETNAM

KAM

LAOS

THAILAND

MALAYSIA

INDONESIA

CHINA

MONGOLIA

BURMA

B'DESH

NEPAL

SRI LANKA

INDIA

PAKISTAN

AFGH

UNION OF SOVIET SOCIALIST REPUBLICS

Proportion of economically active labour force in mining, manufacturing and transport in mid 1970s

over 40%

30.1 — 40%

20.1 — 30%

10.1 — 20%

10% and below

data not available

Extreme range: 51.8% Hong Kong — 1.3% Nepal

IRAN

KUWAIT

IRAQ

SYRIA

OMAN

S. YEMEN

N. YEMEN

SAUDI ARABIA

TURKEY

CYPRUS

GREECE

EGYPT

SOMALIA

MADAGASCAR

ETHIOPIA

KENYA

UG

TANZ

SUDAN

ZAIRE

ZAMBIA

MOZAMBIQUE

MALAWI

SOUTH AFRICA

BOTS

NAMIBIA

ANGOLA

CONGO

GABON

CAM

C A R

CHAD

LIBYA

SWEDEN

NORWAY

FINLAND

DEN

W GER

E GER

POL

CZECH

HUNG

AUST

YUGO

ROM

BUL

ALB

NETH

BEL

LUX

FRANCE

SWITZ

ITALY

IRELAND

UNITED KINGDOM

PORTUGAL

SPAIN

ALGERIA

TUNISIA

MOROCCO

MAURITANIA

MALI

NIGER

NIGERIA

V. VOLTA

GHANA

BENIN

TOGO

IVORY CO.

LIBERIA

SIERRA LEONE

GUINEA

GUINEA BISSAU

SENEGAL

GAMBIA

GREENLAND

ICELAND

BARBADOS

FIJI

HONG KONG

LUXEMBOURG

MAURITIUS

SEYCHELLES

SINGAPORE

WESTERN SAMOA

FALKLAND ISLANDS

URUGUAY

BRAZIL

ARGENTINA

CHILE

PARAGUAY

BOLIVIA

PERU

ECUADOR

COLOMBIA

VENEZUELA

PANAMA

TRINIDAD AND TOBAGO

GUYANA

SURINAM

FRENCH GUIANA

CANADA

UNITED STATES OF AMERICA

MEXICO

GUATEMALA

EL SALVADOR

BELIZE

HONDURAS

NICARAGUA

COSTA RICA

BAHAMAS

CUBA

JAMAICA

HAITI

DOMINICAN REPUBLIC

Source:
I.L.O. Yearbook of Labour Statistics, 1979
I.L.O. Statistical Yearbook, 1977, 1978
UN. Statistical Yearbook, 1976
UN. Statistical Yearbook for Asia and the Pacific, 1977

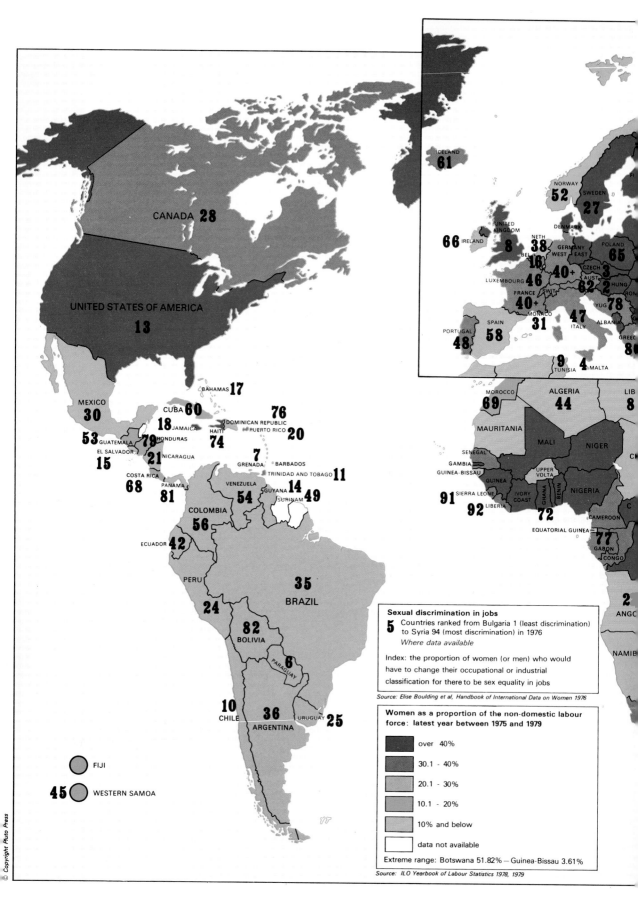

ICELAND **61**

CANADA **28**

NORWAY **52** SWEDEN **27**

UNITED KINGDOM **66** IRELAND **8** DENMARK **38** GERMANY WEST POLAND **65**
NETH BEL **18**
CZECH **3**
LUXEMBOURG **46** **40+** AUST
FRANCE SWIT **62** HUNG **2** ROM
40+ YUG **78**
MONACO **31** **47** ALBANIA
ITALY
PORTUGAL SPAIN **58**
48 GREE
80

UNITED STATES OF AMERICA

13

9 TUNISIA **4** MALTA

MOROCCO **69** ALGERIA **44** LIB **8**

BAHAMAS **17**

MEXICO **30**
CUBA **60**
DOMINICAN REPUBLIC **76**
53 GUATEMALA **18** JAMAICA HAITI **74** PUERTO RICO **20**
EL SALVADOR **79** HONDURAS
15 **21** NICARAGUA
COSTA RICA **68** GRENADA **7** BARBADOS
PANAMA **81** TRINIDAD AND TOBAGO **11**
VENEZUELA **54** GUYANA **14** SURINAM **49**
COLOMBIA **56**

MAURITANIA
SENEGAL MALI NIGER
GAMBIA
GUINEA-BISSAU GUINEA UPPER VOLTA
91 SIERRA LEONE IVORY GHANA BENIN NIGERIA
92 LIBERIA COAST **72** CAMEROON
EQUATORIAL GUINEA
77 GABON CONGO

ECUADOR **42**

PERU

BRAZIL

24 **35**

82 BOLIVIA

PARAGUAY

6

10 **36** URUGUAY
CHILE **25**
ARGENTINA

ANGO
NAMIB
2

Sexual discrimination in jobs

5 Countries ranked from Bulgaria 1 (least discrimination) to Syria 94 (most discrimination) in 1976
Where data available

Index: the proportion of women (or men) who would have to change their occupational or industrial classification for there to be sex equality in jobs

Source: Elise Boulding et al, Handbook of International Data on Women 1976

Women as a proportion of the non-domestic labour force: latest year between 1975 and 1979

▓	over 40%
▓	30.1 - 40%
▒	20.1 - 30%
░	10.1 - 20%
░	10% and below
□	data not available

Extreme range: Botswana 51.82% — Guinea-Bissau 3.61%

Source: ILO Yearbook of Labour Statistics 1978, 1979

○ FIJI

45 ○ WESTERN SAMOA

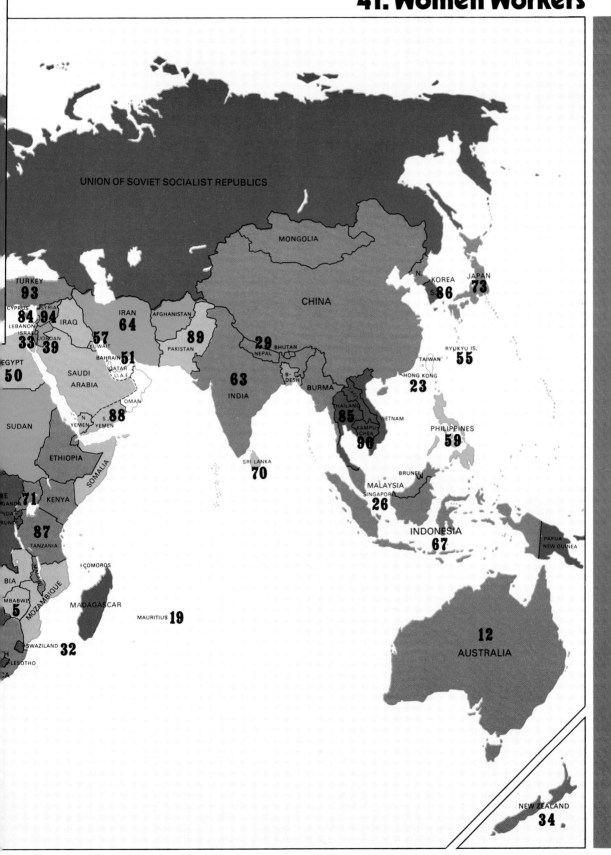

UNION OF SOVIET SOCIALIST REPUBLICS

MONGOLIA

CHINA

TURKEY
93

CYPRUS
84 SYRIA
LEBANON **94** IRAQ
ISRAEL
33 JORDAN
39 KUWAIT

IRAN
64

AFGHANISTAN

57

BAHRAIN **51**
QATAR
U.A.E.

SAUDI
ARABIA

EGYPT
50

SUDAN

N
YEMEN S.
YEMEN **88**

ETHIOPIA

SOMALIA

PAKISTAN

89

29 BHUTAN
NEPAL

B-
DESH

INDIA
63

BURMA

THAILAND
85

VIETNAM

KAMPU-
CHEA
90

N. KOREA
86
S.

JAPAN
73

RYUKYU IS.
55

TAIWAN

HONG KONG
23

PHILIPPINES
59

SRI LANKA
70

RE
UGANDA
71 KENYA
NDA
RUNDI

87
TANZANIA

BIA

MBABWE
5

MOZAMBIQUE

MADAGASCAR

COMOROS

MAURITIUS **19**

SWAZILAND **32**
H
LESOTHO
CA

OMAN

BRUNEI

MALAYSIA
SINGAPORE
26

INDONESIA
67

PAPUA
NEW GUINEA

12
AUSTRALIA

NEW ZEALAND
34

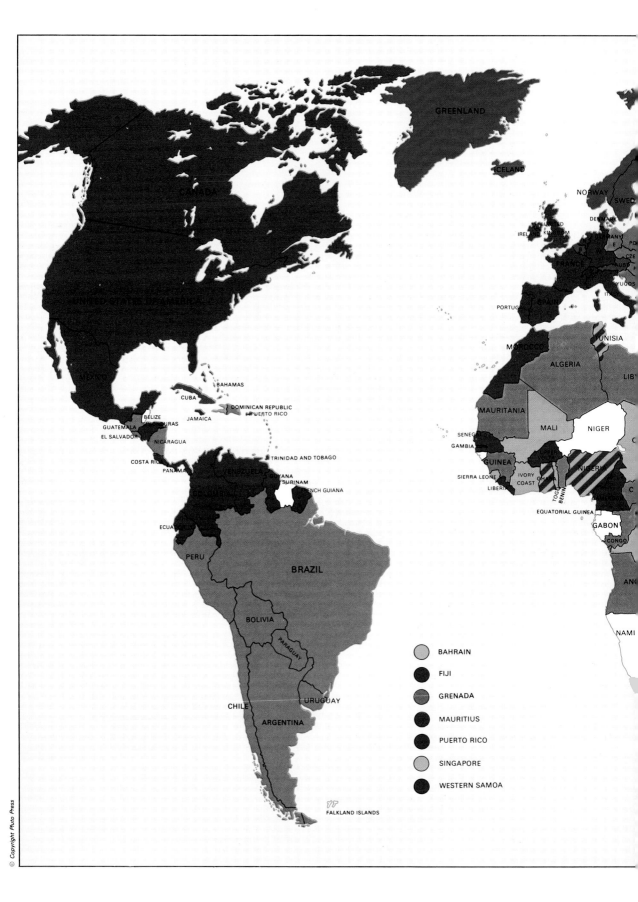

GREENLAND

ICELAND

NORWAY

SWED

DENMARK

UNITED KINGDOM

IRELAND

GERMANY

E PO

CANADA

FRANCE

CZE

AUS

YUGOS

SPAIN

IT

PORTUGAL

TUNISIA

MOROCCO

ALGERIA

LIBY

UNITED STATES OF AMERICA

MAURITANIA

MALI

NIGER

MEXICO

SENEG

GAMBIA

GUINEA

BAHAMAS

CUBA

DOMINICAN REPUBLIC

SIERRA LEONE

IVORY COAST

GHA

NIGERIA

PUERTO RICO

LIBERIA

BELIZE

JAMAICA

TOGO

BENIN

C

GUATEMALA

HONDURAS

EQUATORIAL GUINEA

EL SALVADOR

NICARAGUA

GABON

COSTA RICA

TRINIDAD AND TOBAGO

CONGO

PANAMA

VENEZUELA

GUYANA

SURINAM

FRENCH GUIANA

COLOMBIA

ANG

ECUADOR

PERU

BRAZIL

NAMI

BOLIVIA

PARAGUAY

○ BAHRAIN

● FIJI

◐ GRENADA

● MAURITIUS

CHILE

URUGUAY

● PUERTO RICO

ARGENTINA

◯ SINGAPORE

● WESTERN SAMOA

FALKLAND ISLANDS

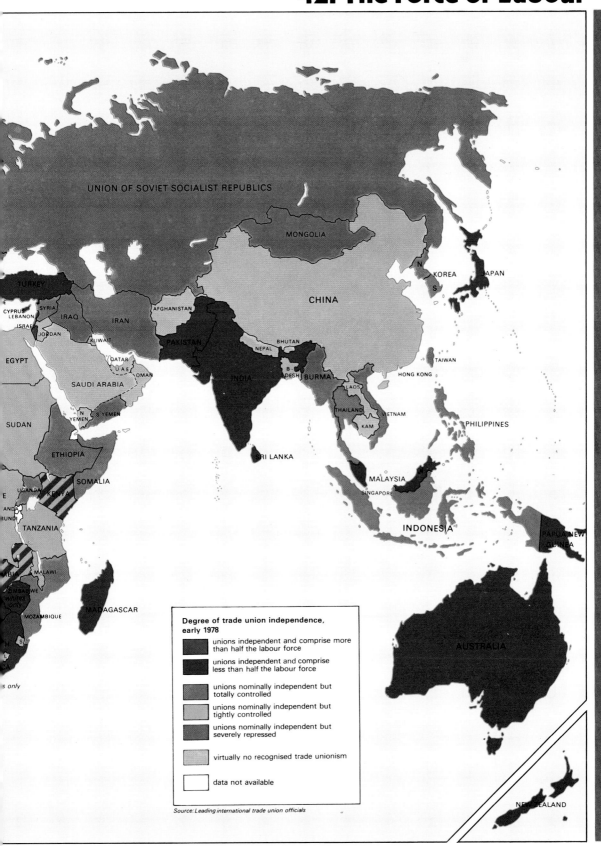

Degree of trade union independence, early 1978

- unions independent and comprise more than half the labour force
- unions independent and comprise less than half the labour force
- unions nominally independent but totally controlled
- unions nominally independent but tightly controlled
- unions nominally independent but severely repressed
- virtually no recognised trade unionism
- data not available

Source: Leading international trade union officials

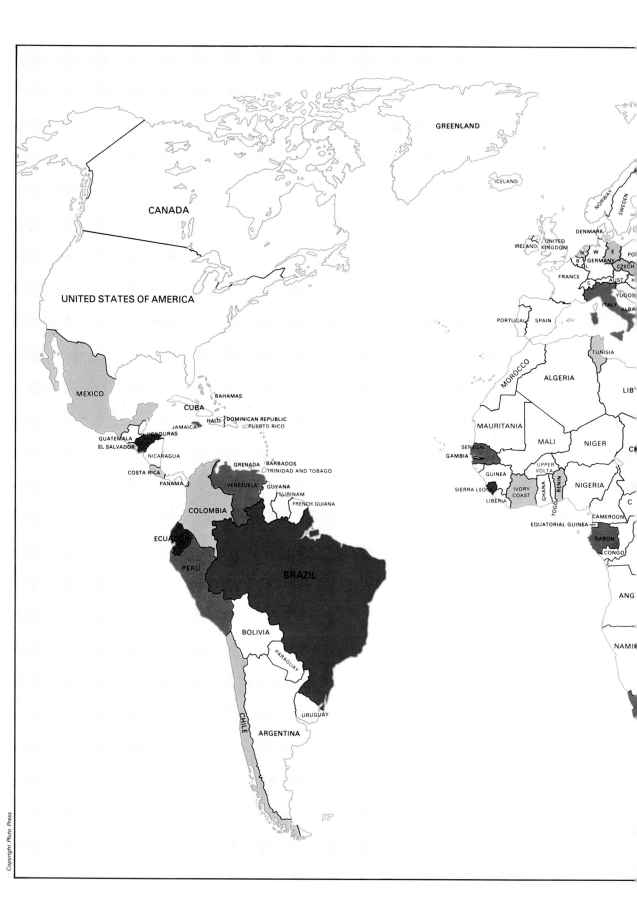

GREENLAND

ICELAND

NORWAY

SWEDEN

CANADA

DENMARK

IRELAND   UNITED
           KINGDOM

N   W   E
B   GERMANY   CZECH   PO

UNITED STATES OF AMERICA

FRANCE   AUST   H

S   YUGOS

ITALY   ALBA

PORTUGAL   SPAIN

TUNISIA

MEXICO

BAHAMAS

CUBA

HAITI   DOMINICAN REPUBLIC
        PUERTO RICO

JAMAICA

GUATEMALA   HONDURAS
EL SALVADOR

NICARAGUA

COSTA RICA

PANAMA

GRENADA   BARBADOS
          TRINIDAD AND TOBAGO

VENEZUELA   GUYANA
            SURINAM
            FRENCH GUIANA

COLOMBIA

ECUADOR

PERU

BRAZIL

BOLIVIA

PARAGUAY

CHILE

URUGUAY

ARGENTINA

MOROCCO

ALGERIA

LIB

MAURITANIA

MALI

NIGER

CH

SENEGAL

GAMBIA

UPPER
VOLTA

GUINEA

BENIN

SIERRA LEONE

IVORY
COAST

GHANA

TOGO

NIGERIA

LIBERIA

C

EQUATORIAL GUINEA

CAMEROON

GABON

CONGO

ANG

NAMI

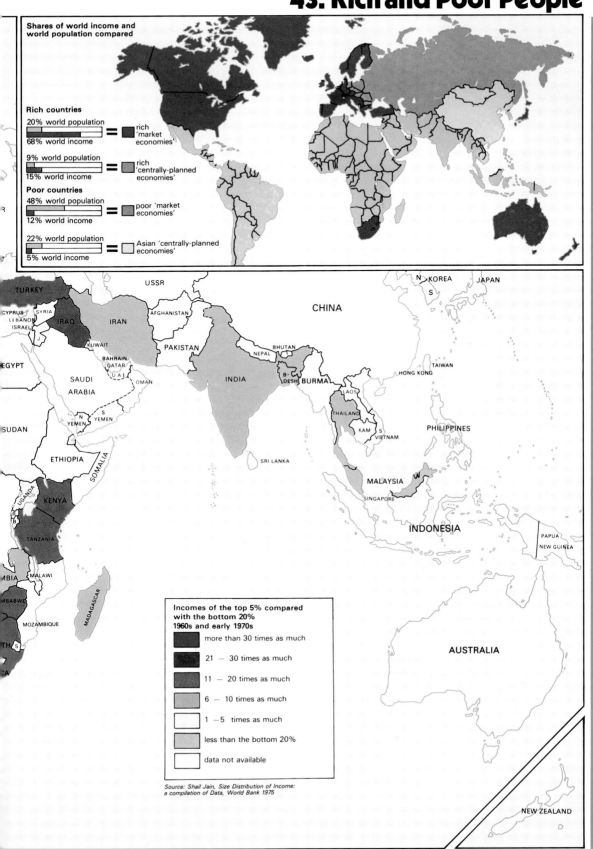

Shares of world income and
world population compared

Rich countries

20% world population
68% world income
= rich 'market economies'

9% world population
15% world income
= rich 'centrally-planned economies'

Poor countries

48% world population
12% world income
= poor 'market economies'

22% world population
5% world income
= Asian 'centrally-planned economies'

**Incomes of the top 5% compared
with the bottom 20%
1960s and early 1970s**

more than 30 times as much

21 — 30 times as much

11 — 20 times as much

6 — 10 times as much

1 — 5 times as much

less than the bottom 20%

data not available

Source: Shail Jain, Size Distribution of Income:
a compilation of Data, World Bank 1975

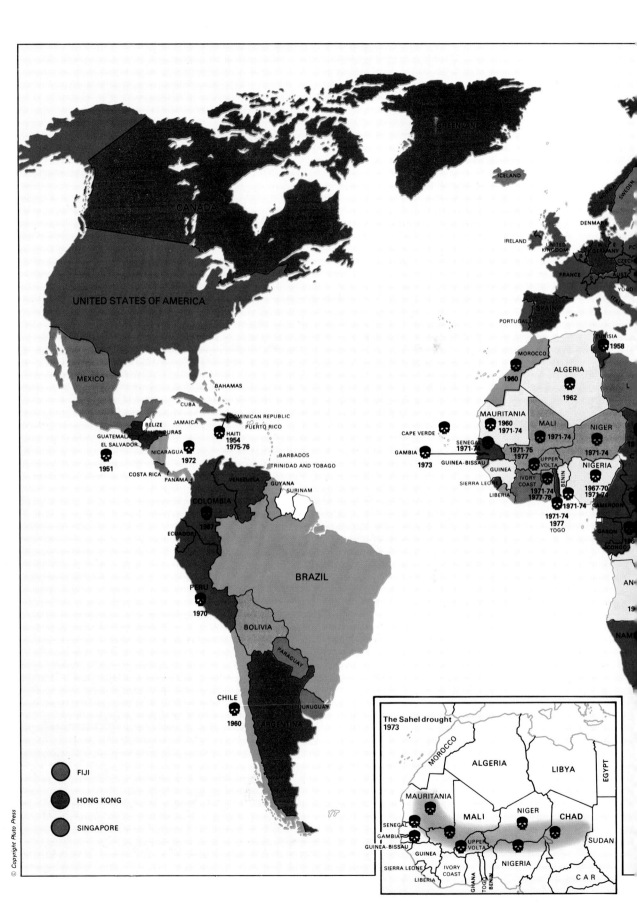

CANADA

GREENLAND

ICELAND

UNITED STATES OF AMERICA

IRELAND

UNITED
KINGDOM

DENMARK

SWEDEN

FRANCE

WEST
GERMANY

CZECH

AUST

YUGO

ITALY

SPAIN

PORTUGAL

MEXICO

BAHAMAS

CUBA

BELIZE

JAMAICA

GUATEMALA

HONDURAS

EL SALVADOR

NICARAGUA

1951

COSTA RICA

PANAMA

DOMINICAN REPUBLIC

PUERTO RICO

HAITI
1954
1975-76

1972

BARBADOS

TRINIDAD AND TOBAGO

VENEZUELA

GUYANA

SURINAM

COLOMBIA

1987

ECUADOR

PERU

1970

BRAZIL

BOLIVIA

PARAGUAY

URUGUAY

CHILE

1960

ARGENTINA

TUNISIA
1958

MOROCCO

1960

ALGERIA

1962

L

MAURITANIA
1960
1971-74

MALI
1971-74

NIGER

1971-74

CAPE VERDE

GAMBIA

1973

SENEGAL
1971-74
1977

GUINEA-BISSAU

UPPER
VOLTA

1971-75
1977

GUINEA

SIERRA LEONE

LIBERIA

IVORY
COAST

1971-74
1977-78

BENIN

1971-74

NIGERIA

1967-70
1971-74

CAMEROON

1971-74
1977
TOGO

GABON

CONGO

AN

NAM

FIJI

HONG KONG

SINGAPORE

The Sahel drought
1973

MOROCCO

ALGERIA

LIBYA

EGYPT

MAURITANIA

SENEGAL

GAMBIA

GUINEA-BISSAU

GUINEA

SIERRA LEONE

LIBERIA

MALI

NIGER

CHAD

SUDAN

UPPER
VOLTA

IVORY
COAST

GHANA

TOGO

BENIN

NIGERIA

CAR

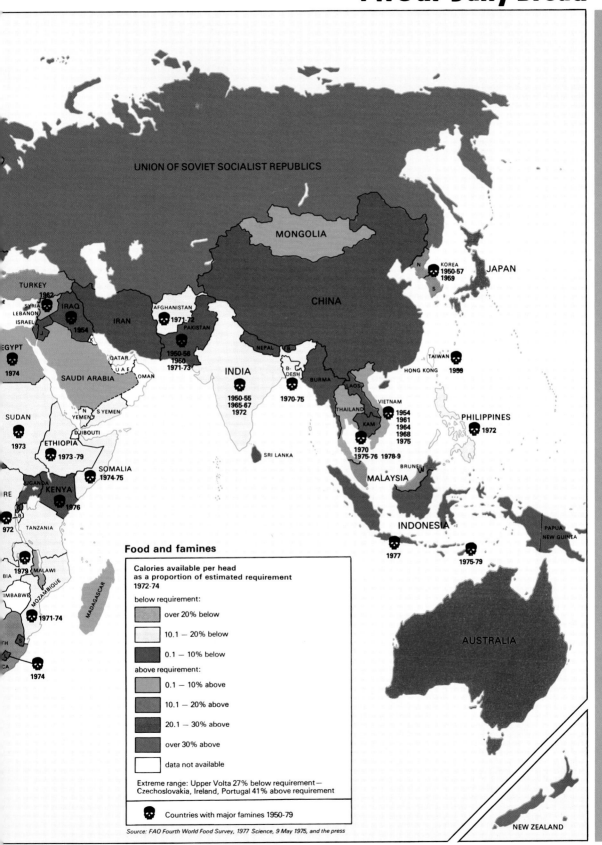

UNION OF SOVIET SOCIALIST REPUBLICS

MONGOLIA

TURKEY
1962

SYRIA
LEBANON
ISRAEL
IRAQ
1954

EGYPT
1974

IRAN

AFGHANISTAN
1971-72

PAKISTAN
1950-56
1960
1971-73

CHINA

KOREA
1950-57
1959

JAPAN

QATAR
U A E
OMAN

SAUDI ARABIA

NEPAL

INDIA
1950-55
1965-67
1972

B-
DESH
1970-75

BURMA

TAIWAN
1959

HONG KONG

SUDAN
1973

N
YEMEN
S YEMEN

DJIBOUTI

ETHIOPIA
1973-79

SOMALIA
1974-75

SRI LANKA

LAOS

THAILAND

VIETNAM
1954
1961
1964
1968
1975

KAM

PHILIPPINES
1972

UGANDA
KENYA
1976

1970
1975-76 **1978-9**

BRUNEI

MALAYSIA

RE

TANZANIA
972

1979 MALAWI

BIA

IMBABWE

MOZAMBIQUE

MADAGASCAR

1971-74

PAPUA
NEW GUINEA

INDONESIA

1977

1975-79

FH
S

CA
1974

AUSTRALIA

Food and famines

Calories available per head
as a proportion of estimated requirement
1972-74

below requirement:

over 20% below

10.1 — 20% below

0.1 — 10% below

above requirement:

0.1 — 10% above

10.1 — 20% above

20.1 — 30% above

over 30% above

data not available

Extreme range: Upper Volta 27% below requirement—
Czechoslovakia, Ireland, Portugal 41% above requirement

☠ Countries with major famines 1950-79

NEW ZEALAND

Source: FAO Fourth World Food Survey, 1977 Science, 9 May 1975, and the press

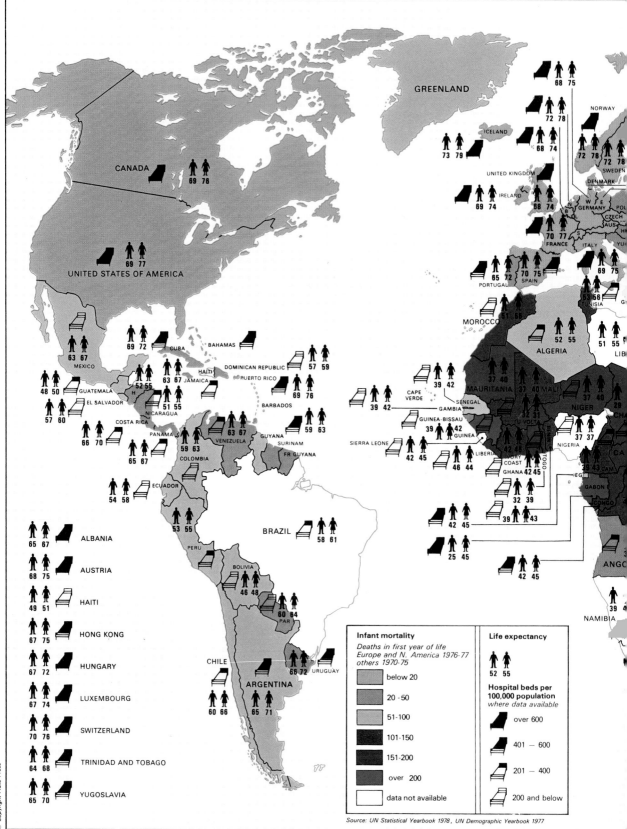

Source: UN Statistical Yearbook 1978, UN Demographic Yearbook 1977

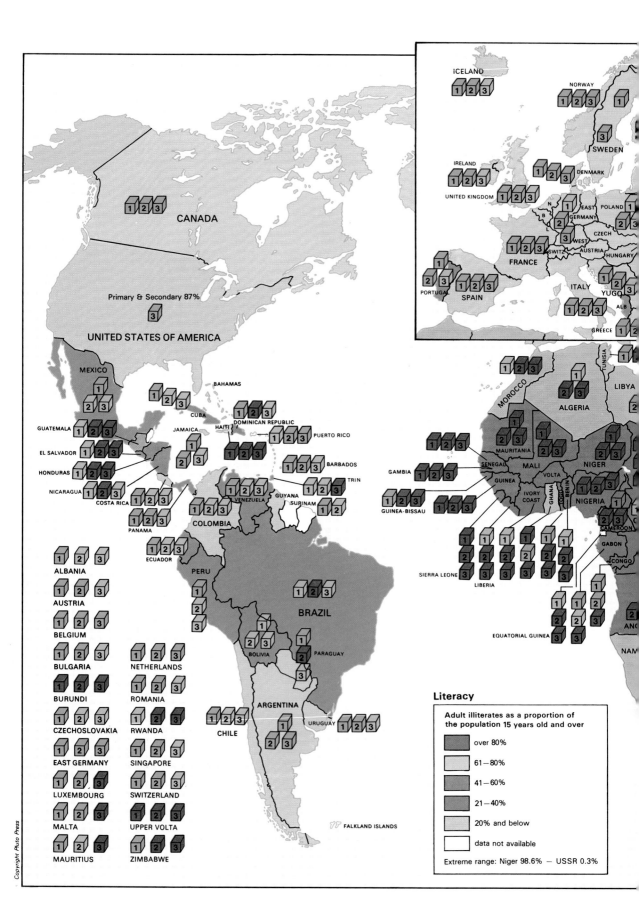

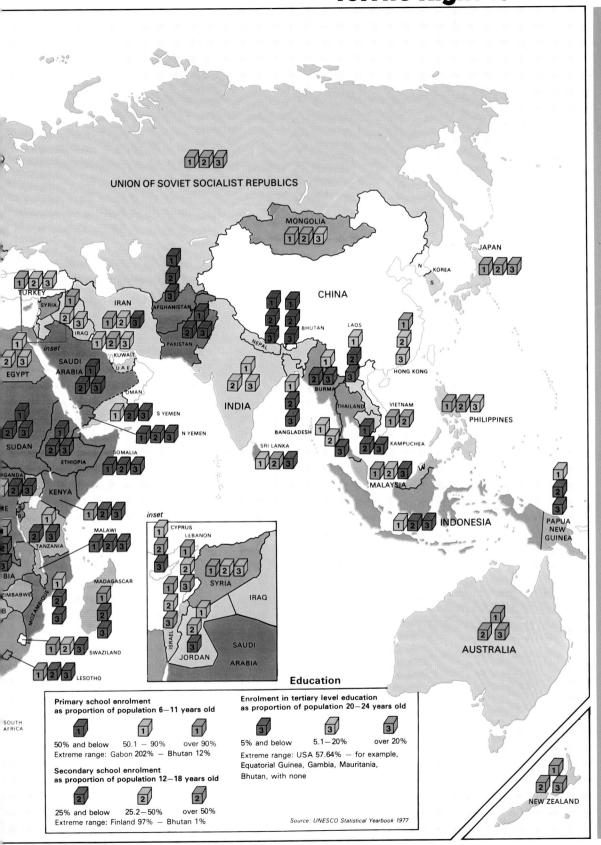

UNION OF SOVIET SOCIALIST REPUBLICS

MONGOLIA

JAPAN

KOREA
N
S

TURKEY

SYRIA

IRAN

AFGHANISTAN

IRAQ

inset

KUWAIT

EGYPT

SAUDI
ARABIA

U.A.E.

OMAN

PAKISTAN

NEPAL

CHINA

BHUTAN

LAOS

HONG KONG

INDIA

BURMA

THAILAND

VIETNAM

PHILIPPINES

S YEMEN

N YEMEN

SUDAN

ETHIOPIA

SOMALIA

BANGLADESH

SRI LANKA

KAMPUCHEA

UGANDA

KENYA

MALAYSIA

INDONESIA

PAPUA
NEW
GUINEA

TANZANIA

MALAWI

MADAGASCAR

ZIMBABWE

MOZAMBIQUE

SWAZILAND

LESOTHO

SOUTH
AFRICA

inset

CYPRUS

LEBANON

SYRIA

IRAQ

ISRAEL

JORDAN

SAUDI
ARABIA

AUSTRALIA

NEW ZEALAND

Education

Primary school enrolment
as proportion of population 6—11 years old

50% and below   50.1 — 90%   over 90%
Extreme range: Gabon 202% — Bhutan 12%

Secondary school enrolment
as proportion of population 12—18 years old

25% and below   25.2—50%   over 50%
Extreme range: Finland 97% — Bhutan 1%

Enrolment in tertiary level education
as proportion of population 20—24 years old

5% and below   5.1—20%   over 20%

Extreme range: USA 57.64% — for example,
Equatorial Guinea, Gambia, Mauritania,
Bhutan, with none

Source: UNESCO Statistical Yearbook 1977

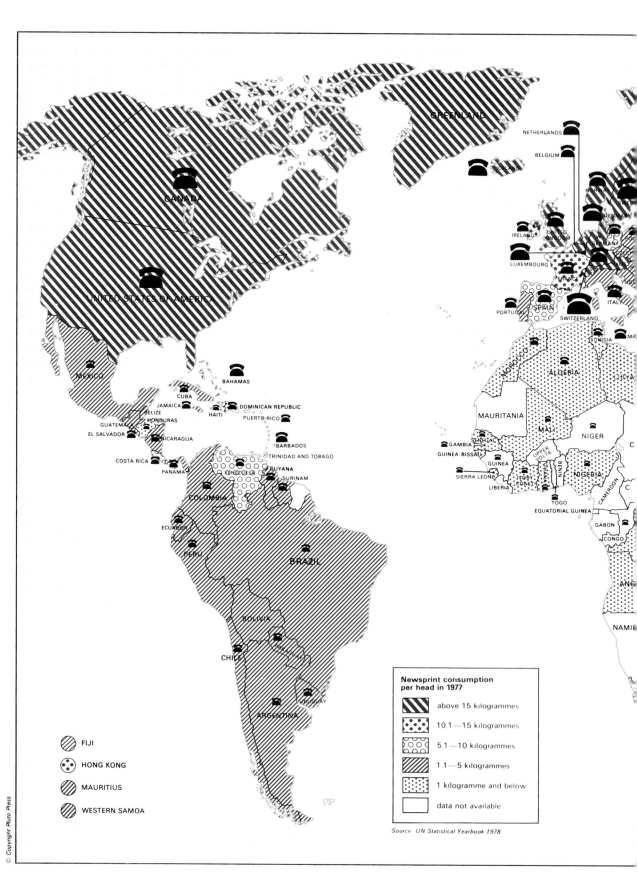

GREENLAND

NETHERLANDS
BELGIUM
SCOTLAND
NORWAY
DENMARK
IRELAND
UNITED KINGDOM
WEST GERMANY
LUXEMBOURG
FRANCE
ITALY
PORTUGAL
SPAIN
SWITZERLAND
TUNISIA
MOROCCO
ALGERIA
LIBYA

CANADA

UNITED STATES OF AMERICA

MEXICO

BAHAMAS

CUBA
JAMAICA
BELIZE
HONDURAS
GUATEMALA
EL SALVADOR
NICARAGUA
COSTA RICA
PANAMA

HAITI
DOMINICAN REPUBLIC
PUERTO RICO

BARBADOS
TRINIDAD AND TOBAGO

MAURITANIA
MALI
NIGER

GAMBIA
SENEGAL
GUINEA-BISSAU
GUINEA
SIERRA LEONE
LIBERIA
UPPER VOLTA
IVORY COAST
GHANA
TOGO
BENIN
NIGERIA
CAMEROON

EQUATORIAL GUINEA
GABON
CONGO

COLOMBIA
VENEZUELA
GUYANA
SURINAM

ECUADOR

PERU

BRAZIL

BOLIVIA

CHILE

PARAGUAY

URUGUAY

ARGENTINA

ANGOLA

NAMIBIA

FIJI

HONG KONG

MAURITIUS

WESTERN SAMOA

**Newsprint consumption
per head in 1977**

	above 15 kilogrammes
	10.1—15 kilogrammes
	5.1—10 kilogrammes
	1.1—5 kilogrammes
	1 kilogramme and below
	data not available

Source UN Statistical Yearbook 1978

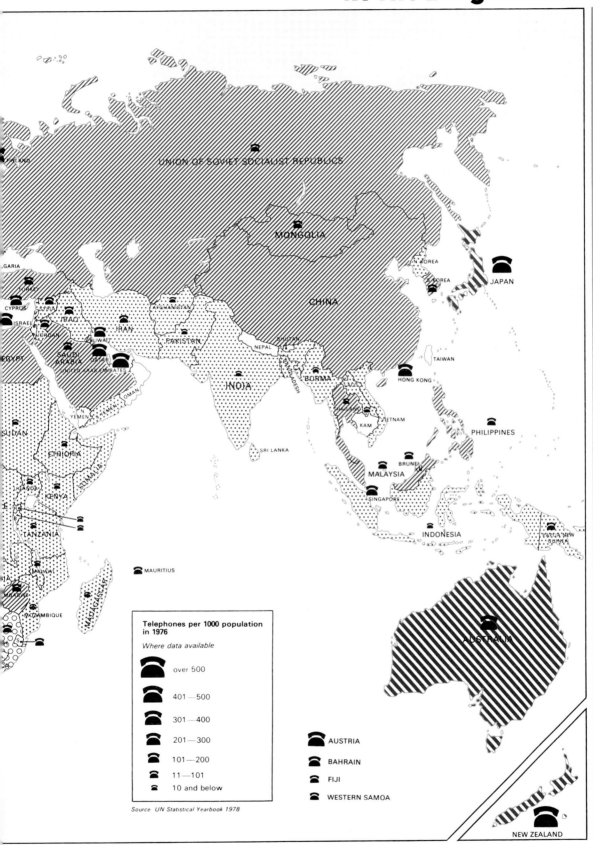

FINLAND

UNION OF SOVIET SOCIALIST REPUBLICS

MONGOLIA

N. KOREA

S. KOREA

JAPAN

GARIA

TURKEY

CYPRUS

SYRIA

ISRAEL

JORDAN

IRAQ

KUWAIT

SAUDI ARABIA

QATAR

UNITED ARAB EMIRATES

EGYPT

N. YEMEN

S. YEMEN

OMAN

IRAN

AFGHANISTAN

PAKISTAN

NEPAL

BHUTAN

INDIA

BANGLADESH

CHINA

TAIWAN

HONG KONG

BURMA

LAOS

THAILAND

KAM

VIETNAM

PHILIPPINES

SRI LANKA

SUDAN

ETHIOPIA

SOMALIA

UGANDA

KENYA

TANZANIA

MALAWI

MAURITIUS

MADAGASCAR

ZIMBABWE

MOZAMBIQUE

BRUNEI

MALAYSIA

SINGAPORE

INDONESIA

PAPUA NEW GUINEA

AUSTRALIA

NEW ZEALAND

Telephones per 1000 population in 1976

Where data available

over 500

401 — 500

301 — 400

201 — 300

101 — 200

11 — 101

10 and below

AUSTRIA

BAHRAIN

FIJI

WESTERN SAMOA

Source UN Statistical Yearbook 1978

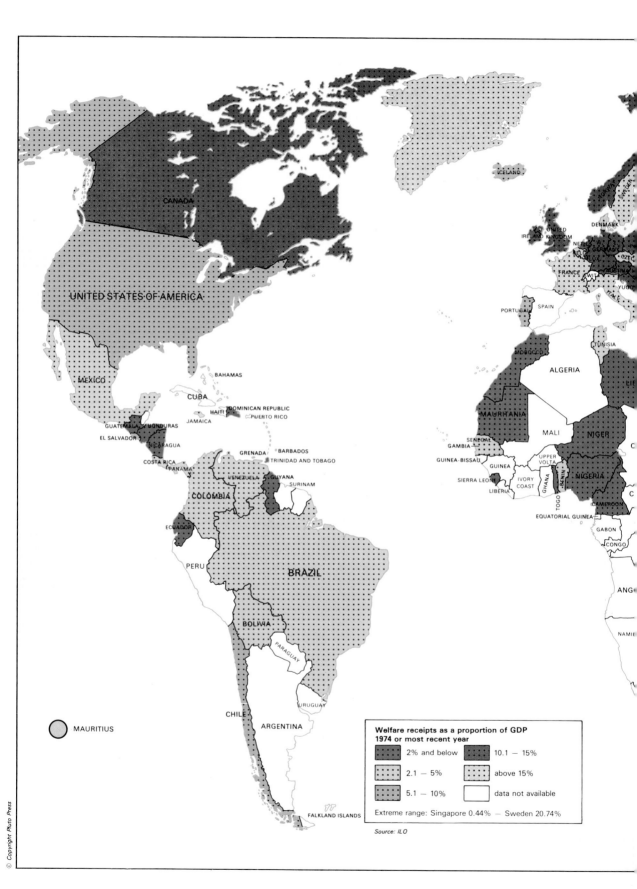

MAURITIUS

Welfare receipts as a proportion of GDP
1974 or most recent year

2% and below		10.1 — 15%
2.1 — 5%		above 15%
5.1 — 10%		data not available

Extreme range: Singapore 0.44% — Sweden 20.74%

Source: ILO

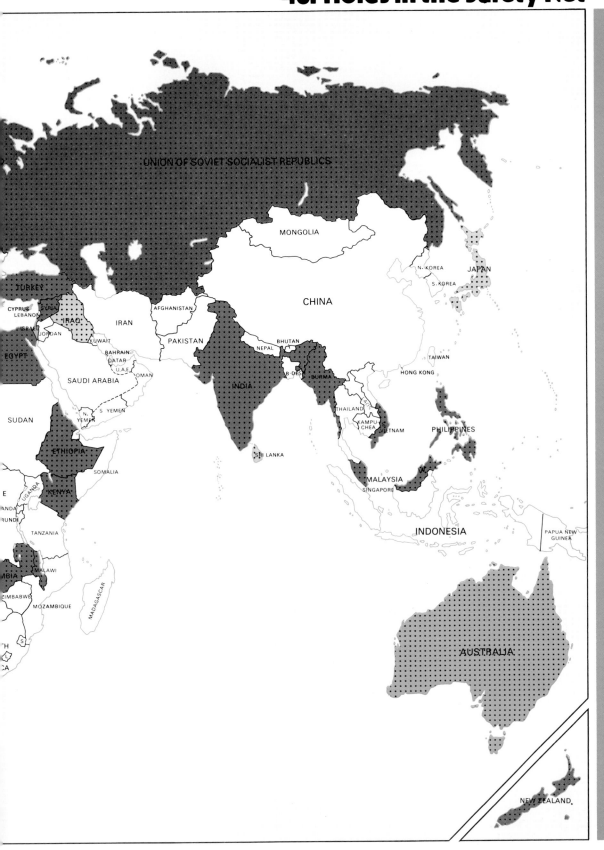

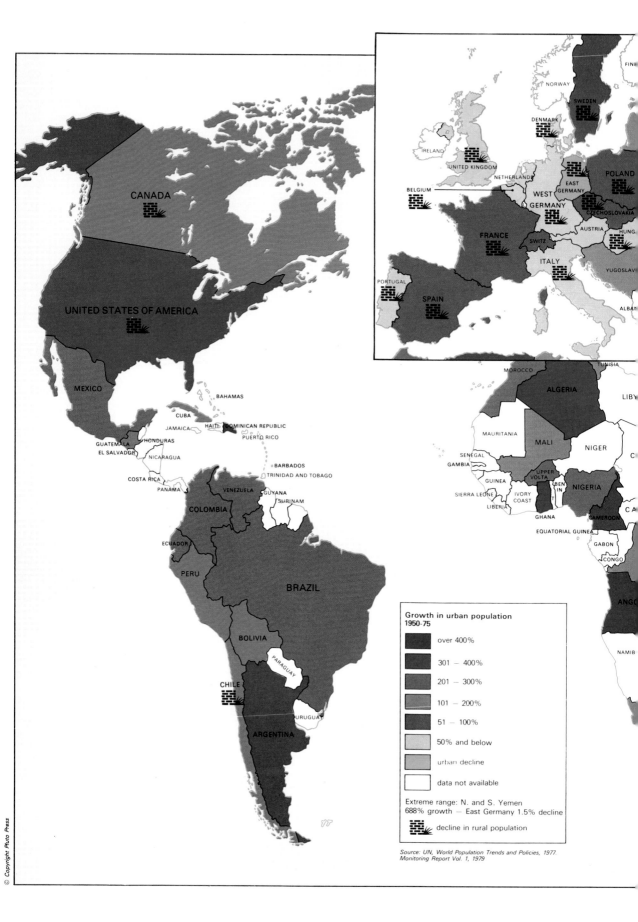

CANADA

UNITED STATES OF AMERICA

MEXICO

BAHAMAS
CUBA
JAMAICA
HAITI DOMINICAN REPUBLIC
PUERTO RICO
GUATEMALA HONDURAS
EL SALVADOR
NICARAGUA
BARBADOS
TRINIDAD AND TOBAGO
COSTA RICA
PANAMA
VENEZUELA
COLOMBIA GUYANA
SURINAM
ECUADOR
PERU
BRAZIL
BOLIVIA
PARAGUAY
CHILE
URUGUAY
ARGENTINA

NORWAY
FINI
SWEDEN
DENMARK
IRELAND
UNITED KINGDOM
NETHERLANDS
BELGIUM
WEST GERMANY
EAST GERMANY
POLAND
CZECHOSLOVAKIA
AUSTRIA
HUNG
FRANCE
SWITZ
ITALY
YUGOSLAVI
PORTUGAL
SPAIN
ALBAN

MOROCCO
TUNISIA
ALGERIA
LIBY
MAURITANIA
MALI
NIGER
SENEGAL
GAMBIA
GUINEA
UPPER VOLTA
BEN IN
NIGERIA
CI
SIERRA LEONE
IVORY COAST
LIBERIA
GHANA
CAMEROON
CA
EQUATORIAL GUINEA
GABON
CONGO
ANGO
NAMIB

Growth in urban population
1950-75

over 400%

301 — 400%

201 — 300%

101 — 200%

51 — 100%

50% and below

urban decline

data not available

Extreme range: N. and S. Yemen
688% growth — East Germany 1.5% decline

decline in rural population

Source: UN, World Population Trends and Policies, 1977.
Monitoring Report Vol. 1, 1979

© Copyright Pluto Press

UNION OF SOVIET SOCIALIST REPUBLICS

MONGOLIA

TURKEY

CYPRUS
LEB
SYRIA
ISRAEL
JORDAN
IRAQ
KUWAIT

IRAN

AFGHANISTAN

CHINA

N KOREA
S

JAPAN

EGYPT

QATAR
U A E
OMAN

PAKISTAN

NEPAL

TAIWAN

HONG KONG

SAUDI ARABIA

N
YEMEN
S YEMEN

INDIA

DESH
BURMA

LAOS

THAILAND

KAM

VIETNAM

PHILIPPINES

SUDAN

ETHIOPIA

SRI LANKA

MALAYSIA

SOMALIA

UGAN
DA
KENYA

INDONESIA

PAPUA
NEW
GUINEA

TANZANIA

MALAWI

BIA

MBABWE
MOZAMBIQUE

MADAGASCAR

AUSTRALIA

TH
S

ICA

NEW ZEALAND

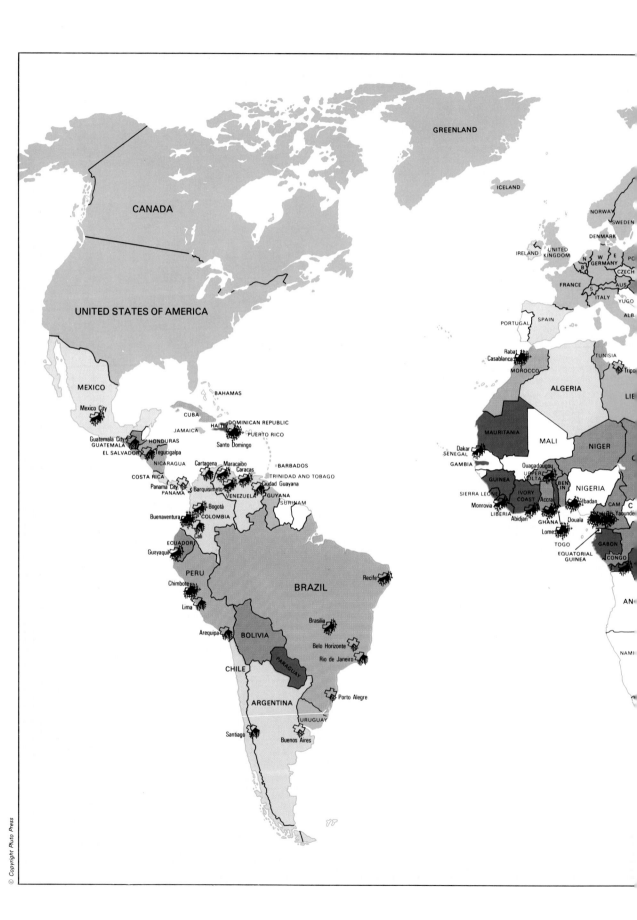

GREENLAND

CANADA

UNITED STATES OF AMERICA

MEXICO

Mexico City

BAHAMAS

CUBA

JAMAICA

HAITI

DOMINICAN REPUBLIC

PUERTO RICO

Santo Domingo

Guatemala City

GUATEMALA

HONDURAS

Tegucigalpa

EL SALVADOR

NICARAGUA

COSTA RICA

Panama City

PANAMA

BARBADOS

TRINIDAD AND TOBAGO

Cartagena

Maracaibo

Caracas

Barquisimeto

Ciudad Guayana

VENEZUELA

GUYANA

SURINAM

Bogotá

Buenaventura

COLOMBIA

Cali

ECUADOR

Guayaquil

PERU

Chimbote

Lima

Arequipa

BOLIVIA

BRAZIL

Recife

Brasilia

Belo Horizonte

Rio de Janeiro

PARAGUAY

CHILE

Porto Alegre

ARGENTINA

URUGUAY

Santiago

Buenos Aires

ICELAND

NORWAY

SWEDEN

DENMARK

IRELAND

UNITED KINGDOM

N

W E

S

B

GERMANY

PO

CZECH

AUS

YUGO

ALB.

FRANCE

ITALY

PORTUGAL

SPAIN

Rabat

Casablanca

MOROCCO

TUNISIA

Tripoli

ALGERIA

LIE

MAURITANIA

MALI

NIGER

Dakar

SENEGAL

GAMBIA

Ouagadougou

UPPER VOLTA

BEN IN

NIGERIA

GUINEA

SIERRA LEONE

IVORY COAST

Accra

Ibadan

CAM

C

Monrovia

LIBERIA

Abidjan

GHANA

Lomé

Douala

Yabundé

TOGO

GABON

EQUATORIAL GUINEA

CONGO

AN

NAMI

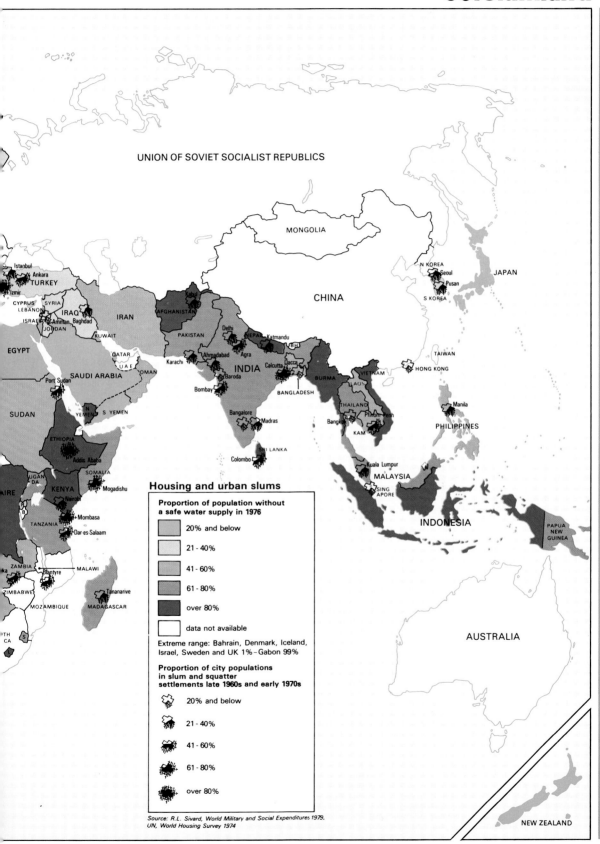

Housing and urban slums

Proportion of population without a safe water supply in 1976

- 20% and below
- 21 - 40%
- 41 - 60%
- 61 - 80%
- over 80%
- data not available

Extreme range: Bahrain, Denmark, Iceland, Israel, Sweden and UK 1% – Gabon 99%

Proportion of city populations in slum and squatter settlements late 1960s and early 1970s

- 20% and below
- 21 - 40%
- 41 - 60%
- 61 - 80%
- over 80%

Source: R.L. Sivard, World Military and Social Expenditures 1979.
UN, World Housing Survey 1974

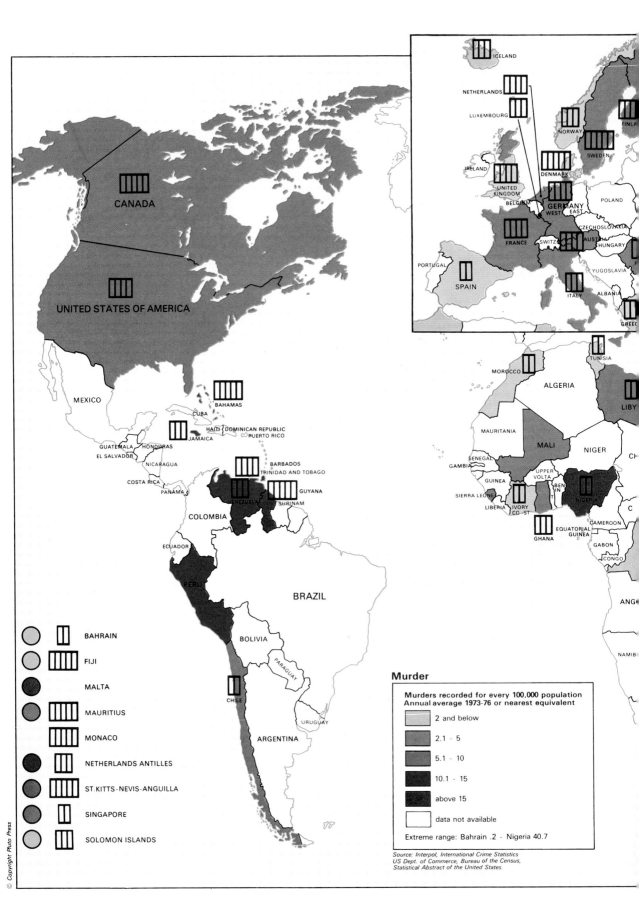

Murder

**Murders recorded for every 100,000 population
Annual average 1973-76 or nearest equivalent**

	2 and below
	2.1 - 5
	5.1 - 10
	10.1 - 15
	above 15
	data not available

Extreme range: Bahrain .2 - Nigeria 40.7

Source: Interpol, International Crime Statistics
US Dept. of Commerce, Bureau of the Census,
Statistical Abstract of the United States.

BAHRAIN

FIJI

MALTA

MAURITIUS

MONACO

NETHERLANDS ANTILLES

ST. KITTS - NEVIS - ANGUILLA

SINGAPORE

SOLOMON ISLANDS

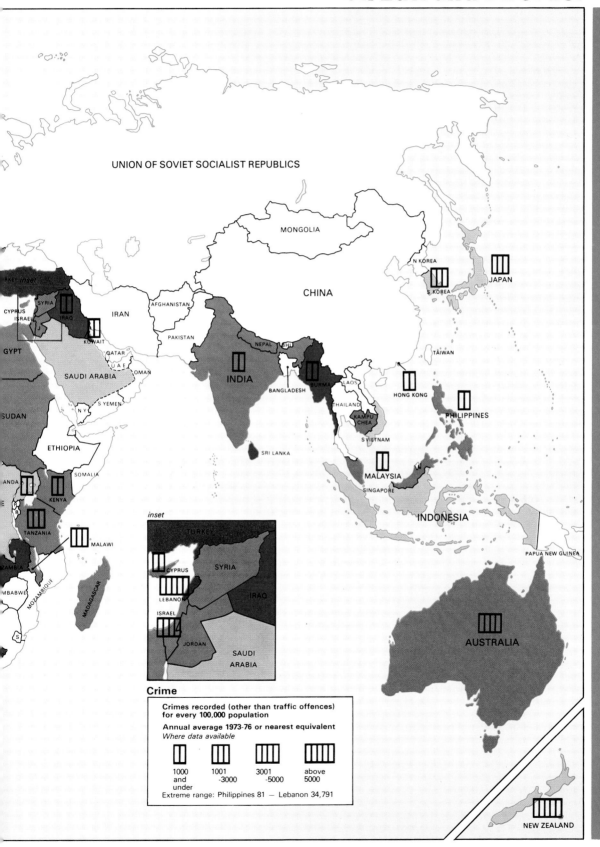

51. Law and Disorder

UNION OF SOVIET SOCIALIST REPUBLICS

MONGOLIA

CHINA

N KOREA

S KOREA

JAPAN

TURKEY *inset*

CYPRUS

SYRIA

ISRAEL

IRAQ

IRAN

AFGHANISTAN

KUWAIT

QATAR

U A E

OMAN

PAKISTAN

NEPAL

BHU

INDIA

BANGLADESH

BURMA

LAOS

TAIWAN

HONG KONG

THAILAND

PHILIPPINES

GYPT

SAUDI ARABIA

N Y

S YEMEN

SUDAN

ETHIOPIA

SOMALIA

ANDA

KENYA

B

TANZANIA

MALAWI

ZAMBIA

MBABWE

MOZAMBIQUE

MADAGASCAR

S

SRI LANKA

KAMPU CHEA

S VIETNAM

MALAYSIA

SINGAPORE

INDONESIA

PAPUA NEW GUINEA

AUSTRALIA

inset

TURKEY

CYPRUS

SYRIA

LEBANON

IRAQ

ISRAEL

JORDAN

SAUDI ARABIA

Crime

Crimes recorded (other than traffic offences) for every 100,000 population

Annual average 1973-76 or nearest equivalent
Where data available

| 1000 and under | 1001 -3000 | 3001 -5000 | above 5000 |

Extreme range: Philippines 81 — Lebanon 34,791

NEW ZEALAND

Unemployment throughout the world is
enormous and growing. This is admitted
everywhere, but official statistics tend to
disguise rather than reveal the extent. For this
reason it has been impossible to produce a
useful map on the problem. Instead this
diagram shows a projected growth in world
population and its division into employed
labour force and inactive population, 1750-2150

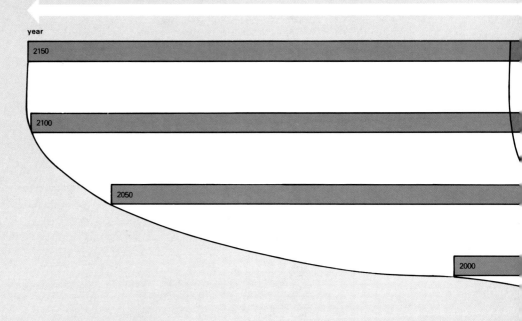

year

2150

2100

2050

2000

**Projected growth in world population
and division into
employed labour force and inactive population**

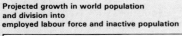
employed labour force

inactive population including unemployed

world population

Source: ILO

people

| 11000 million | 10000 million | 9000 million | 8000 million | 7000 million | 6000 million | 5000 million |

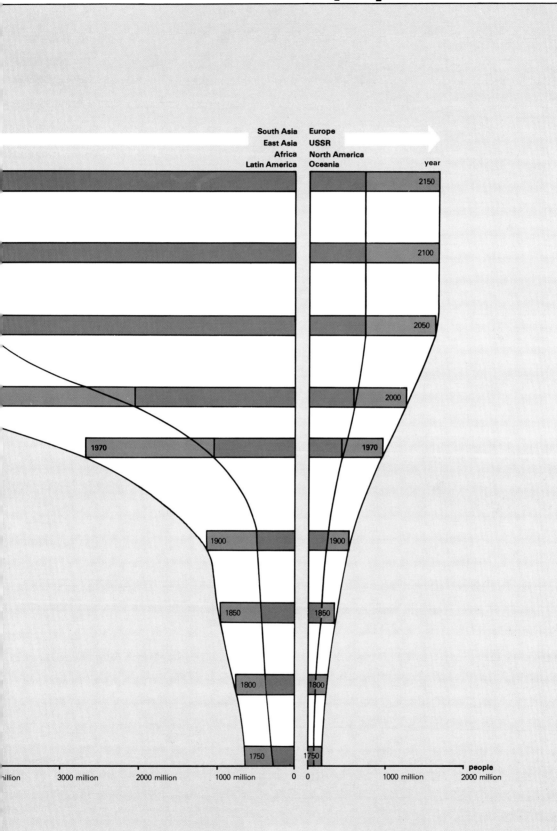

South Asia   Europe
East Asia   USSR
Africa   North America
Latin America   Oceania

year

2150

2100

2050

2000

1970   1970

1900   1900

1850   1850

1800   1800

1750   1750

million   3000 million   2000 million   1000 million   0   0   1000 million   2000 million

people

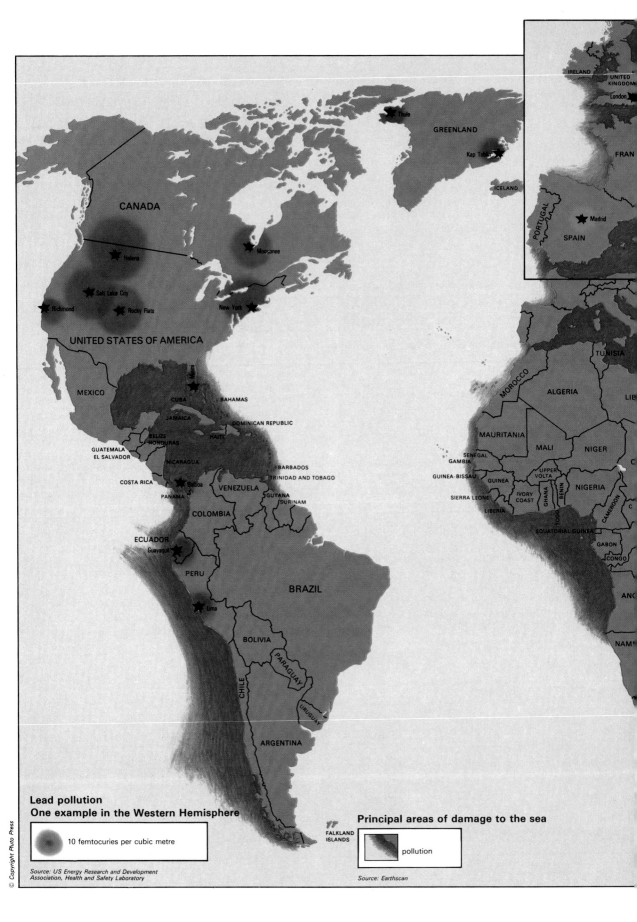

GREENLAND

Thule

Kap Tobin

ICELAND

CANADA

Helena

Moosonee

Salt Lake City

Richmond

Rocky Flats

New York

UNITED STATES OF AMERICA

MEXICO

Miami

CUBA

BAHAMAS

JAMAICA

DOMINICAN REPUBLIC

BELIZE

HONDURAS

HAITI

GUATEMALA

EL SALVADOR

NICARAGUA

BARBADOS

TRINIDAD AND TOBAGO

COSTA RICA

Balboa

VENEZUELA

PANAMA

GUYANA

SURINAM

COLOMBIA

ECUADOR

Guayaquil

PERU

Lima

BRAZIL

BOLIVIA

PARAGUAY

CHILE

URUGUAY

ARGENTINA

FALKLAND

ISLANDS

IRELAND

UNITED

KINGDOM

London

FRAN

PORTUGAL

Madrid

SPAIN

TUNISIA

MOROCCO

ALGERIA

LIB

MAURITANIA

MALI

NIGER

SENEGAL

GAMBIA

GUINEA-BISSAU

GUINEA

UPPER

VOLTA

NIGERIA

SIERRA LEONE

IVORY

COAST

GHANA

TOGO

BENIN

CAMEROON

C

LIBERIA

EQUATORIAL GUINEA

GABON

CONGO

ANG

NAM

Lead pollution
One example in the Western Hemisphere

10 femtocuries per cubic metre

Principal areas of damage to the sea

pollution

Source: US Energy Research and Development
Association, Health and Safety Laboratory

Source: Earthscan

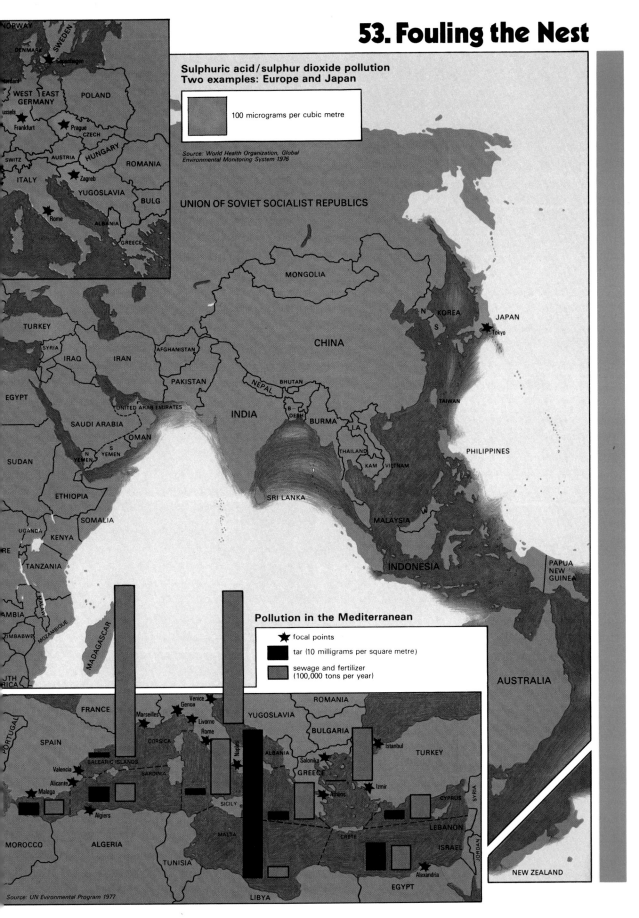

Sulphuric acid/sulphur dioxide pollution
Two examples: Europe and Japan

100 micrograms per cubic metre

*Source: World Health Organization, Global
Environmental Monitoring System 1976*

UNION OF SOVIET SOCIALIST REPUBLICS

Pollution in the Mediterranean

★ focal points

■ tar (10 milligrams per square metre)

▨ sewage and fertilizer
(100,000 tons per year)

Source: UN Evironmental Program 1977

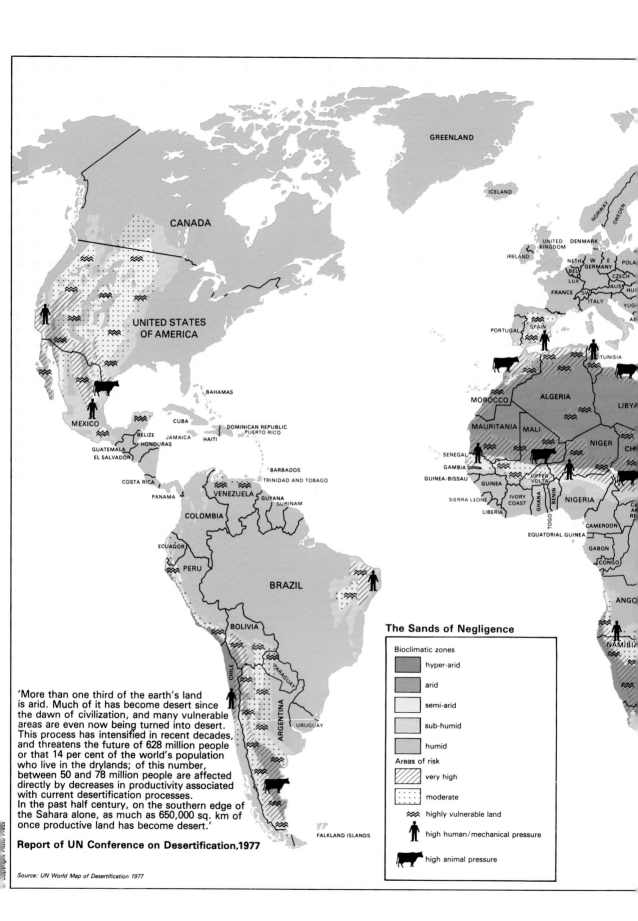

GREENLAND

CANADA

UNITED STATES
OF AMERICA

BAHAMAS

CUBA
DOMINICAN REPUBLIC
PUERTO RICO
JAMAICA HAITI
MEXICO
BELIZE
GUATEMALA HONDURAS
EL SALVADOR

COSTA RICA
PANAMA
BARBADOS
TRINIDAD AND TOBAGO
VENEZUELA
GUYANA
SURINAM
COLOMBIA

ECUADOR
PERU
BRAZIL

BOLIVIA

CHILE
PARAGUAY
ARGENTINA
URUGUAY

FALKLAND ISLANDS

ICELAND

NORWAY SWEDEN

UNITED DENMARK
KINGDOM
IRELAND
NETH
BEL GERMANY POLA
LUX
FRANCE SW CZECH
AUS HU
ITALY
YUG
PORTUGAL SPAIN
TUNISIA

MOROCCO ALGERIA LIBYA

MAURITANIA MALI NIGER CH

SENEGAL
GAMBIA UPPER
GUINEA-BISSAU GUINEA VOLTA NIGERIA
SIERRA LEONE IVORY
COAST GHANA BENIN
LIBERIA TOGO
CAMEROON
EQUATORIAL GUINEA
GABON
CONGO

ANGO

NAMIBIA

The Sands of Negligence

Bioclimatic zones

- hyper-arid
- arid
- semi-arid
- sub-humid
- humid

Areas of risk

- ⟍⟍⟍ very high
- ⋯⋯ moderate
- ≋ highly vulnerable land
- 🧍 high human/mechanical pressure
- 🐄 high animal pressure

'More than one third of the earth's land
is arid. Much of it has become desert since
the dawn of civilization, and many vulnerable
areas are even now being turned into desert.
This process has intensified in recent decades,
and threatens the future of 628 million people
or that 14 per cent of the world's population
who live in the drylands; of this number,
between 50 and 78 million people are affected
directly by decreases in productivity associated
with current desertification processes.
In the past half century, on the southern edge of
the Sahara alone, as much as 650,000 sq. km of
once productive land has become desert.'

Report of UN Conference on Desertification,1977

Source: UN World Map of Desertification 1977

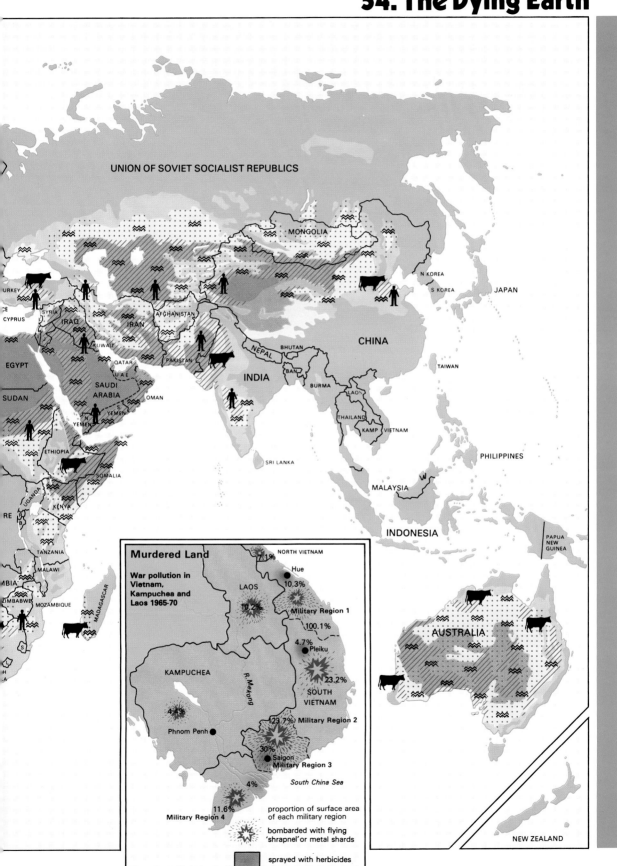

UNION OF SOVIET SOCIALIST REPUBLICS

MONGOLIA

N KOREA

S KOREA

JAPAN

TURKEY

CYPRUS

SYRIA

IRAQ

KUWAIT

QATAR

U.A.E.

OMAN

AFGHANISTAN

IRAN

PAKISTAN

NEPAL

BHUTAN

BAN

CHINA

TAIWAN

EGYPT

SAUDI ARABIA

N YEMEN

YEMEN

SUDAN

INDIA

BURMA

LAOS

THAILAND

KAMP

VIETNAM

SRI LANKA

PHILIPPINES

ETHIOPIA

SOMALIA

UGANDA

KENYA

MALAYSIA

TANZANIA

MALAWI

BIA

ZIMBABWE

MOZAMBIQUE

MADAGASCAR

INDONESIA

PAPUA NEW GUINEA

AUSTRALIA

Murdered Land

War pollution in Vietnam, Kampuchea and Laos 1965-70

NORTH VIETNAM

7.1%

Hue

10.3%

LAOS

10.2%

Military Region 1

100.1%

4.7% Pleiku

23.2%

SOUTH VIETNAM

KAMPUCHEA

R. Mekong

4.4%

23.7% **Military Region 2**

Phnom Penh

30%

Saigon

Military Region 3

4%

South China Sea

11.6%

Military Region 4

proportion of surface area of each military region

bombarded with flying 'shrapnel' or metal shards

sprayed with herbicides

NEW ZEALAND

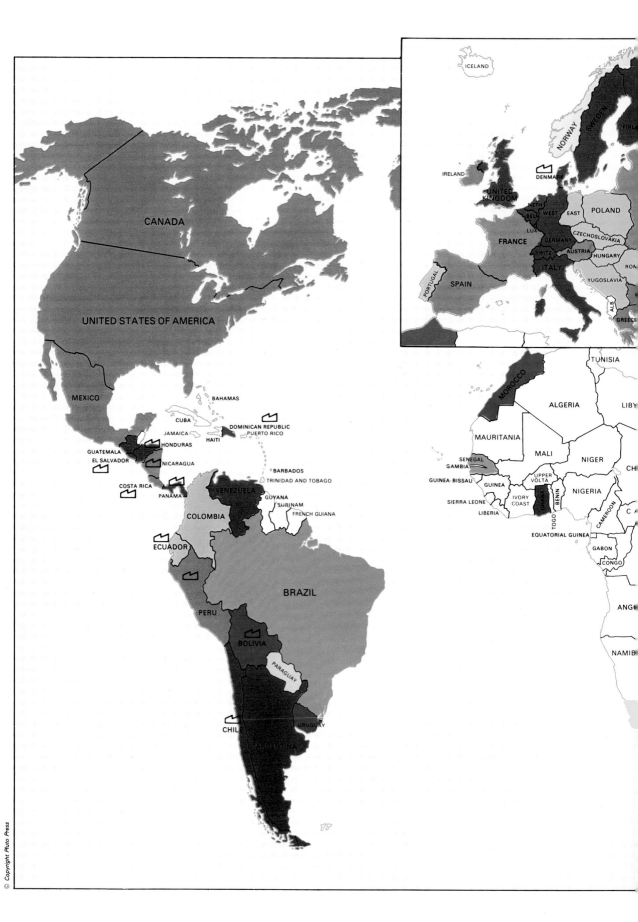

CANADA

UNITED STATES OF AMERICA

MEXICO

BAHAMAS
CUBA
JAMAICA
HAITI
DOMINICAN REPUBLIC
PUERTO RICO
GUATEMALA
HONDURAS
EL SALVADOR
NICARAGUA
COSTA RICA
PANAMA
VENEZUELA
BARBADOS
TRINIDAD AND TOBAGO
GUYANA
SURINAM
FRENCH GUIANA
COLOMBIA
ECUADOR
PERU
BRAZIL
BOLIVIA
PARAGUAY
CHILE
URUGUAY
ARGENTINA

ICELAND
NORWAY
SWEDEN
FINLA
IRELAND
DENMARK
UNITED KINGDOM
NETH
BEL
WEST
EAST
POLAND
LUX
CZECHOSLOVAKIA
FRANCE
GERMANY
AUSTRIA
SWITZ
HUNGARY
ROM
PORTUGAL
ITALY
YUGOSLAVIA
SPAIN
ALB
GREECE

TUNISIA
MOROCCO
ALGERIA
LIBYA
MAURITANIA
MALI
NIGER
CH
SENEGAL
GAMBIA
UPPER
VOLTA
GUINEA-BISSAU
GUINEA
NIGERIA
BENIN
SIERRA LEONE
IVORY
COAST
GHANA
TOGO
LIBERIA
CAMEROON
C A
EQUATORIAL GUINEA
GABON
CONGO
ANG
NAMIB

© Copyright Pluto Press

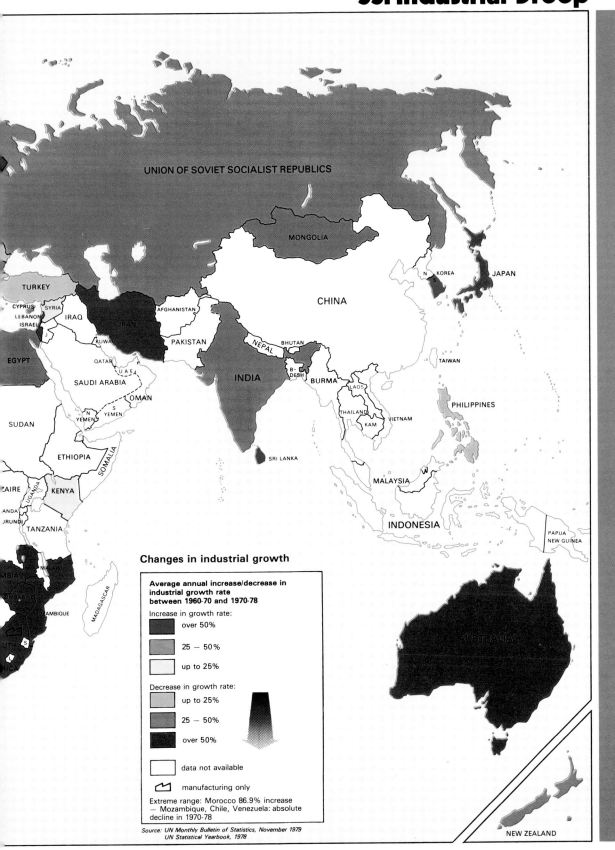

UNION OF SOVIET SOCIALIST REPUBLICS

MONGOLIA

CHINA

N. KOREA JAPAN

TURKEY

CYPRUS
SYRIA
LEBANON
ISRAEL
IRAQ
J
IRAN
AFGHANISTAN

KUWAIT

TAIWAN

EGYPT

QATAR
U.A.E.
SAUDI ARABIA
OMAN
N YEMEN
S YEMEN

PAKISTAN

NEPAL
BHUTAN
B-DESH
BURMA

INDIA

LAOS

THAILAND
KAM
VIETNAM

PHILIPPINES

SUDAN

ETHIOPIA

SOMALIA

SRI LANKA

AIRE UGANDA KENYA

ANDA
JRUNDI
TANZANIA

MADAGASCAR

MALAYSIA

INDONESIA

PAPUA
NEW GUINEA

MBIA MALAWI

BWE

AMBIQUE

UTH
S
RICA

AUSTRALIA

Changes in industrial growth

Average annual increase/decrease in industrial growth rate between 1960-70 and 1970-78

Increase in growth rate:

- over 50%
- 25 — 50%
- up to 25%

Decrease in growth rate:

- up to 25%
- 25 — 50%
- over 50%

- data not available

- manufacturing only

Extreme range: Morocco 86.9% increase — Mozambique, Chile, Venezuela: absolute decline in 1970-78

Source: UN Monthly Bulletin of Statistics, November 1979
UN Statistical Yearbook, 1978

NEW ZEALAND

GREENLAND

ICELAND
FAROE ISLANDS

NORWAY
SWEDEN

DENMARK

IRELAND
UNITED
KINGDOM

N
B
W
E
GERMANY

POL

CZECH

FRANCE
S
AUS
H
YU

ITALY

PORTUGAL
SPAIN

CANADA

UNITED STATES OF AMERICA

MEXICO

BAHAMAS

CUBA

HAITI
DOMINICAN REPUBLIC

BELIZE
JAMAICA
HONDURAS
GUATEMALA
EL SALVADOR
NICARAGUA
PUERTO RICO

COSTA RICA
PANAMA

BARBADOS
TRINIDAD AND TOBAGO

VENEZUELA
GUYANA
SURINAM

COLOMBIA

ECUADOR

PERU

BRAZIL

BOLIVIA

PARAGUAY

CHILE

URUGUAY

ARGENTINA

FALKLAND ISLANDS

TUNISIA

MOROCCO

ALGERIA

LIB

MAURITANIA

MALI

NIGER

CK

CAPE VERDE

SENEGAL
GAMBIA
GUINEA-BISSAU
GUINEA

UPPER
VOLTA

NIGERIA

SIERRA LEONE
IVORY
COAST

GHANA
BENIN
TOGO

C A

LIBERIA

CAMEROON

EQUATORIAL GUINEA

GABON
CONGO

ANG

NAMIE

○ BAHRAIN

● MAURITIUS

○ SINGAPORE

© Copyright Pluto Press

56. The First Inflationary Crest, 1974

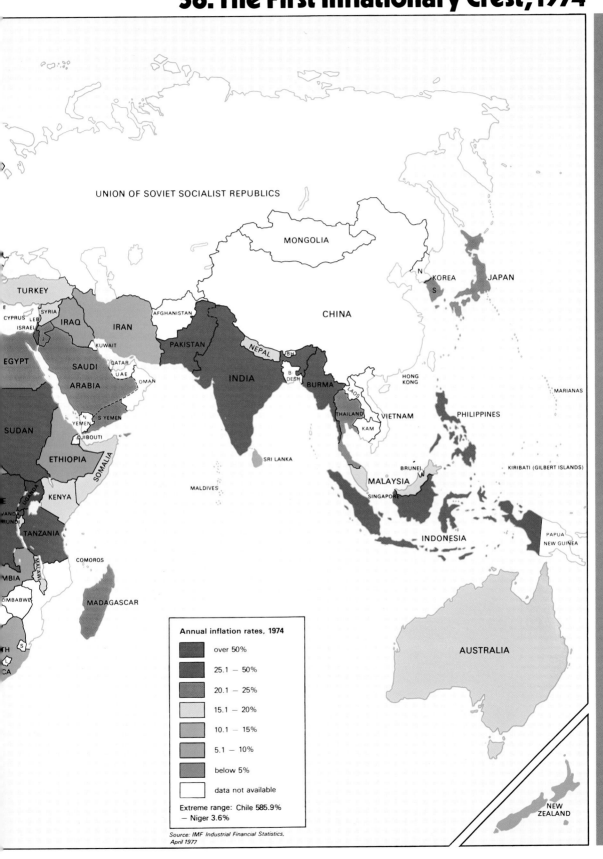

UNION OF SOVIET SOCIALIST REPUBLICS

MONGOLIA

TURKEY

E
CYPRUS LEB SYRIA
ISRAEL IRAQ IRAN
KUWAIT
EGYPT QATAR
SAUDI UAE
ARABIA OMAN
N
YEMEN S YEMEN
DJIBOUTI

SUDAN

ETHIOPIA SOMALIA

E
UGANDA KENYA
VANDA
RUNDI
TANZANIA

MBIA MALAWI COMOROS

ZIMBABWE MADAGASCAR

TH S CA

AFGHANISTAN

PAKISTAN NEPAL
BH
B DESH
INDIA BURMA

CHINA

KOREA JAPAN
N S

HONG KONG

LAOS
THAILAND VIETNAM
KAM

SRI LANKA

MALDIVES

PHILIPPINES

MARIANAS

KIRIBATI (GILBERT ISLANDS)

BRUNEI
MALAYSIA
SINGAPORE

INDONESIA

PAPUA
NEW GUINEA

AUSTRALIA

NEW ZEALAND

Annual inflation rates, 1974

- over 50%
- 25.1 — 50%
- 20.1 — 25%
- 15.1 — 20%
- 10.1 — 15%
- 5.1 — 10%
- below 5%
- data not available

Extreme range: Chile 585.9%
— Niger 3.6%

Source: IMF Industrial Financial Statistics,
April 1977

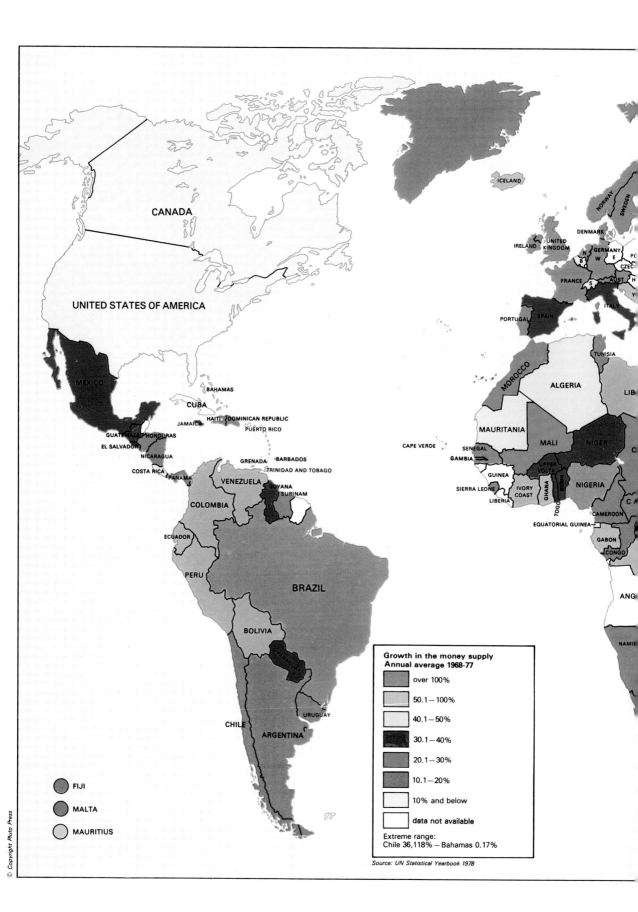

CANADA

ICELAND

NORWAY

SWEDEN

DENMARK

IRELAND UNITED
KINGDOM GERMANY

N
B
W

E

PO

CZEC

UNITED STATES OF AMERICA

FRANCE

S

AUST
H

ITALY

PORTUGAL SPAIN

TUNISIA

MEXICO

BAHAMAS

CUBA

HAITI DOMINICAN REPUBLIC

JAMAICA PUERTO RICO

GUATEMALA HONDURAS

EL SALVADOR

NICARAGUA

COSTA RICA PANAMA

GRENADA BARBADOS

TRINIDAD AND TOBAGO

VENEZUELA GUYANA
SURINAM

COLOMBIA

ECUADOR

PERU

BRAZIL

BOLIVIA

PARAGUAY

URUGUAY

CHILE ARGENTINA

MOROCCO

ALGERIA

LIB

MAURITANIA

MALI NIGER

SENEGAL

GAMBIA

GUINEA

SIERRA LEONE

LIBERIA

IVORY
COAST

UPPER
VOLTA

GHANA

TOGO

BENIN

NIGERIA

CAMEROON

EQUATORIAL GUINEA

GABON

CONGO

C A

CAPE VERDE

ANG

NAMIE

77

FIJI

MALTA

MAURITIUS

Growth in the money supply
Annual average 1968-77

over 100%

50.1 — 100%

40.1 — 50%

30.1 — 40%

20.1 — 30%

10.1 — 20%

10% and below

data not available

Extreme range:
Chile 36,118% — Bahamas 0.17%

Source: UN Statistical Yearbook 1978

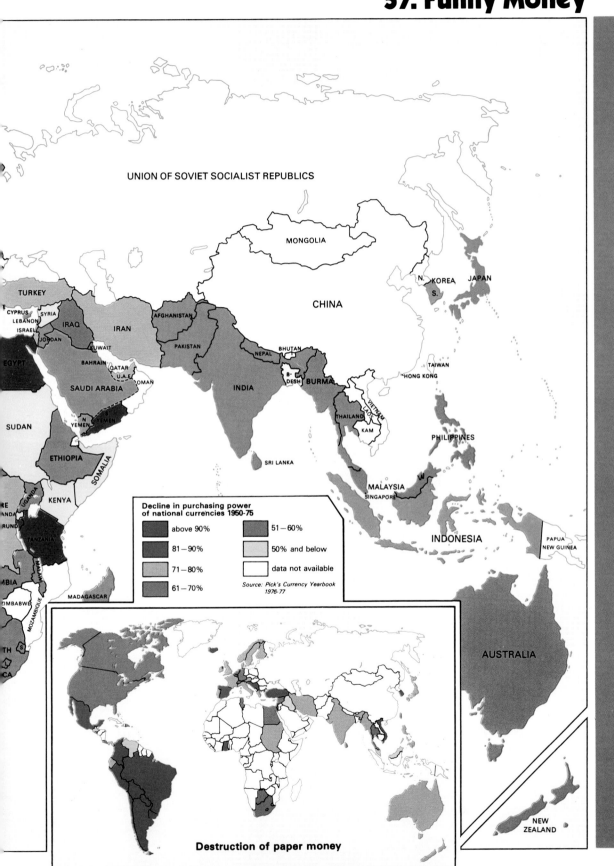

UNION OF SOVIET SOCIALIST REPUBLICS

MONGOLIA

CHINA

N. KOREA
S.

JAPAN

TURKEY

CYPRUS
LEBANON
SYRIA
ISRAEL
JORDAN
IRAQ
IRAN
AFGHANISTAN

KUWAIT

EGYPT

BAHRAIN
QATAR
U.A.E.
OMAN

SAUDI ARABIA

PAKISTAN

NEPAL
BHUTAN
B-
DESH
BURMA

TAIWAN
HONG KONG

SUDAN

N
YEMEN
S
YEMEN

INDIA

THAILAND
VIETNAM
LAOS
KAM

PHILIPPINES

ETHIOPIA

SOMALIA

KENYA

SRI LANKA

MALAYSIA
SINGAPORE

INDONESIA

PAPUA
NEW GUINEA

RE
ANDA
RUND

TANZANIA

MALAWI

MBIA
ZIMBABWE

MOZAMBIQUE

MADAGASCAR

TH
CA

AUSTRALIA

**Decline in purchasing power
of national currencies 1950-75**

above 90%   51—60%

81—90%   50% and below

71—80%   data not available

61—70%

*Source: Pick's Currency Yearbook
1976-77*

Destruction of paper money

NEW
ZEALAND

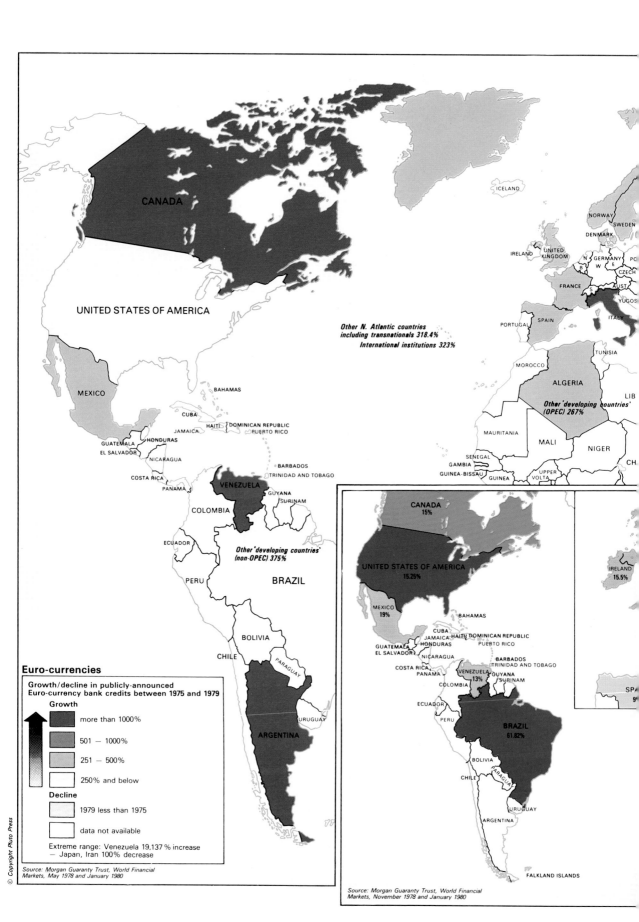

Other N. Atlantic countries
including transnationals 318.4%
International institutions 323%

Other 'developing countries'
(OPEC) 267%

Other 'developing countries'
(non-OPEC) 375%

Euro-currencies

Growth/decline in publicly-announced
Euro-currency bank credits between 1975 and 1979

Growth

- more than 1000%
- 501 — 1000%
- 251 — 500%
- 250% and below

Decline

- 1979 less than 1975
- data not available

Extreme range: Venezuela 19,137 % increase
— Japan, Iran 100% decrease

*Source: Morgan Guaranty Trust, World Financial
Markets, May 1978 and January 1980*

CANADA
15%

UNITED STATES OF AMERICA
15.25%

MEXICO
19%

IRELAND
15.5%

VENEZUELA
13%

BRAZIL
61.82%

SPA
9

*Source: Morgan Guaranty Trust, World Financial
Markets, November 1978 and January 1980*

© Copyright Pluto Press

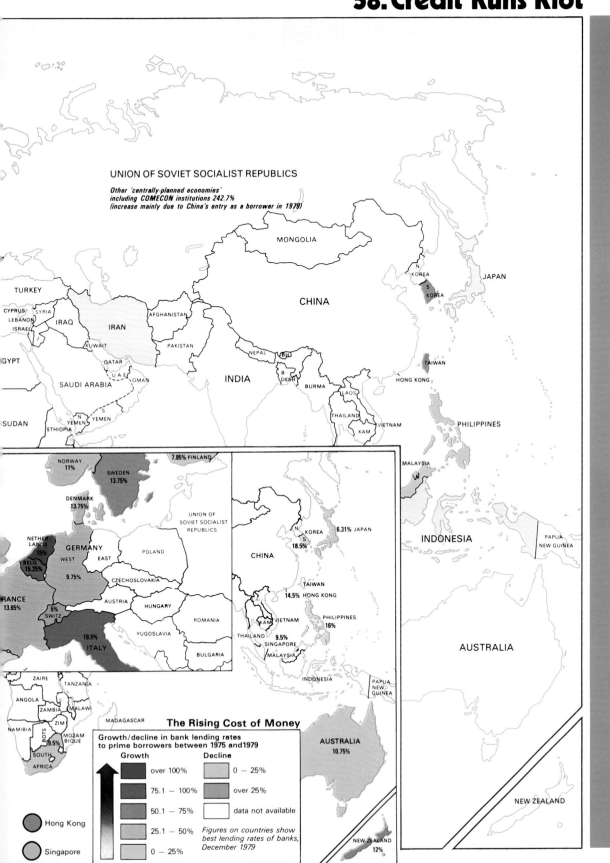

UNION OF SOVIET SOCIALIST REPUBLICS

Other 'centrally-planned economies'
including COMECON institutions 242.7%
(increase mainly due to China's entry as a borrower in 1979)

MONGOLIA

TURKEY
CYPRUS
LEBANON
SYRIA
ISRAEL
IRAQ
IRAN
AFGHANISTAN
KUWAIT
QATAR
U.A.E
OMAN
PAKISTAN
NEPAL
BH
B.
DESH
BURMA
LAOS
THAILAND
KAM
VIETNAM
N
KOREA
S
KOREA
JAPAN
CHINA
TAIWAN
HONG KONG
PHILIPPINES

SAUDI ARABIA
GYPT
SUDAN
N
YEMEN
S
YEMEN
ETHIOPIA

INDIA

MALAYSIA

INDONESIA

PAPUA
NEW GUINEA

AUSTRALIA

NEW ZEALAND

The Rising Cost of Money

NORWAY
11%
SWEDEN
13.75%
7.85% FINLAND
DENMARK
13.75%
NETHER-
LANDS
15%
GERMANY
WEST
9.75%
EAST
POLAND
UNION OF
SOVIET SOCIALIST
REPUBLICS
BELG
15.25%
CZECHOSLOVAKIA
RANCE
13.65%
5%
SWITZ
AUSTRIA
HUNGARY
19.5%
ITALY
YUGOSLAVIA
ROMANIA
BULGARIA

N
KOREA
S
18.5%
6.31% JAPAN
CHINA
TAIWAN
14.5%
HONG KONG
KAM
VIETNAM
THAILAND
9.5%
SINGAPORE
MALAYSIA
PHILIPPINES
16%
INDONESIA
PAPUA
NEW
GUINEA

ZAIRE
TANZANIA
ANGOLA
ZAMBIA
MALAWI
NAMIBIA
BOTS
ZIM
MOZAM
BIQUE
9.5%
SOUTH
AFRICA
MADAGASCAR

AUSTRALIA
10.75%

NEW ZEALAND
12%

Growth/decline in bank lending rates
to prime borrowers between 1975 and 1979

Growth		Decline	
	over 100%		0 – 25%
	75.1 – 100%		over 25%
	50.1 – 75%		data not available
	25.1 – 50%		
	0 – 25%		

*Figures on countries show
best lending rates of banks,
December 1979*

Hong Kong

Singapore

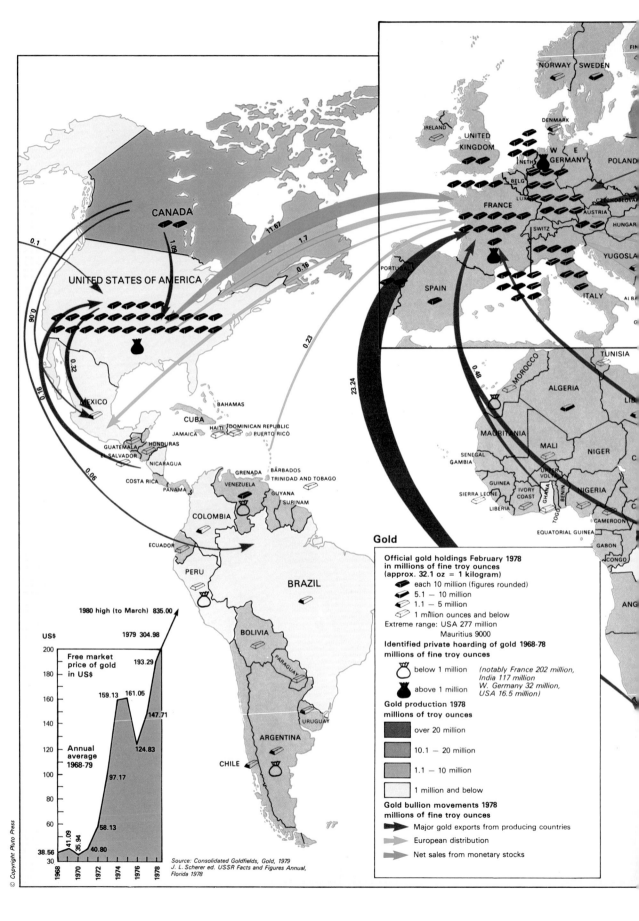

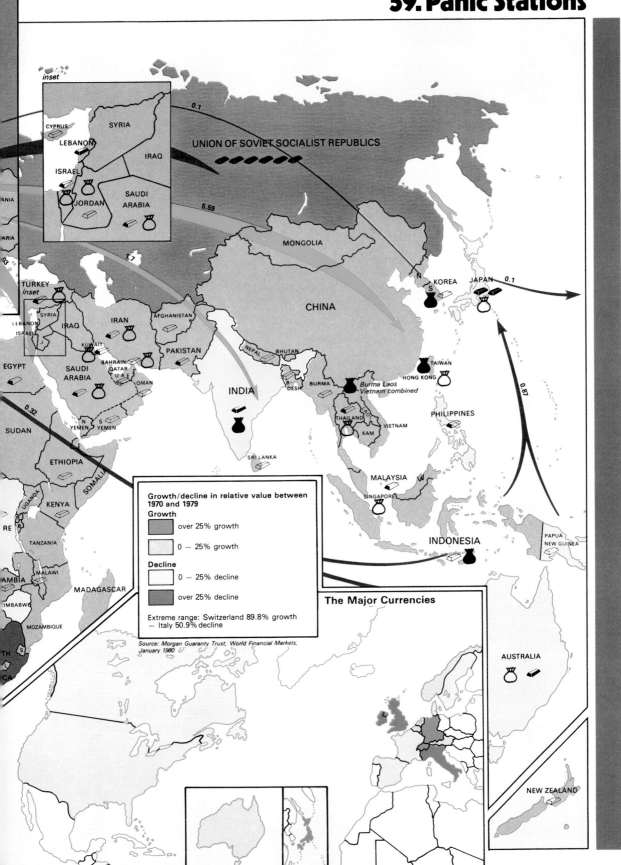

inset

0.1

UNION OF SOVIET SOCIALIST REPUBLICS

Inset:
CYPRUS
SYRIA
LEBANON
IRAQ
ISRAEL
JORDAN
SAUDI ARABIA

5.59

1.7

MONGOLIA

N
S KOREA
JAPAN 0.1

TURKEY
inset
LEBANON
SYRIA
ISRAEL
IRAQ
IRAN
AFGHANISTAN
CHINA

EGYPT
KUWAIT
PAKISTAN
BAHRAIN
QATAR
U.A.E.
OMAN
SAUDI ARABIA
N YEMEN
S YEMEN

NEPAL
BHUTAN
B-DESH
BURMA
INDIA

TAIWAN
HONG KONG

0.32

SUDAN

ETHIOPIA

SOMALIA

UGANDA
KENYA
RE
B
TANZANIA

AMBIA
MALAWI
IMBABWE
MOZAMBIQUE
MADAGASCAR
TH
S
CA

Burma Laos Vietnam combined

THAILAND
KAM
VIETNAM

PHILIPPINES

0.87

SRI LANKA

MALAYSIA
W
SINGAPORE

INDONESIA

PAPUA NEW GUINEA

Growth/decline in relative value between 1970 and 1979

Growth

over 25% growth

0 — 25% growth

Decline

0 — 25% decline

over 25% decline

Extreme range: Switzerland 89.8% growth
— Italy 50.9% decline

Source: Morgan Guaranty Trust, World Financial Markets, January 1980

The Major Currencies

AUSTRALIA

L

NEW ZEALAND

Nuclear Power States

present

planned (by 1984)

CANADA

Gentilly

Darlington

F. Covington
Edwards

Vernon
Montague Seabrook
Rowe
Berlin

New York
Harrisburg Reading
Parsippany
Atlanta
County

Big Rock

Seattle
Satsop

Trojan

UNITED STATES OF AMERICA

Washington
Richmond

Diablo Canyon

San Luis Obispo

Rocky Flats

Marble Hill Bailly

Inola
Russellville
Barnwell

Grants

MEXICO

CUBA

CHINA

Onagawa

JAPAN
Tokyo

Sasebo City Koji

Nagasaki

Darwin

AUSTRALIA

Brisbane

Lugo

PORTUGAL
Peniche

Badajoz

Adelaide

Sydney

Canberra

Melbourne

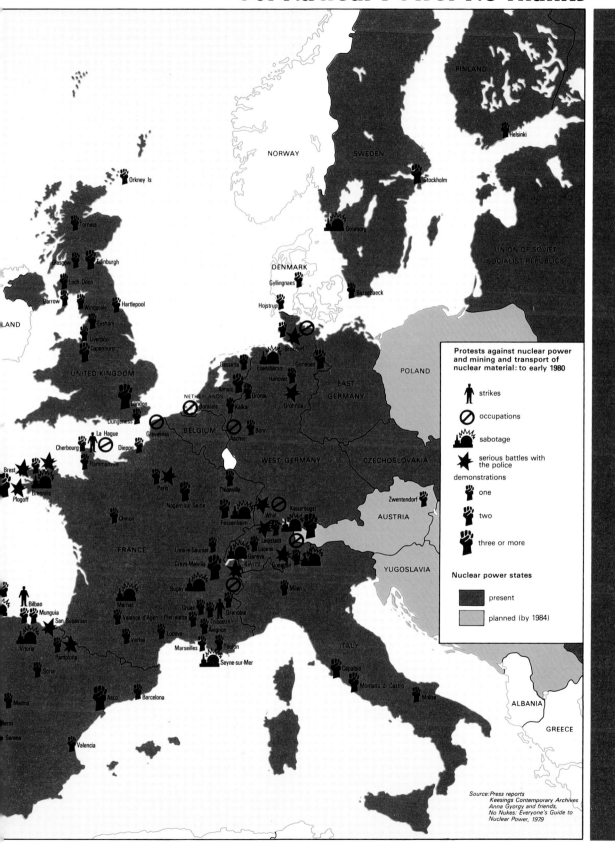

NORWAY

SWEDEN

FINLAND

Helsinki

Orkney Is

Stockholm

Torness

Goteborg

Glasgow   Edinburgh

Loch Doon

UNION OF SOVIET
SOCIALIST REPUBLICS

Barrow   Hartlepool

Windscale

DENMARK

Eysham

Gyllingnaes

Liverpool

Barsebaeck

Capenhurst

Hojstrup

UNITED KINGDOM

Gassette   Brokdorf

Esenshamm   Gorleben

NETHERLANDS   Almelo   Hanover

London

Gronau

POLAND

Borssele   Kalkar

Dungeness

EAST
GERMANY

BELGIUM   Grohnde

Gravelines   Bonn

La Hague

Aachen

Cherbourg   Dieppe

WEST GERMANY

CZECHOSLOVAKIA

Flammanville

Brest

Paris   Thionville

Plogoff   Brennilis

Nogent-sur-Seine

Whyl   Kaiseraugst

Zwentendorf

Chinon

Fassenheim

AUSTRIA

Leibstadt

FRANCE

Lons-le-Saunier

Lucens

Geneva   SWITZ.   Bugano

Creys-Malville

YUGOSLAVIA

Bugey   Milan

Marnac   Granoble

Bilbao

Cruas

Munguia   Valence-d'Agen   Pierrelatte

San Sebastian   Tricastin

Lodeve   Avignon

Vitoria   Verfeil

ITALY

Pamplona   Marseilles   Toulon

Soria   Seyne-sur-Mer   Capalbio

Montalto di Castro

Madrid

Molise

leros   Asco   Barcelona

ALBANIA

Serena

GREECE

Valencia

Protests against nuclear power and mining and transport of nuclear material: to early 1980

- strikes
- ⊘ occupations
- sabotage
- ★ serious battles with the police

demonstrations
- one
- two
- three or more

Nuclear power states

- present
- planned (by 1984)

Source: Press reports
Keesings Contemporary Archives
Anna Gyorgy and friends,
No Nukes: Everyone's Guide to
Nuclear Power, 1979

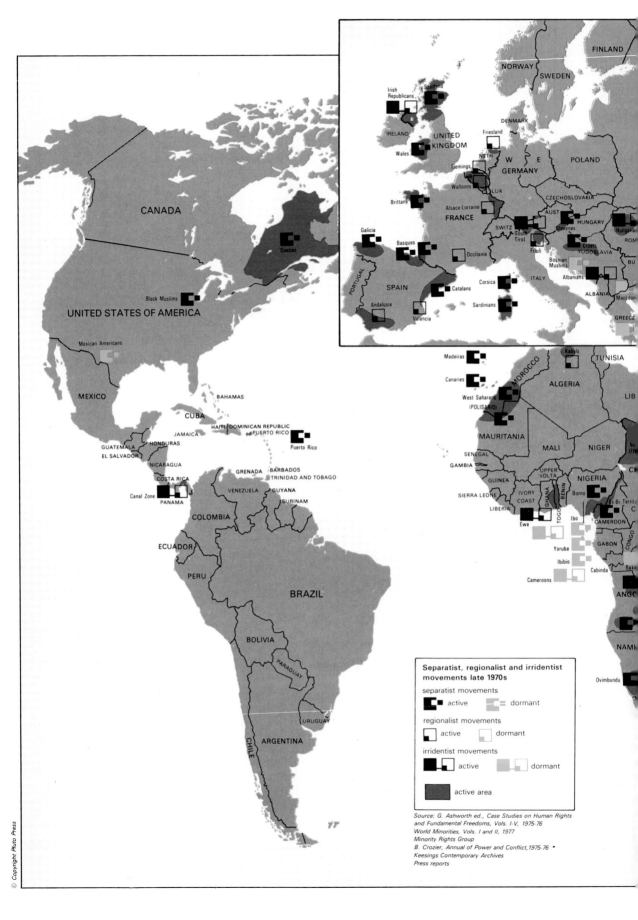

CANADA

Quebec

UNITED STATES OF AMERICA

Black Muslims

Mexican Americans

MEXICO

BAHAMAS

CUBA

JAMAICA

HAITI / DOMINICAN REPUBLIC
PUERTO RICO

Puerto Rico

GUATEMALA
EL SALVADOR

HONDURAS

NICARAGUA

COSTA RICA

Canal Zone

PANAMA

GRENADA
BARBADOS
TRINIDAD AND TOBAGO

VENEZUELA

GUYANA

SURINAM

COLOMBIA

ECUADOR

PERU

BRAZIL

BOLIVIA

PARAGUAY

URUGUAY

CHILE

ARGENTINA

NORWAY

SWEDEN

FINLAND

Irish
Republicans

Scotland

IRELAND

UNITED
KINGDOM

DENMARK

Friesland

Wales

NETH

Flemings

LUX

W
GERMANY

E

POLAND

Walloons

CZECHOSLOVAKIA

Brittany

FRANCE

Alsace-Lorraine

AUST

HUNGARY

Galicia

SWITZ

South
Tirol

Slovenes

Friuli

Hungaria

ROM

Basques

YUGOSLAVIA

Croats

BU

Occitanie

Bosnian
Mushms

ITALY

Corsica

Albanians

SPAIN

Catalans

ALBANIA

Macedon

Andalusia

Sardinians

GREECE

Valencia

Madeiras

Kabyls

TUNISIA

Canaries

MOROCCO

ALGERIA

LIB

West Saharans
(POLISARIO)

MAURITANIA

MALI

NIGER

No
(FR

SENEGAL

GAMBIA

UPPER
VOLTA

CI

GUINEA

NIGERIA

SIERRA LEONE

IVORY
COAST

GHANA

BENIN

Borno

LIBERIA

TOGO

Ibo

Ex-Br. Territo

C

Ewe

CAMEROON

Yoruba

GABON

CONGO

Ibibio

Cabinda

Bak

Cameroons

ANGC

NAMI

Ovimbundu

Separatist, regionalist and irridentist movements late 1970s

separatist movements

active   dormant

regionalist movements

active   dormant

irridentist movements

active   dormant

active area

Source: G. Ashworth ed., Case Studies on Human Rights
and Fundamental Freedoms, Vols. I-V, 1975-76
World Minorities, Vols. I and II, 1977
Minority Rights Group
B. Crozier, Annual of Power and Conflict, 1975-76 •
Keesings Contemporary Archives
Press reports

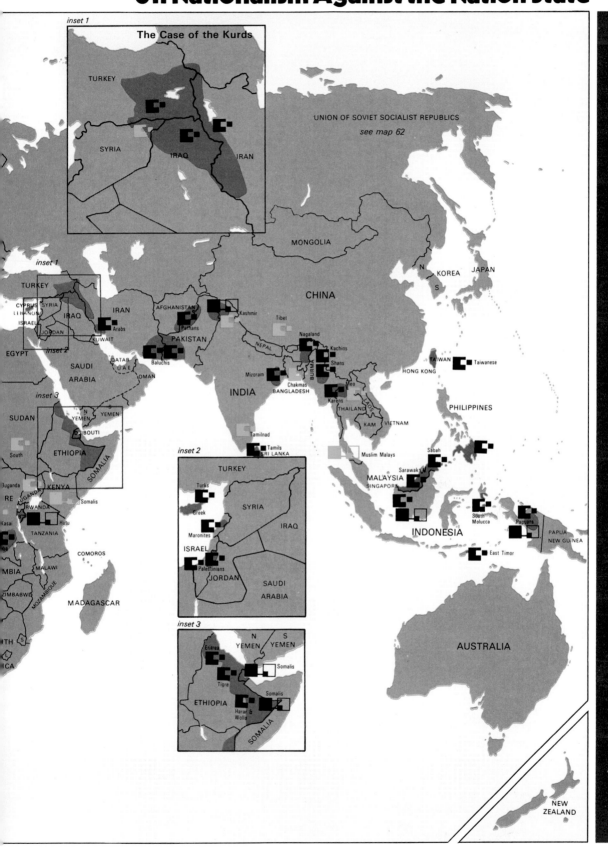

inset 1

The Case of the Kurds

TURKEY

SYRIA

IRAQ

IRAN

UNION OF SOVIET SOCIALIST REPUBLICS

see map 62

MONGOLIA

inset 1

TURKEY

CYPRUS
LEBANON
ISRAEL
JORDAN

SYRIA

IRAQ

IRAN

Arabs

KUWAIT

AFGHANISTAN

Pathans

PAKISTAN

Baluchis

EGYPT

inset 2

SAUDI ARABIA

QATAR
U.A.E.

OMAN

CHINA

Kashmir

Tibet

NEPAL

Nagaland

Kachins

Shans

BURMA

Mizoram

Chakmas

BANGLADESH

INDIA

Karens

THAILAND

Meo

LAOS

KAM

VIETNAM

N KOREA

S

JAPAN

TAIWAN Taiwanese

HONG KONG

PHILIPPINES

Tamilnad

Tamils
SRI LANKA

Muslim Malays

Sabah

Sarawak

MALAYSIA

SINGAPORE

South Molucca

Papuans

PAPUA NEW GUINEA

INDONESIA

East Timor

inset 3

SUDAN

N YEMEN YEMEN

DJIBOUTI

ETHIOPIA

SOMALIA

South

Buganda

UGANDA

KENYA

RWANDA

Hutu

Somalis

TANZANIA

Kasai

COMOROS

MALAWI

MBIA

ZIMBABWE

MOZAMBIQUE

MADAGASCAR

TH

CA

inset 2

TURKEY

Turks

Greek

SYRIA

IRAQ

Maronites

ISRAEL

Palestinians

JORDAN

SAUDI ARABIA

inset 3

Eritrea

N YEMEN S YEMEN

Somalis

Tigre

ETHIOPIA

Harar & Wollo

Somalis

SOMALIA

AUSTRALIA

NEW ZEALAND

East Siberian Sea

Laptev Sea

o Ukta

R Kolyma

R Indigirka

R Lena

YAKUT

R Aldan

Petropavlosk-Kamchatskiy o

oYakutsk

Sea of Okhotsk

Lower Tunguska

Stony Tunguska

JEWS to Jewish Autonomous Oblast

R Amur

Birobidjan
o ►Khabarovsk
BURYAT   o Blagoveshchensk

L Baykal

Irkutsk o   ▥ Ulan-Ude

Vladivostok

o Kyzyl
TUVA

ESTONIANS
LATVIANS
LITHS
SAAMI
KARELS
BYELO–
RUSSIANS
UKRAINIANS
RUSSIANS
KOMI
MANSI
KHANTY
YAKUTS
BASHKIRS
KAZAKHS
BURYATS
BURYATS
GEORGIANS
ARMENIANS
AJERS
KAZAKHS
TURKMEN
UZBEKS
KAZAKHS
KIRGIZ
TURKMEN
TADZHIKS

...monstrations

...t show trials

...s on nationalism

...and prison camps

...spitals

	Balts		Paleo-Asiatics
	Caucasians		Slavs
	Finno-Ugrians		Turkic
	Iranians		sparsely populated
	Mongols		

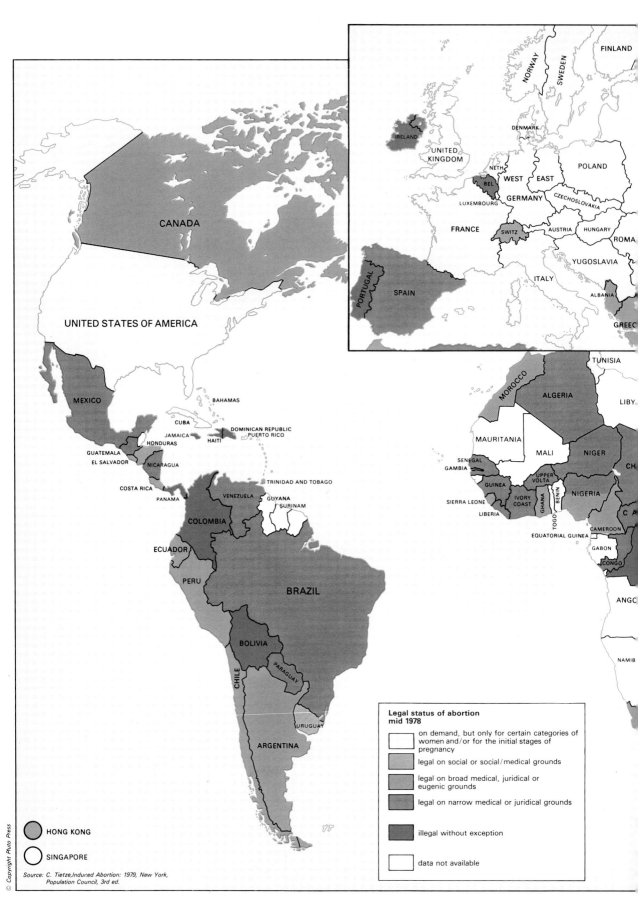

CANADA

UNITED STATES OF AMERICA

MEXICO

BAHAMAS

CUBA

JAMAICA
HONDURAS
GUATEMALA
EL SALVADOR
NICARAGUA

DOMINICAN REPUBLIC
PUERTO RICO
HAITI

COSTA RICA
PANAMA

VENEZUELA

TRINIDAD AND TOBAGO

GUYANA
SURINAM

COLOMBIA

ECUADOR

PERU

BRAZIL

BOLIVIA

PARAGUAY

CHILE

URUGUAY

ARGENTINA

NORWAY
SWEDEN
FINLAND

DENMARK

IRELAND
UNITED
KINGDOM

POLAND

NETH.
BEL
LUXEMBOURG

WEST
GERMANY

EAST

CZECHOSLOVAKIA

FRANCE

SWITZ.

AUSTRIA
HUNGARY

ROMA

PORTUGAL
SPAIN

YUGOSLAVIA

ITALY

ALBANIA

GREEC

TUNISIA

MOROCCO

ALGERIA

LIBY.

MAURITANIA

MALI

NIGER

CH

SENEGAL
GAMBIA

GUINEA

UPPER
VOLTA

BENIN

NIGERIA

SIERRA LEONE
LIBERIA

IVORY
COAST

GHANA

TOGO

C A

EQUATORIAL GUINEA

CAMEROON

GABON

CONGO

ANGC

NAMIB

**Legal status of abortion
mid 1978**

on demand, but only for certain categories of
women and/or for the initial stages of
pregnancy

legal on social or social/medical grounds

legal on broad medical, juridical or
eugenic grounds

legal on narrow medical or juridical grounds

illegal without exception

data not available

HONG KONG

SINGAPORE

Source: C. Tietze, Induced Abortion: 1979, New York,
Population Council, 3rd ed.

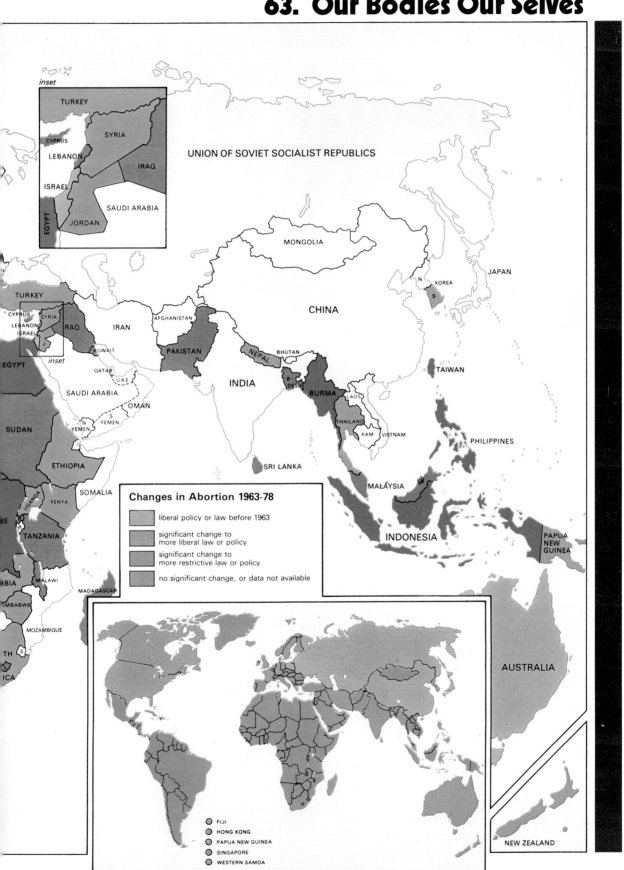

inset

TURKEY
CYPRUS
SYRIA
LEBANON
ISRAEL
EGYPT
JORDAN
IRAQ
SAUDI ARABIA

UNION OF SOVIET SOCIALIST REPUBLICS

MONGOLIA

JAPAN

N KOREA S

CHINA

TURKEY
CYPRUS
LEBANON SYRIA
ISRAEL
IRAQ
inset

IRAN

AFGHANISTAN

KUWAIT

QATAR
UAE

EGYPT

SAUDI ARABIA

OMAN

N YEMEN
S YEMEN

SUDAN

ETHIOPIA

SOMALIA

UGANDA
KENYA

TANZANIA

MALAWI

MADAGASCAR

IMBABWE

MOZAMBIQUE

TH S

ICA

BIA

PAKISTAN

NEPAL

BHUTAN

B-DESH

BURMA

INDIA

SRI LANKA

TAIWAN

LAOS

THAILAND

KAM VIETNAM

PHILIPPINES

MALAYSIA W

INDONESIA

PAPUA NEW GUINEA

AUSTRALIA

Changes in Abortion 1963-78

liberal policy or law before 1963

significant change to more liberal law or policy

significant change to more restrictive law or policy

no significant change, or data not available

⬤ FIJI
⬤ HONG KONG
⬤ PAPUA NEW GUINEA
⬤ SINGAPORE
⬤ WESTERN SAMOA

NEW ZEALAND

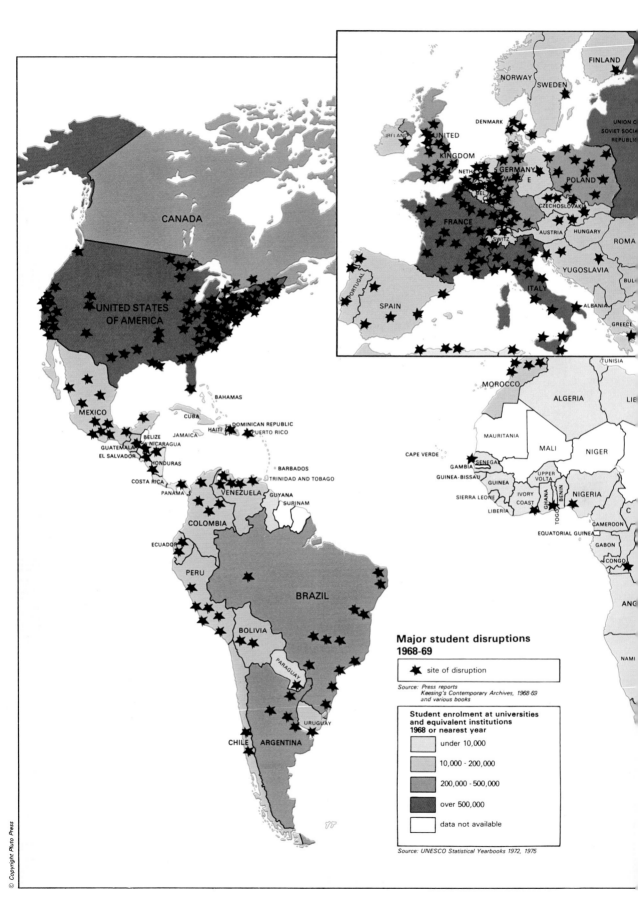

CANADA

UNITED STATES
OF AMERICA

MEXICO

BAHAMAS

CUBA
JAMAICA   DOMINICAN REPUBLIC
HAITI   PUERTO RICO
BELIZE
GUATEMALA   NICARAGUA
EL SALVADOR   HONDURAS
COSTA RICA
PANAMA   VENEZUELA   GUYANA
BARBADOS
TRINIDAD AND TOBAGO
SURINAM

COLOMBIA

ECUADOR

PERU

BRAZIL

BOLIVIA

PARAGUAY

CHILE   ARGENTINA

URUGUAY

NORWAY   SWEDEN   FINLAND

DENMARK

IRELAND   UNITED
KINGDOM
NETH   GERMANY
BEL   W   E   POLAND

UNION C
SOVIET SOCIA
REPUBLIC

CZECHOSLOVAKIA

FRANCE

SWITZ   AUSTRIA   HUNGARY
ROMA

YUGOSLAVIA   BUL

ITALY

PORTUGAL
SPAIN

ALBANIA
GREECE

TUNISIA

MOROCCO   ALGERIA   LIE

MAURITANIA

CAPE VERDE
GAMBIA   SENEGA   MALI   NIGER

GUINEA-BISSAU
GUINEA   UPPER
VOLTA
SIERRA LEONE   IVORY   GHANA   BENIN   NIGERIA
COAST   TOGO
LIBERIA

CAMEROON
EQUATORIAL GUINEA

GABON
CONGO   ANG

NAMI

Major student disruptions
1968-69

★ site of disruption

Source: Press reports
Keesing's Contemporary Archives, 1968-69
and various books

Student enrolment at universities
and equivalent institutions
1968 or nearest year

under 10,000

10,000 - 200,000

200,000 - 500,000

over 500,000

data not available

Source: UNESCO Statistical Yearbooks 1972, 1975

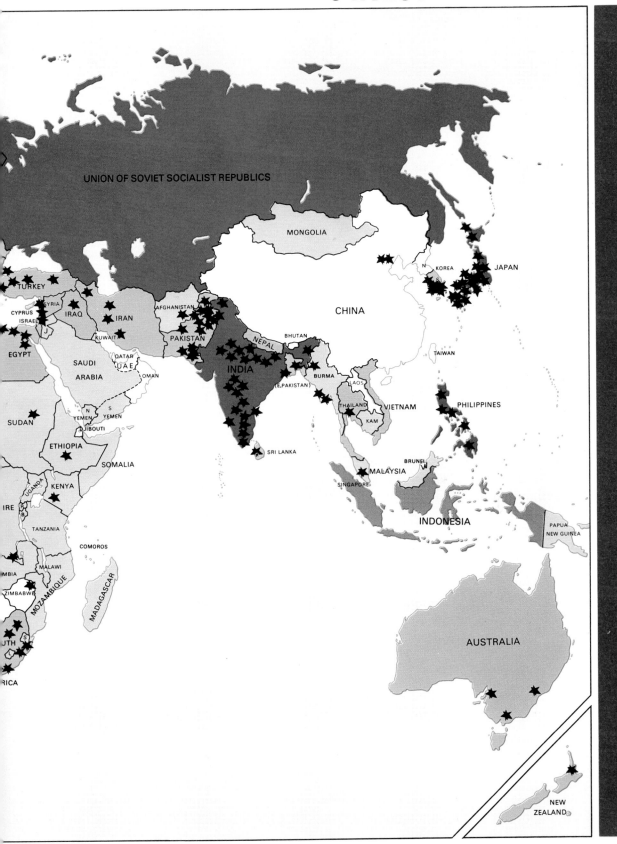

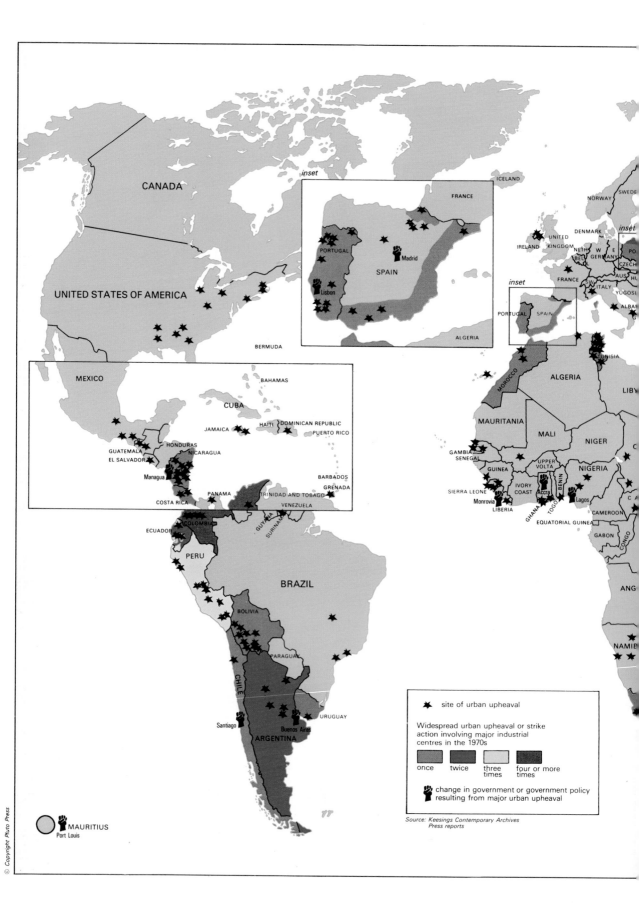

CANADA

inset

UNITED STATES OF AMERICA

BERMUDA

ICELAND

NORWAY   SWEDE

FRANCE

PORTUGAL

SPAIN

Madrid

Lisbon

ALGERIA

DENMARK

IRELAND   UNITED
           KINGDOM
                    NETH
                    BEL GERMANY W E
                                   PO
                    LUX
                         CZECH
                         AUS HU
                    FRANCE SWI
                              ITALY YUGOSL
                                     ALBAN
                                         G

inset

inset

PORTUGAL   SPAIN

MOROCCO

TUNISIA

ALGERIA

LIBY

MEXICO

BAHAMAS

CUBA

JAMAICA   HAITI   DOMINICAN REPUBLIC
                             PUERTO RICO

HONDURAS
GUATEMALA   NICARAGUA
EL SALVADOR

Managua

COSTA RICA   PANAMA

BARBADOS
GRENADA

TRINIDAD AND TOBAGO
VENEZUELA

ECUADOR   COLOMBIA
                    GUYANA
                    SURINAM

PERU

BRAZIL

BOLIVIA

PARAGUAY

CHILE

URUGUAY

Santiago   Buenos Aires

ARGENTINA

MAURITANIA

MALI

NIGER

GAMBIA
SENEGAL

GUINEA

SIERRA LEONE   IVORY
                COAST
Monrovia   Accra
LIBERIA   GHANA TOGO BENIN

NIGERIA

Lagos

CAMEROON

C A

EQUATORIAL GUINEA

GABON   CONGO

ANG

NAMIB

MAURITIUS
Port Louis

★ site of urban upheaval

Widespread urban upheaval or strike
action involving major industrial
centres in the 1970s

| once | twice | three times | four or more times |

change in government or government policy
resulting from major urban upheaval

Source: Keesings Contemporary Archives
Press reports

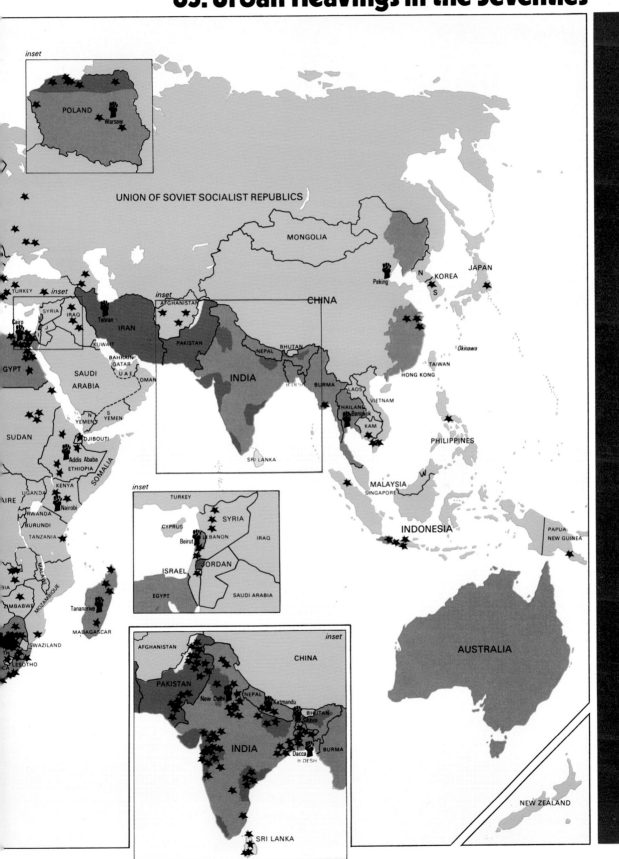

The States of the World

Sovereign states and dependent territories referred to in this atlas
*Dependent territories

Afghanistan	Democratic Republic of Afghánistán
Albania	Republika Popullore Socialiste e Shqipërisë
Algeria	El Djemhouria El Djazaïria Eddemokratia Echaabia
Andorra	Les Vallées d'Andorra
	Valls d'Andorra
Angola	Angola
Antigua	Antigua
Argentina	República Argentina
Australia	Australia
Austria	Republik Österreich
Bahamas	The Commonwealth of the Bahamas*
Bahrain	Bahrain
Bangladesh	People's Republic of Bangladesh
Barbados	Barbados
Belgium	Royaume de Belgique
	Koninkrijk België
Belize	Belize*
Benin	République Populaire du Benin
Bermuda	Bermuda*
Bhutan	Druk-yul
Bolivia	República de Bolivia
Botswana	Botswana
Brazil	República Federativa do Brasil
Brunei	Brunei
Bulgaria	Narodna Republika Bulgaria
Burma	Pyidaungsu Socialist Thammada Myanma Naingngandaw
Burundi	Burundi
Cambodia *see* **Kampuchea**	
Cameroon	République Unie du Cameroun
Canada	Canada
Cape Verde	República de Cabo Verde
Cayman Islands	Cayman Islands*
Central African Republic	Central African Republic
Chad	République du Tchad
Chile	República de Chile
China	Zhonghua Renmin Gonghe Guo (People's Republic of China)
Colombia	República de Colombia
Comoros	Etat Comorien
Congo	République Populaire du Congo
Costa Rica	República de Costa Rica
Cuba	República de Cuba
Cyprus	Kypriaki Dimokratia
	Kibris Cumhuriyeti
Czechoslovakia	Ceskoslovenská Socialistická Republika
Denmark	Kongeriget Danmark
Djibouti	Republic of Djibouti
Dominica	Commonwealth of Dominica
Dominican Republic	República Dominicana
Ecuador	República del Ecuador
Egypt	Arab Republic of Egypt
El Salvador	República de El Salvador

Equatorial Guinea	República de Guinea Ecuatorial
Ethiopia	Ethiopia
Falkland Islands	Falklands Islands and Dependencies*
Fiji	Fiji
Finland	Suomen Tasavalta
	Republiken Finland
France	République Française
French Guiana	Guyane Française*
Gabon	République Gabonaise
Gambia	The Gambia
Guadeloupe	Guadeloupe*
Germany, East	Deutsche Demokratische Republik
	(German Democratic Republic)
Germany, West	Bundesrepublik Deutschland
	(Federal Republic of Germany)
Ghana	Ghana
Gilbert Islands *see* Kiribati	
Greece	Elliniki Dimokratia
Greenland	Grønland*
Grenada	Grenada
Guatemala	República de Guatemala
Guinea	République Populaire at Révolutionnaire de Guinée
Guinea-Bissau	Guinea-Bissau
Guyana	Guyana
Haiti	République d'Haiti
Honduras	República de Honduras
Hong Kong	Hong Kong*
Hungary	Magyar Népköztársaság
Iceland	Lýðveldið Ísland
India	Bharat
Indonesia	Republik Indonesia
Iran	Jumhouriy Islamiy Irân
	Islamic Republic of Iran
Iraq	al Jumhouriya al 'Iraqia
Ireland	Éire
Israel	Medinat Israel
	(State of Israel)
Italy	Repubblica Italiana
Ivory Coast	République de Côte d'Ivoire
Jamaica	Jamaica
Japan	Nippon (or Nihon)
Jordan	Al Mamlaka al Urduniya al Hashemiyah
	(The Hashemite Kingdom of Jordan)
Kampuchea	Democratic Kampuchea (formerly Cambodia)
Kenya	Djumhuri ya Kenya
Kiribati	Kiribati (formerly Gilbert Islands)
Korea, North	Chosun Minchu-chui Inmin Konghwa-guk
Korea, South	Han Kook
Kuwait	Dowlat al Kuwait
Laos	Laos
Lebanon	al-Jumhouriya al-Lubnaniya
Lesotho	Lesotho
Liberia	Liberia
Libya	Al-Jamahirayah Al-Arabiya
	Al Libya Al Shabiya Al-Ishtirakiya
	(Socialist People's Libyan Arab Jamahiriyah)

Liechtenstein	Liechenstein
Luxembourg	Grand-Duché de Luxembourg
Madagascar	The Democratic Republic of Madagascar
Malawi	Malawi
Malaysia	Malaysia
Maldives	Republic of Maldives
Mali	République du Mali
Malta	Republika Ta Malta
Martinique	Martinique*
Mauritania	République Islamique de Mauritanie
Mauritius	Mauritius
Mexico	Estados Unidos Mexicanos
Monaco	Monaco
Mongolia	Bügd Nayramdakh Mongol Ard Uls
	(Mongolian People's Republic)
Morocco	al-Mamlaka al-Maghrebia
Mozambique	The People's Republic of Mozambique
Namibia	South-West Africa*
	Suidwes-Afrika*
Nauru	Nauru
Nepal	Népal
Netherlands	Koninkrijk de Nederlanden
New Hebrides *see* **Vanuatu Republic**	
New Zealand	New Zealand
Nicaragua	República de Nicaragua
Niger	République du Niger
Nigeria	Federal Republic of Nigeria
Norway	Kongeriket Norge
Oman	Saltanat Oman
Pakistan	Islamic Republic of Pakistan
Panama	República de Panamá
Papua New Guinea	Papua New Guinea
Paraguay	República del Paraguay
Peru	República del Perú
Philippines	República de Filipinas
	Republika ñg Pilipinas
Poland	Polska Rzeczpospolita Ludowa
Portugal	República Portuguesa
Puerto Rico	Puerto Rico*
Qatar	State of Qatar
Reunion	La Réunion*
Rhodesia *see* **Zimbabwe**	
Romania	Republica Socialistă România
Rwanda	Rwanda
St Christopher (St Kitts)-Nevis-Anguilla	St Christopher (St Kitts)-Nevis-Anguilla*
St Lucia	St Lucia*
St Vincent	St Vincent and the Grenadines*
San Marino	Repubblica di San Marino
Sao Tome and Principe	São Tomé e Principe
Saudi Arabia	al-Mamlaka al-'Arabiya as-Sa'udiya
Senegal	République du Sénégal
Seychelles	Seychelles
Sierra Leone	Sierra Leone
Singapore	Republic of Singapore
Solomon Islands	Solomon Islands
Somalia	Al-Jumhouriya As-Somaliya Al-Democradia
	(Somali Democratic Republic)

South Africa	Republiek van Suid-Afrika
	Republic of South Africa
South-West Africa *see* Namibia	
Spain	Estado Español
Sri Lanka	Sri Lanka
Sudan	Jamhuryat es-Sudan Al Democratia
	(The Democratic Republic of the Sudan)
Surinam	Suriname
Swaziland	Swaziland
Sweden	Konungariket Sverige
Switzerland	Suisse
	Svizzera
	Schweiz
Syria	al-Jamhouriya al Arabia as-Souriya
Taiwan	Republic of China
Tanzania	United Republic of Tanzania
Thailand	Prathes Thai
	Muang-Thai
Togo	République Togolaise
Tonga	Tonga (Friendly Islands)
Trinidad and Tobago	Trinidad and Tobago
Tunisia	Al-Djoumhouria Attunusia
Turkey	Türkiye Cumhuriyeti
Tuvalu	Tuvalu
Uganda	Uganda
Union of Soviet Socialist Republics (USSR)	Soyuz Sovyetskikh Sotsialisticheskikh Respublik
United Arab Emirates	United Arab Emirates
United Kingdom	United Kingdom of Great Britain and Northern Ireland
United States of America (USA)	United States of America
Upper Volta	République de Haute-Volta
Uruguay	República Oriental del Uruguay
Vanuatu Republic	Vanuatu Republic (formerly New Hebrides)
Vatican City	Vatican City State
Venezuela	República de Venezuela
Vietnam	Công Hòa Xã Hôi Chu Nghĩa Viêt Nam
	(The Socialist Republic of Vietnam)
Virgin Islands (British)	British Virgin Islands
Western Samoa	Samoa i Sisifo
Yemen, North	al Jamhuriya al Arabiya al Yamaniya
	(Yemen Arab Republic)
Yemen, South	Jumhurijah al-Yemen al Dimuqratiyah al Sha'abijah
	The People's Democratic Republic of Yemen
Yugoslavia	Socijalisticka Federativna Republika Jugoslavija
	(Socialist Federal Republic of Yugoslavia)
Zaire	République du Zaïre
Zambia	Zambia
Zimbabwe	Zimbabwe

Source: Statesman's Yearbook 1980–81, with amendments indicated by changed circumstances, e.g. Vanuatu, Iran; or by different interpretations of unchanged circumstances, e.g. Namibia

Notes to the Maps

2. The Proliferation of States

This map shows the proliferation of states since 1945, when much of the world was still run from Europe. A further state, Vanuatu (the New Hebrides), became independent in July 1980, and the existence of powerful separatist movements (see *Map 61: Nationalism Against the Nation State*) suggests that the process of proliferation is still far from over.

A list of the many states with a population of less than a million is given on the map. For comparison, the estimated population of China in 1979 was 850 million, and that of India in 1979, 605 million.

Sovereign states are those that are generally accepted as such by other sovereign states and by international agencies. Thus Taiwan is included, although the governments of both China and Taiwan continue to insist that the island is an integral part of China. Similarly, both the Transkei and the Ukraine are excluded: the first is recognized only by South Africa, and the second, while recognized by the UN, is not deemed independent by any member state. In addition, there are border regions held by one sovereign state and claimed by another. The most notable example is Kashmir, which though incorporated into India is still claimed by Pakistan. No judgement is made on such disputes within this atlas and all states and boundaries conform to those given in *The Times Atlas of the World*.

The two Germanies are shown as new states because neither existed in its present form before 1945. It would have been even more misleading to have shown them as both existing, independently sovereign, in 1945.

Although Greenland is named to distinguish it from the neighbouring Canadian land mass, it is constitutionally part of Denmark. Likewise, Guadeloupe and Martinique, in the Caribbean, are constitutionally part of France.

Some longstanding European statelets, shown as insets on the left of the map, allow their foreign affairs to be controlled by powerful neighbours. They are not really states in the accepted sense at all.

3. The State by Population

This map compares the populations of the world's states in 1979 and gives their annual average growth rate during the seventies.

Population is shown by a graphic distortion which preserves the geographical relationship between states. What emerges is an idea of how very different the world would look if the size of each state corresponded to its population. States with less than a million inhabitants have been excluded. A list of these is given on *Map 2: The Proliferation of States*.

Population growth rates are shown in colour. On current trends, a map of this kind produced year after year would show a marked and continuing decrease in the size of the rich states relative to the rest.

For other graphically distorted maps, which give a different view of the world, see for example *Map 23: National Income* or *Map 26: Government Income*.

For many states, population figures are no better than inspired guesses. In the US, for example, the existence of a large illegal immigrant society, officially estimated at between two and twelve million (see note to *Map 38: The Flight to Work*) is among the many factors in the widely recognized under-recording of population. In others, recording and non-recording of population forms part of the political tussle between its constituent parts — as between the states in Nigeria. In yet others there are simply no provisions for a separate census administration and population figures are supplied by officials engaged in other, seemingly more pressing, business and who have not necessarily been appointed for their numeracy.

4. The State Invades Antarctica

These four maps show the gathering invasion by the state system of the last large unpossessed land mass. They show Antarctica's potential mineral wealth, which states are claimants to its territory, and where each of those claimants has set up scientific stations. One US settlement, the Amundsen–Scott base at the South Pole, is at the meeting point of all the territorial claims in the continent, as if to underline the USA's refusal to recognize them.

Antarctica is rich in resources. It is already a major source of protein in the form of fish, whale meat and increasingly, krill (the many species of oceanic shrimp which constitute the basic food of whales). It holds promise of being a major source of the many minerals already mined in Southern Africa, Australia and South America with which Antarctica shares a common geological past. It is suspected of being rich in mineral oil and gas deposits. It also harbours 70 per cent of the world's fresh water which, in the form of ice, could be detached, towed and made available to the world's arid zones.

Antarctica is attractive in other ways. Scientifically, it is an isolated, relatively clean place from which to monitor global climatic conditions and changes, or levels of atmospheric pollution. It is also a useful base for research into human adaptability to extreme cold and dryness. Its remoteness is causing it to be viewed as a potential nuclear dustbin, able to absorb the radioactive waste that is too dangerous to store or to hide in the populated areas of the world. Militarily, it is attractive for its relative distance from likely theatres of war and its closeness to the only sea link between the Pacific, Atlantic and Indian Oceans other than the vulnerable Suez and Panama Canals.

5. The State Invades the Sea

'If a new and broadly accepted law of the sea does not emerge through international agreement, we face the prospect of each state determining its own view, with ever-widening claims to ocean space and resources. The acceptance of such a situation, favouring as it would power at the expense of justice, and risking unforeseeable possibilities of conflict, is unthinkable.' Kurt Waldheim, Secretary General, opening the sixth annual session of the Third United Nations Conference on the Law of the Sea, 15 May 1979.

This map shows how an extension of national jurisdiction to 200 nautical miles off all coasts, including those of islands, could affect as much as one-third of the sea area that covers some 70 per cent of the globe. Most littoral states have already claimed an Exclusive Economic Zone (EEZ) of 200 miles and, in some cases, the greater riches of the continental shelf have led to claims of 350 miles or more.

The many areas where EEZs overlap are areas of potential conflict. Some of these have caused disputes not yet resolved, and they are shown on the map. Where agreements have been reached (as between Britain and France for example) they have not been included.

The map also shows the areas of major fishing disputes between states, some of which date from pre-EEZ times. Such disputes, and similar disputes concerning sea-bed and undersea-bed resources, can only be fuelled by the new claims to hitherto free resources.

In the process of establishing and extending EEZs, small island territories have a special value. Some zones shown on the map have no apparent territorial source. This is because the islands which extend these EEZs are too small to show up on a map of this scale.

6. Invasions of the Sky

No state has so far claimed territorial rights to the stratosphere, and very few have invaded any part of it with people or materials. But the drive to do so is strong. By the end of the seventies, the pattern of satellite launches had become relatively fixed from year to year and this illustration gives an impressionistic view of launches made in 1978.

Two important and menacing developments took place in that year: the launching of the first hunter-killer satellite, and the contamination of a part of the earth's surface with radioactive debris from a satellite crash.

The satellite illustrated in the bottom right-hand corner of the map is one launched by the European Space Agency, which has eleven member states, whose shares range from Denmark's 2.19 per cent to West Germany's 25 per cent.

The relatively large number of Russian launches reflects the short life span of their satellites which, in contrast to US satellites, is usually measured in days rather than months.

It has been estimated that to the end of the seventies there have been roughly 2,000 launches, through which more than 11,300 man-made objects have been put into space: satellites, rockets, nose cones, shields, capsules and the like, along with fragments from the various space shots that went wrong.

Satellite tracking stations on earth have been overwhelmingly American. However, these are now becoming redundant as new techniques permit surveillance from fixed satellites, without the risk and dependence upon foreign governments and their citizens.

7. Foreign Military Presence

This map records all foreign air, land and sea bases at the end of the seventies. By its very nature, the subject is one on which those who have the information are most reluctant to part with it. It is also one in which abrupt changes in political alignment may lead to equally abrupt rearrangements of the bases which express and support them.

As a whole, the map shows that the global disposition of military forces not only reflects interstate alliances and old imperial interests, but also the fundamental confrontation between Western and Soviet bloc states.

Army bases are distinguished according to whether troops are stationed there primarily for fighting purposes or primarily for training, advisory or surveillance ones. Combat forces are divided into major and minor presences, namely, large self-contained forces organized as divisions of 10,000 or more (and occasionally, as in the case of Britain, 8,500 or more) and smaller forces of battalion strength or more.

It has been impossible to locate the precise sites of many foreign bases other than those of the Americans. Lack of information has also made it impossible to record the changes in tenancy of landing, refuelling and servicing facilities in the Middle East and the Horn of Africa, as Russians gave way to Americans in the last months of the seventies and the early months of 1980.

8. Military Spending

This map shows in colour, how much of each state's gross national product (GNP) is spent on military uses. Symbols are used to show the proportion of central government expenditure so employed. A regional summary is given in the inset map.

The source of these statistics is the US Arms Control and Development Agency, which tends to understate US arms expenditure (see the note to *Map 11: Arms for the Sake of the Profit*).

There is little correspondence between military spending and the nature of individual regimes. Many military regimes or regimes with a substantial military presence, as in Latin America for example, spend a relatively small proportion of their income on military purposes (see *Map 28: Military Government*). The financial cost of domestic repression over unarmed populations is small.

The real impulse to high military spending lies in global or regional confrontation between states. What the map shows overall is how much of the world's resources are devoted to unproductive preparations for war and to mutual destruction.

9. The Nuclear Club

This map shows the extent to which individual states are armed with deliverable nuclear weapons – on their own account or at the behest of an allied state.

A 'known nuclear weapons state' is one which has manufactured and exploded a nuclear weapon or other nuclear explosive device. A 'suspected nuclear weapons state' is one which is widely reputed to have constructed already, or to be able to construct within a very short time, several nuclear weapons. A 'near nuclear weapons state' is one which could develop this capability by the year 2000. An important component of this capability is the commissioning of a nuclear reactor, either for research or for the generation of electricity (see *Map 17: Nuclear Power*).

The danger in the proliferation of nuclear weapons has been underlined by Pakistan's public commitment to construct a nuclear weapon, despite considerable pressure from the main nuclear powers. This commitment is reportedly financed by Libya on the understanding that Libya would share in the result. And during the preparation of this atlas, Pakistan has leapt from being a rather distant candidate for the 'nuclear club' to being an imminent member.

10. Air Power

This map shows the comparative potency of individual states in conventional warfare. It uses the single but important index, numbers of combat aircraft. All naval and army combat aircraft are included, but not training, counter-insurgency and troop-carrying planes, or helicopters.

Numbers are by no means an invariable measure of potency. China's huge combat air force is seriously obsolescent; many of Egypt's aircraft, supplied by the Russians, are grounded for lack of spare parts; Iran's air force is increasingly understaffed and demoralized.

Yet the map provides the best comparison of potency in conventional warfare currently available. To have compared numbers of soldiers would have been to ignore the capacity of the weapons available to them, and this is often more material than the quantity of military personnel. Ownership of warships is limited to littoral states and is likely to be further influenced by the apparent vulnerability of coastal regions. As for land vehicles, it proved difficult to distinguish adequately between tanks and fighting vehicles; and among tanks, difficult to distinguish heavy, medium and light from one another.

11. Arms for the Sake of the Profit

This graphically distorted map shows the relative amounts spent by states on the purchase of foreign arms. Major arms exporters are distinguished from major external arms importers and, in the case of the latter, the major source of arms is shown in colour. The colour breakdown in the figures at the bottom of the map provides a regional summary of the size and source of arms imports.

The acquisition of weapons is an expensive business, and for those who are able to supply them, an extremely profitable one. Although even major arms suppliers, such as France and the United Kingdom, seem to dwindle beside the two giants in arms supply, the USA and the USSR, it does not follow that their trade is unimportant for them, or for their particular markets. Exports are, in fact, less crucial to the arms industry in the USA and USSR, which have huge domestic arms markets, than to states large parts of whose arms production is often ultimately dependent on the existence of export markets to supplement domestic ones.

Available statistics give different impressions of the USA's share of the arms market. The official US statistics which we have used, from the US Arms Control and Disarmament Agency, estimates the USA's share of world arms sales in 1976 at 39 per cent. While Tom Gervasi, in *Arsenal of Democracy* (New York, Grove Press 1977) attributes more than 50 per cent of such sales to the USA, and the *SIPRI Yearbook 1979*, 48 per cent.

The choice of major arms supplier is, for some states, not a static one. Since the statistics for this map were collected, for instance, both Egypt and Somalia have elected to buy the majority of their arms from the USA rather than the USSR.

This map is concerned solely with armed conflict between independent states in the seventies which involved uniformed personnel of the regular armed forces. It shows both the participants in such wars and the actual area of conflict. For internal armed conflict, see *Map 61: Nationalism Against the Nation State.*

Of course, the nature of such conflicts and their impact on the protagonists has differed enormously: from minor border clashes, as between Libya and Egypt, to the so-called Yom Kippur war in the Middle East, the wars between India and Pakistan and the long Vietnam war which was fought as well in both Kampuchea and Laos.

States are depicted as they were in early 1980; they may not have existed or existed in their current form at the time of some of the conflicts shown. Bangladesh was not an independent state during one of the wars between India and Pakistan. And it was the armed forces of Rhodesia that were engaged against Zambia and Mozambique before Zimbabwe was recognized as an independent state in 1980.

12. States at War in the 1970s

Thirteen minerals of generally accepted economic and strategic importance have been chosen to illustrate the disparity in the distribution of the world's mineral resources among states. Three of the most important minerals are dealt with elsewhere: in an inset map to *Map 15: Energy Power* (coal); *Map 16: Oil Power*; and *Map 59: Panic Stations* (gold). Of the minerals included in these two maps: antimony is used in the manufacture of batteries and, increasingly, as a flame retardant; and manganese is important not only as a steel hardening agent but also in the chemical industry.

Possession of a large quantity of a single important mineral does not necessarily convey a corresponding economic strength. In many instances, mines may be owned by foreign-based transnational corporations (see *Map 36: The Nationality of Transnationals*) which as far as possible dispose of resources in their own interests. Furthermore, market forces may so adjust the current value of particular minerals as to turn a major mine from a highly prized and profitable operation into a vulnerable, loss-making one. None the less, there are five states (shown in Map 14) whose abundance and diversity of mineral resources makes it appropriate to term them mineral powers: Australia, Canada, South Africa, the USA and the USSR.

In some states, the statistics for diamond production do not distinguish between gem and industrial stones. For this reason, the combined figure is given in all cases. South Africa dominates the international market in gem stones: partly through its own important share of world production; partly through its control of the Namibian mines; and not least because, through the Central Selling Organization, it commands an effective world monopoly to whose operations the USSR, amongst others, is party.

A reservation must be made with regard to the figures for chrome. During the period of UDI, from 1964 to 1980, some chrome mined in Zimbabwe, then Rhodesia, was almost certainly exported via South Africa and included in that country's statistics.

13. Mineral Power

14. The World Mineral Powers

This map shows the relationship between each state's energy consumption and production. States with a small or large energy surplus (those which produce more than they consume) are contrasted with states which have a small or large energy deficit (those which consume more than they produce).

The existence of an energy deficiency helps to explain certain policies. The enormous dependence of Japan on imported sources of energy has led to the Japanese government committing itself to a doubling of nuclear power generating capacity within the next few years. (See *Map 17: Nuclear Power*.)

Since the statistics for this map were prepared, the exploitation of rich oil deposits has been substantially changing the ratios of energy pro-

15. Energy Power

duction and consumption for some states: for instance, Mexico, Norway and the United Kingdom. However, this process has not affected the usefulness of the broad categories employed in the map.

Some comment on the statistics used is necessary:

Renewable energy sources, such as solar, tidal and wind power, which require advanced technology for their development, have been so neglected as to be considered negligible and are excluded by the source of the map, *UN World Energy Supplies 1973–77*. Traditional sources, such as wood and dung, are also excluded. Where their contribution is important, as in India and some African states, no accurate figures are available. Where such figures are available, as for some European states, their relative contribution is unimportant.

Production data are based on the production of coal, lignite, crude petroleum, natural gas, natural gas liquids, hydro- and nuclear electricity. Where peat is important as fuel, it is included.

Consumption data are based on the apparent consumption of coal, lignite, petroleum products, natural gas, hydro- and nuclear electricity. Coke, manufactured gas, and electricity traded internationally are considered to have been consumed by importing countries.

Comparison between coal and other sources of energy is based on calorific value. One metric ton of coal is equivalent to 1.47 metric tons of crude petroleum or 1.67 metric tons of natural gas liquid.

The steeply rising price of oil has caused renewed interest in the world's coal resources. Coal can be used as a substitute fuel for power stations and is itself a source of oil. The inset map compares coal production and consumption in all states where it is above 10 million metric tons a year.

16. Oil Power

This map compares the oil production and consumption of individual states where it amounts to more than 0.5 per cent of the world's total. Annual average rates of growth or decline are shown in colour and major oil movements, in proportion to their size, are shown in all cases where they are above 5 million metric tons.

The soaring price of oil during the seventies has given the major oil-exporting states enormous economic power. The Organization of Petroleum Exporting Countries (OPEC) first used its united weight in 1973. Since then, even those oil exporters which have remained outside the cartel, such as Mexico and the United Kingdom, have effectively accepted its leadership in setting prices. Saudi Arabia is by far the largest oil exporter in the world and among OPEC members it is by far the most influential. The United States has publicly and repeatedly pressed Saudi Arabia to use this influence to hold down oil prices. But fear of damaging the cartel and other regional political constraints have qualified Saudi Arabia's ability to do so.

The increasing dependence of the United States on imported oil has been a crucial factor in its persistently enormous trade deficit in the post war period. This has led to the depreciation of the US dollar against many currencies, the erosion of confidence in the dollar as a reserve currency, and an international monetary upheaval without precedent since the second world war. This upheaval is the subject of *Map 59: Panic Stations*.

At present the USSR is still a major oil exporter. But reliable estimates suggest that within a few years it will, like the USA, be an oil importer on an increasing scale. The economic and political consequences of a scramble by the two superpowers for scarce and costly oil supplies are unlikely to be comfortable.

17. Nuclear Power

Two major factors contribute to the current rush by states to develop nuclear power stations. First, growing energy deficits exacerbated by the rising price of oil, and second, the access that such programmes offer to the production of nuclear weapons (see *Map 10: The Nuclear Club*). There is no doubt that the latter is a significant inducement for some poor states, with a relatively low energy consumption, to undertake ambitious nuclear power programmes.

By 1978, 5.85 per cent of the world's total electricity generating power already came from nuclear power stations. This proportion will increase dramatically if all the power stations planned are put into operation.

Only nuclear power reactors likely to produce more than 20 megawatts (mW(e)) per year are included and the information on planned nuclear reactors is, of course, liable to rapid change.

For public response to the dangers of such programmes, see *Map 60: Nuclear Power No Thanks.*

18. Food Power

In this graphically distorted map, colour is used to show whether states have a small or large deficit in food trade. The size of each state is related to its share of world food trade in 1977; if a state is a net exporter, its size is determined by its share of world food exports; if a net importer, by its share of world food imports.

The main exporters of staple grains — the USA, Canada, Australia and Argentina — can use their food surplus as an instrument of considerable power. The US Secretary of State for Agriculture, Earl Butz, said in 1974, 'Food is a weapon. It is now one of the principal weapons in our negotiating kit.' In 1980, in response to the Russian invasion of Afghanistan, the USA embargoed all sales of grain to the USSR not already pledged by contract.

Some states may well show an overall surplus in food trade and yet be unable to nourish their populations at all adequately. Such surpluses are in many cases created by large exports of a single food or beverage commodity, especially coffee, cocoa, sugar and honey, or tropical fruits (see *Map 21: Dependence and Diversity*). Comparison should also be made with *Map 44: Our Daily Bread*. Colombia, a major coffee exporter, is shown here to have a substantial surplus in food trade. Yet the number of calories available per head of population is below requirement and there was a famine in Colombia in 1967. Africa's case is even more ironic. Here it is shown to have an overall surplus in food trade as a result of major exports of coffee, cocoa and tropical fruits. Yet it remains one of the world's most desperate areas of undernourishment and even starvation.

19. Industrial Power

This map shows the enormous discrepancies in industrial wealth, and the power associated with it, between a relatively small number, and the vast mass of the world's states. Canada, for example, with a population of 23 million has more industrial power than the whole of Africa and India combined. The map shows too, the enormous industrial dominance of the USA, although it is diminishing in relation to Japan and the main industrial states of Western Europe. (See also *Map 55: Industrial Droop* which shows the generally decreasing rates of industrial growth between the sixties and the seventies.)

In this map, as elsewhere in this atlas, the need for manageable bands of comparison produces a low band which contains considerable disparities. As an extreme example, the Central African Republic, with an industrial output of US$46 million per year in the mid-seventies is bracketed with Egypt, whose annual industrial output was US$4,000 million.

The statistics available for industrial output are surprisingly inadequate in a number of ways. The only comprehensive figures are given in the UN *Yearbook of Industrial Statistics*, but these apply to different years, many states are omitted altogether, and different criteria are employed. They also demonstrate the distortions inevitable when local values are translated into some international standard, in this case the US dollar. Several East European states have two separate and official dollar conversion rates for their currencies: a 'basic' one, and a non-commercial rate, generally for tourists. The UN statistics have been calculated according to the basic rate, but if these were comparable, the value of manufacturing output in Poland, for example, would have been close to that of West Germany. For the purposes of this map such figures have been converted according to the non-commercial rate.

20. Technological Power

The number of scientists and engineers which each state has in relation to its total population is clearly linked to the size of its manufacturing output – as comparison with *Map 19: Industrial Power* shows. Industrial powers have much greater resources with which to sustain and promote research and development. The inset map, *Brain Drain*, adds the point that there is an international flow of skilled professional and technical labour from the poor states to the rich – labour which is trained at the expense of the poor to benefit the rich.

Given the lacklustre performance in manufacturing output of some East European states, such as Poland and Czechoslovakia, it may seem strange that they should possess so high a proportion of scientists and engineers: as high as Japan and twice as high as West Germany. The answer must lie in their wasteful use of all resources, human as well as material, under the dominion of a distended bureaucracy.

One important aspect of technological power not portrayed on the map is ownership of patents and trademarks. The rich states extend their dominion in technology by either preventing access to certain processes or by exacting a high price for them. Of the patents granted to foreigners in 50 poor states in 1972, no less than 40.6 per cent were owned in the USA, 11.5 per cent in West Germany, 9.6 per cent in Switzerland and 8.9 per cent in the United Kingdom. Of the trademarks registered by foreigners in 54 poor states in 1974, no less than 34.3 per cent were owned in the USA, 15.1 per cent in Japan, 12.2 per cent in the United Kingdom, 9.2 per cent in West Germany and 7 per cent in France. (UNCTAD, *The Role of the Patent System*, 1975 and *The Impact of Trademarks on the Development Process of Developing Countries*, 1977).

21. Dependence and Diversity

This map shows how many states are dependent, for the majority of their export income, on the sale of either one product or a very small number of products. The most extreme case is Oman, where the whole of its export income comes from oil.

The economic weakness of a state dependent upon a single major export is self-evident, especially when it is poor, in competition with other poor states and with the rich as well, and when the product is an agricultural commodity. Not only is there the persistent threat of bad or too bountiful harvests, there is also the threat that access to major traditional markets might be denied: when major customers are also a producer, as with sugar for example, they can take steps to protect their own production at others' expense.

Some poor countries appear to have a stronger, more diversified economic base than they have in reality, since their principal export also takes a partly manufactured form. Bangladesh offers a striking example: 25 per cent of its export income comes from raw jute; but another 25 per cent comes from textile products made mainly from jute and a further 33 per cent comes from woven non-cotton textiles, which are also mainly made of jute. A rare example among rich states is New Zealand: fully two-thirds of New Zealand's exports are animal products.

It should be noted that the statistics do not include tourism nor do they include income from the services offered by tax havens (see *Map 37: The Islands of the Blessed*). For some states, notably in the Caribbean, these are a substantial source of foreign income.

22. Trade Power

This is a graphically distorted map which reveals the extent to which international trade is dominated by a relatively few rich states. In 1978, the whole of Africa emerges as less powerful in trading terms than the

United Kingdom; and the whole of South and Central America as less powerful than the Netherlands.

By comparing this map with *Map 19: Industrial Power* and *Map 23: National Income*, it can be seen that the United States is comparatively weaker in international trade than it is either in manufacturing output, or in the value of its gross national product.

The USSR's relative weakness as a trading power – compared, say, with population (see *Map 3: The State by Population*) with industrial output (see *Map 19: Industrial Power*) or with military power (see *Map 8: Military Spending*) – is also apparent.

As *Map 21: Dependence and Diversity* shows, the weakness of the small trading states is compounded by their dependence on one or two export commodities. Because the poor countries are marginal to international trade, they remain poor; because they are poor, they remain marginal.

23. National Income

The gross national product (GNP) of states in 1977 is shown by a graphic distortion which preserves, as in other maps of this kind, the geographical relationship between states. The annual average rate of growth or decline in GNP per head is shown in colour. (GNP measures a country's total annual income including net earnings from abroad.) What the map underlines is the vast discrepancies between states in both national income and rate of growth.

The most notable increases in the growth rate of GNPs during the seventies have generally been due to one of two factors: either the possession of oil (see *Map 16: Oil Power*); or, participation in the international assembly line of manufacture, where much of the processing has increasingly gone to states able to provide a skilled, controlled, and relatively low-paid labour force, along with tax concessions (see *Map 37: Islands of the Blessed*).

The inset map, *People and Purses*, shows the amount of GNP, or national income, available per head of population. Of course, the greater a state's population, the more it must earn to sustain the well-being of its people.

National income statistics must be viewed with particular caution as pointed out in the Introduction. They do not measure adequately either the value of subsistence production or the value of domestic labour. Further, the measure of national income statistics is the national currency of a single state, the USA, which is vulnerable to movements in foreign exchange rates. To say that the national income of Switzerland, for instance, has increased within a few days by 1 per cent because the Swiss franc has risen in that proportion against the US dollar is manifestly absurd. Yet it is standard practice in national income comparisons.

24. The Debt-Laden South

It is by now well-known that most poor states, generally situated in the southern part of the world, are becoming poorer in relation to the rich, generally situated in the northern part of the world. This map measures the extent of the accumulated debt of poor states, and the degree to which that debt has recently grown or declined. The inset map shows the drain on export income of debt servicing charges and debt repayments.

What the map as a whole shows is the increasing instability of an international economic system in which many states are unable to live within their straitened means, let alone develop their economies – and in which the related fear of debt repudiation and state bankruptcy fuels the further growth of debt. (For manifestations of this increasing instability see *Map 58: Credit Runs Riot* and *Map 59: Panic Stations*.)

In many instances, obligations to foreign creditors can be met only by contracting new debts, thereby increasing the overall burden with its corresponding drain on future income. When creditors are unwilling to provide more loans, as has happened already to both Zaire and Turkey, formal bankruptcy can only be avoided by postponing debt repayments.

An increase in debt does not invariably mean an increase in economic vulnerability. Mexico and Venezuela, for example, have found no difficulty in borrowing huge sums of money in the expectation (shared by their creditors) of future income from oil exports. At the same time, however, the oil price rises that enhance the economic prospects of a Mexico or a Venezuela add correspondingly to the difficulties and costs of other states.

To be sure, among the states affected by the weight of debt are many in the rich northern part of the world. And likewise, such states are driven to increase their external public debt. But the problems of rich industrial states are of a different order from those of the poor states. They are better able to regain a surplus in their balance of payments by increasing exports, especially to the oil exporting states.

25. Margins of Safety

This map shows the size of the gold and foreign currency reserves held by each state in relation to its monthly imports bill: how long each state could sustain its current level of imports without additional earnings from exports.

It must be emphasized that the same figure has a different significance for the rich and for the poor. States whose sources of export income are diverse have much greater flexibility than those dependent on income from one or very few products (see *Map 21: Dependence and Diversity*).

Gold and foreign exchange reserves represent a form of liquid capital to meet deficits in current payments and to repay debt. The gold content of reserves in the map was valued, according to the practice of the World Bank, at the 'official' price of US$ 42.2 per ounce. This is well below the average market price in the recent past. Some governments have accordingly revalued their gold holdings, but while this would make very little difference to the value of reserves held by the poor, it would greatly increase the value of reserves held by the rich — especially the USA, West Germany, France, the Netherlands, Italy and, of course, South Africa.

For reasons best known to themselves, the USSR and states in Eastern Europe do not disclose the value or content of their reserves.

26. Government Income

This graphically distorted map shows each state's share of total world-wide government income from taxes, levies and direct production. The annual average rate of growth or decline of this share is shown in colour.

Gross domestic product (GDP) measures the total wealth generated within a state each year. By comparison with gross national product (GNP), the subject of *Map 23: National Income*, it excludes income payable abroad and excludes income from foreign sources. Reservations on GNP statistics, given in the note to Map 23, apply equally to GDP figures, but additional reservations are needed here. Although the data for most states has been averaged out over a period of three years, 1975–77, for some states three-year comparisons were not available, and for others statistics had to be taken for earlier years. Further, in some cases the figure for a government's share of GDP dates from a different year to that of the GDP figure itself. It is very unlikely though that this invalidates the comparison.

Figures for the USSR and similar states are based differently from those for the rest of the world. We have used those that are closest to UN national income accounting practice.

The wealth of governments, of course, does not necessarily corres-pond to the wealth, let alone the size, of their respective populations. For comparison, see *Map 3: The State by Population* and *Map 23: National Income*.

27. The State Apparatus

This map shows the number of people, as a proportion of total popula-tion, employed by each state for the purpose of internal security.

Some states appear to include in their definition all those who perform police functions of any kind and this must explain the extra-ordinarily high figure for Sweden, for example – 3,655 members of internal security forces for each 100,000 population.

States which include various forms of people's militia or home guard in their statistics are identified on the map. Such forces are used to supplement conventional police. East Germany, for instance, has less than one hundred conventional police for every 100,000 inhabitants, but when the people's militia is included the figure soars to 2,443. Another interesting example is the United States, where a National Guard is used in such circumstances as serious rioting. In the USA, the number of conventional police is 299 per 100,000 population, but when the National Guard are included the figure rises to 515. Both Denmark and Portugal have sizeable 'home guards'. Finally, Switzerland's internal security forces include a large force of reservists which leads to the enormous figure of 7,766 for every 100,000 people. To show how such inclusions may distort the statistics one need only compare with these examples the figure for the United Kingdom of 44.7.

We would have preferred to portray the state apparatus in terms of administrative employment by central and local government, but astonishingly, relevant figures of any kind are available for very few states and when they are, they involve widely different definitions of government employees. In some cases workers in nationalized industries are included, along with teachers and soldiers; in others teachers and soldiers are included, but not workers in nationalized industries; in still others, only those directly involved in government administration are included, even excluding those administering state welfare schemes. As examples of the wide discrepancies in the statistics, official Russian figures for 1978 suggest that some two and a half million out of a total labour force of 109 million (or 2.16 per cent) belong to the apparatus of government, economic and cooperative management and public organizations. While official Danish figures suggest there are some 678,000 public employees out of an economically active population of two and a half million – over 26 per cent.

Such material as is available, and could be made consistent, is shown in the inset map. It includes employees in state health and welfare schemes, but excludes teachers, soldiers and workers in state or para-statal industries.

This map shows the involvement of the military in the government of states, wherever it is substantial, at the end of 1978. The military have not stood still since then, of course. Idi Amin's regime in Uganda was overthrown only for its civilian successor to be displaced by a military coup. Liberia and Surinam both acquired military regimes in 1980 and South Korea, while retaining a civilian government facade, entered the eighties under military command.

A state under martial law is one in which the law governing the armed forces applies to the entire population. A military regime is one in which members of the armed forces compose the principal agency of government. A regime with 'substantial military participation' is one in which the principal agency of government may have a majority of civilians, but crucial positions, including some not directly connected with the armed forces, are held by members of the military. States with 'regimes (as at the end of 1978) established by military coup' have governments which have been essentially continuous since the coup which determined the regime.

Some states, for example Malawi, have civilian or largely civilian dictatorships which are to a greater or lesser degree dependent on military backing. These have not been included since they are not primarily instances of military government.

This map shows the relative importance attached by states to invest-ment in soldiers and investment in teachers. It also shows the number of

28. Military Government

29. Bullets and Blackboards

soldiers employed by each state in relation to its population.

The ratio of soldiers to population gives no indication of the size of individual armies. For such an impression, comparison should be made with *Map 3: The State by Population*. China, for example, may have a low ratio of soldiers to population, but so large is its population that it has more soldiers than any other state. Nor does a low ratio of soldiers to population necessarily denote a relatively libertarian regime or a relatively contented populace. The sustenance of oppression or the control of discontent often call on the employment not of soldiers but of special methods (see *Map 31: Scourges of the State*) and special agents (see *Map 27: The State Apparatus*).

Particular events may radically alter or at least temporarily distort information on individual states. For example, the overthrow of the fascist regime in Portugal ended a system of military conscription, for warfare abroad, which had made Portugal's ratio of soldiers to population among the highest in the world. And since 1974, the changing situation in South-East Asia produced first a large reduction and then a large increase in the relative sizes of the armies in the area.

30. Conscription and Conscience

This map shows the extent of compulsory military service for men in the mid seventies and the status of conscientious objection in the early seventies. In some states, military service is compulsory but selective and the colour for these has been cross-hatched with the colour for the appropriate period of service. Reserve duty is also shown.

In some states, for example Poland and the Netherlands, the length of compulsory service in the army differs from that in other branches of the armed forces. In such cases, it is the length of army service which has been taken as the standard. In other states, notably Sweden and Portugal, a flexible period of military service applies and here the shorter has been used.

In Israel and Burma conscription applies to women as well as men. There are signs that other states may adopt this practice. In some cases conscription applies to only a section of the population: in South Africa, only to whites; in Cyprus, only to Greeks; in Israel only to Jews and Druzes.

No state accepts political opinion as sufficient grounds for release from military service: conscientious objection is essentially regarded by states as a concession to be restricted as far as possible rather than as a right to be enjoyed. In many, even religious grounds are so circumscribed that only members of a particular sect qualify — for example, the Mennonites in Mexico, Bolivia and Paraguay.

31. Scourges of the State

A healthy society, Plato believed, would have no use for doctors or lawyers. By analogy, it may be argued that a world without states would have no need for the prisons, the torture chambers and the places of execution that this map records.

States rarely acknowledge the application of torture or the existence of political prisoners and in the reporting of these the work of Amnesty International is crucial. For this reason, though, it is important to emphasize that the absence of individual symbols on this map may only mean that there have been no reported instances in the years covered.

The law on the death penalty is sometimes misleading for a number of reasons. In the United Kingdom, for example, the death penalty remains on the statute book but for use only in cases of treason and certain forms of piracy. It has not been imposed since 1964 and is popularly believed to have been abolished altogether. The fact that it remains on the statute book, however, means that it may be much more readily reinstated. In other states, for example Australia and the USA, the death penalty comes within the jurisdiction of constituent states rather than the federal government. In both cases, some state governments have abolished the death penalty while others have retained it.

The number of prisoners in relation to total population is shown in colour. Some of the statistics are confusingly low and may well denote the very opposite of the contented, peaceful conditions they appear to indicate. In Amin's Uganda and Pol Pot's Kampuchea, for example, there were less protracted ways of dealing with opponents than confining them in jails.

32. Refugees

The world refugee population is large, fluctuating and poorly recorded. This map shows the numbers of new refugees between 1972 and 1979. Such refugees may either have been displaced within their own state or have been obliged to move to others across state frontiers.

Major refugee movements both before and since this period have not been included. For example, the Nigerian civil war over Biafra in 1967–1970 led to a major internal displacement of population; substantial flows of refugees have moved from Cuba to the USA both before and after the period; and since 1979 there have been regular reports of large numbers leaving Afghanistan and various provincial states in north-east India. A single exception has been made. The Palestinians have been included because of their continuing political importance and because, unlike so many other refugees, they have scarcely been resettled or absorbed.

33. Languages of Rule

A language of rule is one which is used by a political and/or economic elite to reinforce its control and sustain its cohesion. It effectively helps to deny participation in government or administration by those who do not speak it. It promotes, most notably in Africa, a closer association between the elites of individual states than with their own populations.

The map identifies the varying status of languages imported or created by such elites. It shows where such languages are official, where they are not official but widely used in government and business, and where they merely have status as old imperial languages. It also shows where popular, creole forms of old imperial languages have developed, particularly in the Caribbean, and where the majority of the poor are unable to speak the official language, as is the case with poor, indigenous Indian populations in parts of South America.

Where languages of rule have been imported their status as official languages may be temporary, as proved the case in Morocco (French) or as may happen throughout Malaysia (English), where in 1980, only Sarawak maintains English as an official language. In some countries – Ireland, the Lebanon and Tanzania – there are two or more official languages, only one of which is the language of the majority. This is shown by cross-hatching colours and adding symbols for the minority language or languages.

Greenland does not appear on this map but as a province of Denmark, Danish is its official language, while the majority of its population of 48,000 speak an Eskimo language.

The map is a contemporary rather than historical record. Portuguese, for example, was brought by conquest to what is now called Brazil. It then so far displaced the indigenous languages as to no longer constitute a language of rule.

34. Religions of Rule

The belief in future fulfilment, prosperity and security; the representation of that belief in ritual; its supporting justification by reference to holy writ, interpreted by a special category of people; and its accommodation within state-supported or state-associated institutions: such are the hallmarks of many religions. In this sense, official Marxism-Leninism is such a religion: with its concentration on the benefits of the future from the sacrifices of the present; its conventional parades and ceremonies; its revealed truths, whose texts are to be interpreted only by those appointed to do so; and its association with the power of the state. Furthermore, like some other religions, it has its own schismatic orthodoxies (the Moscow and the Peking denominations); its populist low church heterodoxies (Titoism in Yugoslavia); its anathematized heresy (Trotskyism); and its fundamentalist sects (revolutionary Marxism).

A religion of rule is defined as one which is professed by the governing classes and which sustains their solidarity. Poland provides a good example of the first case, since official Marxism-Leninism, of the Moscow denomination, rules over a population almost entirely Roman Catholic in allegiance. An example of the second case is the United Kingdom. Here the majority of the population is either secular or holds a variety of religious beliefs. But the Church of England is the official state religion, its bishops are automatically members of the upper house of parliament and it retains control through its official status.

In dealing with Christianity, Catholicism and Protestantism are distinguished only where one of these is clearly dominant, and no distinction is made between different versions of Protestantism. As far as Islam is concerned, the only distinction made is between Sunni and Shia, such variants as do exist being accommodated within each dominant strain.

Sites of recent religious conflict are shown on the map, but only where there is current violence on religious grounds, or where there is a significant religious component. In Kampuchea, this reflects the struggle between Peking- and Moscow-backed forces; in Afghanistan, between Islam and Moscow.

35. The Public and the Private

These two maps *Big Money* and *Big Business*, are intended to show the wealth, and therefore power, of some of the world's major banks and some of the largest transnationals compared with many independent states.

Big Money shows the gold and foreign currency reserves of individual states in relation to the assets of banks in the private sector (that is, not central banks). While it is normal for a bank's assets to be almost entirely equalled by its liabilities, it is almost always true that a state's national reserves are more than matched by its foreign debts.

Since the map was prepared, the Crédit Agricole de France replaced the Bank of America as the world's largest bank, with assets of US$105,000 million. Yet in 1976, no state had assets larger than the Bank of America and only one, West Germany, had assets above those of the National Westminster Bank, then only the twentieth in size. At the same time, although the Cantonal Bank of St Gall, in Switzerland, was the world's 300th bank in size, many states, especially in South America and Africa, had reserves lower than its assets.

The reserve figures for the United Kingdom are now considerably higher for a number of reasons: partly because the British government has pursued a tighter monetary policy with related high interest rates, and partly because North Sea oil and oil price rises have produced a strong currency and an enormous inflow of funds.

As with *Map 25: Margins of Safety*, it has been impossible to compare the national reserves of the USSR and associated states because they are not declared.

Big Business compares the gross national product of individual states with the sales income of a range of US transnationals, or multinationals, in 1977. While a corporation's turnover is not the precise equivalent of a state's GNP, the two are close enough for useful comparison. Both Guyana and Surinam, together with many states in Africa, had GNPs lower than the sales income of the US owned company, Time Inc.

36. The Nationality of Transnationals

This map demonstrates the dichotomy in the nature of transnational enterprise. While their name and their method of functioning would suggest allegiance to no particular state interests, they remain tied to the state where they are officially based. The pressures of world-wide competition lead transnational companies to cross state boundaries. The drive for power and the need for support from the state means that their 'nationality' should never be overlooked.

The map confirms common knowledge, that the majority of transnationals are owned in the states of Western Europe and, in particular, the United States, home base of the largest transnationals in the world.

This map shows some of the many ways in which corporations and business generally seek to avoid state taxation. It also shows how many states, especially islands in the Atlantic and the Pacific, find legal means of benefiting from this search. To emphasize the role of islands, all the states involved have been artificially depicted as such.

The map isolates tax havens, flags of convenience, free production zones and offshore manufacturing zones as the primary means of tax avoidance. It is in the nature of the topic that such a map cannot be exhaustive; private capital's search for havens of one sort or another is relentless, inventive, and often successfully cloaked in secrecy.

The difference between major and minor tax havens is one of financial importance, as judged by the private banking sources consulted.

States offering registration of flags of convenience are those which provide shipping companies with the advantages of nominal or low taxation, and little or no regulation of safety or working conditions on board.

Free production zones are areas set aside for offshore manufacturing or assembly plants. Major zones are defined as those in which 10,000 or more workers were employed in 1975. Offshore plants may operate both inside and outside free production zones. They are based on local labour but export all their output. They enjoy tax and customs privileges. The free production zones featured on this map relate to Africa, Asia and Latin America only. Others, in Ireland and, increasingly Eastern Europe, have been excluded on the grounds that they are as yet unimportant in their economic and social effect on their host economies.

37. The Islands of the Blessed

This map shows the numbers of people prepared to go abroad in search of work, their states of origin and the states to which they are drawn.

While international agencies such as the United Nations and the International Labour Office in Geneva are permanently working to compile and publish statistics on population movements and employment, there is no single world-wide study of people seeking work across national frontiers. As a result this map has been produced in the full knowledge that it is incomplete, dependent as it is on occasional regional statistics and personal estimates of individuals. Some states, such as Australia, Venezuela and north-east India, are known to attract immigrant workers, but no figures or estimates were available.

One of the difficulties is that in some cases most of the people who enter a state in search of work do so illegally. This is particularly true of the United States where most illegal entrants do so from Mexico and most of these, perhaps two-thirds of the total, are Mexican citizens. Estimates of the illegal migrant population 'range from two to twelve million' according to a *White House Fact Sheet*, 4 August 1977. The figure on this map of three million migrant workers in the US is an estimate prepared by Roger Böhning of the ILO.

Migrant labour is a major source of income to both the families left behind and their states of origin. At the end of 1973, West Germany was paying children's allowances for some 850,000 children who were living abroad and who had at least one parent working in West Germany. These were going to the following:

38. The Flight to Work

Turkey	515,200
Yugoslavia	148,100
Italy	80,900
Spain	42,500
Portugal	32,600
Greece	28,700

The number of foreign children who were resident in West Germany and receiving payments at the same time came to 154,400. (UN, *The Welfare of Migrant Workers and Their Families*, Report of a seminar in Yugoslavia, New York 1976.)

A further example of the value of migrant labour to their states of origin relates to African migrant workers in France. In 1973, transfers from migrant workers in France contributed 24.7 per cent of Morocco's total revenue from external sources, 20 per cent of Algeria's and 11.6 per cent of Tunisia's. (Roberto Aliboni ed., *Arab Industrialization and Economic Integration*, London, Croom Helm 1979.)

39. Exploitation

Ideally, a measure of exploitation would compare the output of all productive workers (i.e. workers whose labour results in essential ingredients for further production) with their income. Such a measure does not exist, since productive and unproductive workers are not differentiated analytically or statistically; since inessential is not differentiated from essential output; since statistics do not cover all economic activity, but only part of it; and since they are not truly international in their scope.

So instead of using a formula such as: value added in productive activity divided by wages in cash and kind for productive activity, we have had to settle for the following: value of gross output in manufacturing, less wages and salaries in manufacturing, divided by wages and salaries in manufacturing.

The results of applying the latter formula were divided into five levels of exploitation: first level — below 4; second level — 4 to 6.99; third level — 7 to 9.99; fourth level — 10 to 12.99; and fifth level — over 12.

The data itself presented certain problems. Some governments report the value of gross output at factor cost, the cost to the producer of the elements of production excluding indirect taxes but including subsidies; some, at producers' prices, including indirect taxes, but excluding subsidies; and some adopt hybrid definitions. Some governments make an attempt to quantify non-wage payments, most do not. In some states — the richer ones — salaries form a large component of the labour bill, in most they do not. In some states, manufacturing covers a far wider range of economic activity than in others. In most but not all cases, a three-year average was used, in others, the three most recent years available, and occasionally, less than three years.

Overall, it must be admitted, we believe that the available data gives a biased picture. Exploitation in rich states appears to be lower than exploitation in poor states, when the opposite may well be the case. It is to be hoped that this first world map of exploitation may lead to a more refined study.

40. The Labour Force

These two maps describe the nature of the labour force in individual states: *Workers on the Land* and *Workers in Industry*. Neither includes the service sector which, everywhere, although for very different reasons, is both large and growing.

Both maps confirm the dependence of poor states on agricultural labour and production. But some poor states, for example Zambia and Uganda, show a surprisingly small percentage of their population to be working in agriculture, together with an equally, and not surprising, small percentage working in industry. This is because in many poor states, much of what is termed 'economically active population' is actually unemployed or is engaged on the fringes of the economy in a multitude of subsistence 'service' capacities. Although this would appear to be a subject on which there would be fairly reliable and complete statistics, this is far from the case. Many African states clearly have great difficulty in establishing the nature of their workforces and may even be reluctant to reveal information.

Figures for China, which are not otherwise available, have been taken from estimates provided by Jon Sigurdson, in *Rural Industrialization in China*, Harvard 1977.

This map shows the percentage of women workers in the non-domestic labour force and gives an index of the degree of sexual discrimination in jobs.

In many states whose workforce is employed primarily in agriculture (see *Map 40: The Labour Force*), women workers inhabit a twilight zone between agricultural and domestic labour. This often leads to strange statistical conclusions such as the apparently low percentage of women workers in both Equatorial Guinea and Guinea-Bissau, and where the actual numbers are known to be high. By comparison, it would be expected that the number of women workers in Islamic states would be low and this is borne out by the map.

The index of sexual discrimination in jobs is based on the proportion of women (or men) who would have to change their occupational or industrial classification for there to be sex equality in employment. Inevitably, the definition of inequality involves an important component of status and this must reflect in some way the personal judgement of its source, Elise Boulding *et al.*, *Handbook of International Data on Women*, 1976. Yet the ranking confirms general knowledge: that women enjoy greater job equality in Eastern Europe than in Western Europe and that there is most discrimination in the Islamic states of the Middle East.

There is one major reservation to be made. Absence of discrimination in dangerous or debilitatingly heavy manual labour is not necessarily a sign of equality. In many Asian states, women act as unskilled assistants to more skilled male workers.

In this map we have attempted to peer behind the single concept of trade unionism to the widely differing realities of trade union freedom and confinement. In some states, trade unions are more or less independent bodies, able to take most decisions related to their interests without interference from the state, except in times of national emergency. In most states, whatever the official pretensions, independent trade unionism does not exist.

As far as we are aware, no such map has previously been attempted. The categories and definitions were determined on the advice of leading international trade union officials. Although the first two categories divide states into those where independent trade unions comprise more than and less than half the labour force, it was not our intention to quantify in detail the numbers of workers in trade unions. In fact, in the United Kingdom for instance, almost half of all employed workers are in unions and the trend is upwards. In the United States, for comparison, only about a quarter of the workforce is unionized and the proportion is declining.

Trade unions that are totally controlled, as in the USSR, Eastern Europe and a number of Asian and African states, are essentially organs of government with no independence of decision. Trade unions that are tightly controlled, as in many other African states, have independence of decision in form, but are in fact permitted such independence only when there is no conflict with major government policies.

There was some disagreement between trade union experts on the appropriate category for trade unionism in certain African states, such as Zambia, Nigeria, Ghana and Kenya and also others in Latin America.

This map compares the incomes of the top 5 per cent in individual states, with the bottom 20 per cent. Although the statistics used relate to the sixties and the early seventies, no later information was available.

The disparity is large, but in reality may be even greater. For a number of reasons, the incomes of the rich are systematically understated by the statistics. It is now widely recognized that the rich enjoy various forms of consumption outside the expenditure of their official after-tax incomes. In Western capitalist societies and their imitators elsewhere, executives, for instance, are provided with forms of untaxed income in kind: the use of company-owned apartments, cars and even planes; participation in company-subsidized schemes for private medical treatment and the private education of children; and a whole multitude of minor benefits which can be broadly described as expense-account entertainment. In addition, instead of salary increases which bring with them a high rate of tax, they are frequently offered option and other equity allowances likely to produce a capital gain and be taxed at a much lower rate, if at all.

Although figures are not available for incomes in the USSR and Eastern Europe, bureaucrats there also have access to privileged consumption beyond their official incomes: through state-supplied living quarters and transport, special medical facilities, special schools or places at schools, and their own shops which make available rare or subsidized goods.

The inset map shows the dramatic division between rich and poor within groups of economies determined by its source, UNCTAD, and which includes Yugoslavia among the 'developed market economies' and Cuba among the 'developed centrally planned' ones.

44. Our Daily Bread

This map shows the number of calories available per head of population in each state and the incidence of famines between 1950 and 1979.

The minimum calorie intake, as defined by the World Health Organization, takes into account climatic conditions, types of work, sex and average weight, and has been incorporated into the figures on which this map is based.

The most extreme cases of states with mass calorie deprivation correspond with the Sahel region of West Africa which suffered severe drought and famine between 1972 and 1974 and which reached their peak in 1973. The Sahel drought is illustrated in the inset map.

Although some rich states, such as Canada, West Germany and Sweden, appear to be less privileged than the USSR and Czechoslovakia, it should be remembered that calorie intake is the most simple of food measures. The diet of the former may involve a higher intake of protein, vitamins and other food values.

The following table provides comparative information on protein deficiency. It appeared in the Food and Agricultural Organization's *Fourth World Survey*, 1977.

state	year of survey	age group (in years)	% suffering from protein energy malnutrition		
			Severe	Moderate	Total
India		1–5	2.0	52.7	54.7
Rwanda	1971	0–5	9.8	44.9	54.7
Cameroon	1973	0–5	4.4	36.4	40.8
Cen. Af. Rep.	1972	0–5	3.0	36.4	39.4
Guatemala	1967	0–4	5.9	26.5	32.4
Guyana	1971	0–4	1.3	30.8	32.1
Haiti	1971	0–5	6.0	25.0	31.0
Burundi	1972	0–5	2.2	28.7	30.4
El Salvador	1967	0–4	3.1	22.9	26.0
Kenya	1968		1.0	25.0	26.0
Brazil	1970	0–4	6.3	18.9	25.2
Colombia	1968		1.7	19.3	21.0
Jamaica	1970	0–3	1.4	18.0	19.4
Barbados	1969	0–4	1.2	15.3	16.5
Venezuela	1971	1–6	0.9	14.5	15.4

For Barbados, El Salvador, Guatemala, Guyana, Jamaica and Venezuela, these were national samples; for Cameroon, the sample was limited to Douala; for the remainder, no further details are given.

Protein deficiency is permanently damaging to small children since it affects the development of the brain.

During the Sahel famine 1972–74, whole populations were uprooted and people died in hundreds of thousands. Exceptionally low rainfall had aggravated the cumulative effects of unrestrained grazing, excessive cultivation and short-sighted social policies.

Early reports suggest that the current famine (1980) in East Africa, the result of civil conflict and war, as well as agricultural neglect and inadequate rainfall, may claim even more victims.

Susan George, citing a National Geographic magazine report of a satellite photograph of the Sahel region, provides a useful correction to the 'climatic' explanation for the tragedy. The photograph shows 'a hexagonal island of green in the tan sea of the Sahel. Inspection revealed it to be a quarter-million acre modern ranch, fenced off with barbed-wire from the surrounding desert. Inside, other fences divide the ranch into five sectors, with cattle grazing a single sector at a time. Though the ranch has been in operation only seven years, the rotational grazing has made the difference between pasture and desert. (Susan George, *How the Other Half Dies: The Real Reasons for World Hunger*, Penguin 1976, page 45.)

45. Bill of Health

This map shows infant mortality rates, life expectancy figures for both men and women and also the number of hospital beds in proportion to population.

Infant mortality is the single most important factor in the measurement of life expectancy at birth and a high rate of infant mortality will reduce significantly figures for life expectancy.

Incidence of hospital beds as an index of medical provision should not be taken to imply a judgement on the value of Western allopathic medicine compared with traditional homeopathic systems. There is no means of telling the extent of provision of traditional systems of medicine, and therefore no way of using them for international comparison; and Western medicine is internationally dominant.

46. The Right to Learn

This map shows the extent of illiteracy in individual states. It also shows the percentage enrolment of the population of appropriate age in primary, secondary and tertiary education. In some states, children of secondary school age are still at primary schools, thus inflating the percentage in primary education and reducing the percentage in secondary education. In Gabon, the Lebanon and Hong Kong for example, this pushes the primary school figure to above 100 per cent.

The limited resources that poor states are able to devote to higher education are in many cases ultimately diverted abroad (see *Map 20: Technological Power* and *Map 38: The Flight to Work*), or into the service of local subsidiaries of transnational corporations whose profits are exported (see *Map 36: The Nationality of Transnationals*). What remains is often the more irrelevant for being too closely modelled on imported curricula which reflect the needs and conditions of alien societies. The predictable result is a high drop-out rate and the explosive resentment that go with it.

47. The Longer Reach

There are few ways in which the citizen can reach out from immediate circumstances to give and receive news, ideas and opinions, in exchanges which constitute the vital source of intellectual emancipation and which so many governments see as a challenge and even a threat. The two such instruments chosen are the telephone, an essentially private form of communication, and newsprint, essentially a means of public communication.

It is certainly true that in many societies poverty is principally responsible for the lack of both. But, as the map reveals, there are some states, the Soviet Union for example, where neither economic backwardness nor widespread illiteracy can explain the relatively small number of telephones available or the relatively low consumption of newsprint.

Of course, newsprint consumption levels can give no indication of who owns or controls the press, or show degrees of press freedom. Nor does access to a telephone guarantee private and free communication.

48. Holes in the Safety Net

This map shows the percentage of welfare payments made by states to individuals, as a percentage of gross domestic product. The data for the map have been taken from the eighth and ninth international inquiries into *The Cost of Social Security*, conducted by the International Labour Office and covering the years 1971–74 in the eighth inquiry and 1976–1979 in the ninth inquiry. Most data comes from the ninth inquiry, except in the case of fourteen states.

A comparison of the results of the two inquiries confirms the truth of that most uncharitable of injunctions 'to those who have, let more be given'. Where comparison between 1971 and 1974 was possible, the proportion of net welfare receipts to gross domestic product fell in every state in Africa, every state in Asia apart from Japan; and every state in South America, except for oil-rich Venezuela. The proportion rose only in Oceania, and throughout Europe except for Czechoslovakia and Greece.

49. The Swelling Cities

This map deals with the internal migration of people. It shows that in most states there is a persistent net migration of country dwellers to towns and cities. Since the total populations of all states except East Germany have increased (see *Map 3: The State by Population*) this has usually been accompanied by a less significant rise in rural population. In East Germany both urban and rural populations have declined, partly as a result of large-scale migration to West Germany in the period before the Berlin Wall was built. In Western and Eastern Europe and North America there has been an actual decline in rural population and this is shown on the map.

A UN monitoring report, *World Population Trends and policies 1977*, 1979, has compared the attitudes of various governments towards population distribution between cities and countryside and the policies pursued.

Out of the 146 governments surveyed, 112 regarded the rate of urbanization as either 'substantially unacceptable' or 'extremely unacceptable'. Yet only 80 of these claim to have policies directed at decelerating – not reversing – the process and 16 had policies of no intervention whatsoever.

The survey produced some strange anomalies. Bhutan and Cyprus regarded their spatial distribution as 'slightly unacceptable', Brazil and Saudi Arabia as 'substantially unacceptable', yet all four were pursuing policies of 'acceleration' of urban growth. On the other hand, East Germany, Hungary, Czechoslovakia and Sweden regarded their spatial distribution as 'entirely acceptable', while at the same time they were pursuing attempts to decelerate the process.

50. Slumland

This map uses access to safe water supplies as the most unambiguous index available of urban health. Other indices, such as area of floor space per person or the number of people per room or dwelling unit are clearly open to misinterpretation when compared internationally.

The map also shows percentage areas of slums in many of the world's major cities. Since the source of information was the United Nations *Second World Housing Survey*, 1974, the most recent available, and only selected cities were included, there appear to be obvious omissions: perhaps Kingston (Jamaica), Port of Spain (Trinidad), La Paz (Bolivia), Jakarta (Indonesia) and Soweto (South Africa) – to name but a few examples. And since economic growth rates are now declining almost everywhere, and the proportion of slum dwellers in the urban population was increasing even in the period of high economic growth, it is reasonable to assume that the situation today is substantially worse than is conveyed by the map.

This map deals with criminal activity as defined by state authorities and also with murder as the supreme human crime. Definitions of crime are obviously open to varieties of interpretation by individual states but in general all crimes which come to the attention of the police, other than traffic offences, are included. Murder is defined as any act performed (successfully) with the intention of taking human life. This definition excludes manslaughter and abortion, but not infanticide.

The fact that statistics can be very misleading is exemplified by definitions of crime in South Africa. There are serious crimes in South Africa which would not be regarded as crimes at all by other states, notably sexual relations between members of different races as defined by South Africa's Immorality Act. Figures for murder, while high, are in reality much higher still, since murders within the black community are sometimes not brought to the attention of the police. And although the numbers may be numerically marginal, statistics for murder do not include those who have died under police interrogation from allegedly natural causes. The peculiarly high figure for murder in the Lebanon may be explained by the escalating political violence that preceded the civil war.

The principal source of statistics used for this map, the International Criminal Police Organization (Interpol) offers some words of caution:

'The General Secretariat simply reproduces the information given on the forms from each country . . . The information . . . is unsophisticated but uniform . . .

'We emphasize the fact that the data given in this report is [sic] in no way intended to be used as a basis for comparison between different countries. Our statistics cannot take account of the differences which exist between the definitions of what constitutes an indictable offence in the various national legislatures considered, of the different methods of calculation, nor of any changes in legal definitions, the structure of the various services engaged in criminal investigation and the conditions under which it is carried out, which may have occurred during the period covered by the report. Bearing in mind all these unknown factors, together with others which influence police investigation, the figures which appear in this report must be considered approximate and should therefore be interpreted with great caution.'

We felt compelled to abandon our original plan for a map on recent rates of unemployment throughout the world for reasons explained in the Introduction.

This chart is taken from one produced by the International Labour Office in 1974. It uses current UN population projections and a rule-of-thumb correlation between total population and economically active population, to present the likely profile of unemployment in rich and poor states up to the year 2150.

Such projections are frequently subject to sudden amendment or refinement which may be caused by new evidence or even new theories. And the chart itself is clearly based on economic trends in the past that may well not be reflected in the future. The difficulties and instabilities of the present world economic system (see Maps 55–59 in particular) point to a period of much slower economic growth than has been known since the second world war, if not to a period of stagnation or even contraction. Such a period, if significantly prolonged, would significantly reduce the economically active proportion to the whole.

At the very least, this chart warns of the blighted future that could affect many millions of lives.

Given the reluctance of the world's states to acknowledge the damage being done to its most basic resources, this map can evoke only some of the worst known examples of pollution to air and sea.

Sea pollution is a phenomenon more recognized than measured. Therefore the map, though based on the data available, remains essentially impressionistic and concentrates on those areas known to be most heavily affected.

In the Mediterranean, the problem has reached emergency dimensions and more detailed information is available which is shown in the inset map. But in addition to the pollutants included, there are at least two other major industrial sources of pollution in the Mediterranean: mercury waste and pesticides.

Air pollution is shown by two limited regional studies of the most commonly dangerous industrial pollutants: sulphur dioxide, which becomes sulphuric acid when combined with water vapour and which is a prime cause of chronic lung disease; and lead, which can seriously and permanently damage the nervous system and is particularly dangerous for children.

It is important to emphasize that pollution is neither local nor isolated. For this reason individual, though dramatic, instances of pollution disasters, such as the mercury poisoning at Minimata (Japan), first officially identified in 1956, and the dioxin poisoning in Seveso (Italy) in 1976 have not been included.

54. The Dying Earth

The purpose of this map is to demonstrate not only the steady increase in desert across the earth, but also the part played in this increase by neglect and deliberate injury.

The map identifies bioclimatic zones, shows areas where there is very high or moderate risk of intensifying or extending aridity and some of the major causes. Vulnerable land includes stony or rocky surfaces, areas subject to soil stripping and gully erosion, areas subject to sand movement, and land with excess salt or bad soil structure. Human and animal pressure refers to density of human population and livestock. Human pressure also includes intense pressure of cultivation associated with mechanization.

It has taken thousands of years for large tracts of desert and semi-desert land to develop out of what were once fertile regions: years in which haphazard human encroachment has upset the delicate balance on which ecological renewal depends.

In recent years this encroachment has become more violent. In large parts of Africa for example, population pressure, patterns of land ownership and war have intensified the destruction of land, increased blight to a virtually endemic condition and produced almost permanent famine (see *Map 44: Our Daily Bread*).

Technology has made possible more deliberate large-scale encroachment and drastic changes in land use can be effected. Vast tracts of rain forest in Brazil are now being turned into grazing land, creating a potential desert of the future.

The extension of desert and arid zones has more than local and regional significance. Large-scale changes in land patterns and use can have major effects on both the weather and the renewal of the world's oxygen supply.

In times of war, even more powerful techniques of destruction are employed, and employed deliberately. The inset map shows the extent of war pollution in Vietnam, Kampuchea and Laos. Whole regions have been poisoned and destroyed through the spraying of herbicides and defoliants and bombardment with shrapnel.

The report of the UN Conference on Desertification 1977, concluded that although more than one-third of the earth's land is already arid, declining fertility and productivity, caused by current levels of intensification, will affect the livelihood of well over 600 million people, most of whom live in poor states.

55. Industrial Droop

This map introduces a section on the emerging symptoms of crisis within the world economic system. What it shows specifically is the decline in the growth rates of industrial production between the sixties and the seventies — a decline which continues to accelerate.

The causes are both complex and arguable. The consequences are momentous (see, for example, *Map 56: The First Inflationary Crest, 1974; Map 59: Panic Stations* and *Map 65: Urban Heavings in the Seventies*).

56. The First Inflationary Crest, 1974

There is no more effective form of undermining the social order than through the unexpected and apparently remedyless inequities induced by a high and rising cost of inflation. In so far as there is a single dominant symptom of crisis in the world system, it is precisely this problem of inflation, which governments freely acknowledge but are patently unable to solve.

A huge rise in the price of oil was made by OPEC in September 1973. But this was itself in large measure a response to the surge of inflation from the end of the sixties. By 1971, world inflation was running at an annual 6.6 per cent, and by 1973 at an annual 9.5 per cent. In 1974, it reached 15.1 per cent overall. In some states, notably the United Kingdom, inflation did not crest until 1975, but in the majority of states, inflation had done so in the previous year.

Figures for inflation are not provided by the Soviet Union or states in Eastern Europe. But if the rates of inflation there were, as claimed, lower than in the industrial West, this was at least in part because consumer queues were appreciably longer.

That the world inflationary crisis in 1974 was no isolated phenomenon is already evident. There was a further inflationary surge in the late seventies, a surge that had not yet crested at the start of 1980. At the end of 1979, inflation figures in many states, notably in such major industrial ones as the USA, Canada and the United Kingdom, were already running above the rate in 1974.

57. Funny Money

Whatever the causes of inflation, there can be no doubt that significant among them is a substantial rise in the supply of money, unmatched by a rise in the production of goods and services.

This map shows the growth in the money supply in individual states over a ten-year period, 1968–77. The figures for a few states do not cover the full ten years, because the statistical series of which they were a part changed their bases during the period. Figures for the United States, the dominant state in the world monetary system, appear peculiarly low. But alongside this low increase in the domestic supply of dollars, there was a massive increase in the supply of expatriate dollars, primarily located in what is known as the Euro-dollar market (see *Map 58: Credit Runs Riot*).

The inset map shows how far the purchasing power of the major currencies was eroded between 1950 and 1975.

58. Credit Runs Riot

If inflation is one symptom of increasing economic instability (see *Map 56: The First Inflationary Crest, 1974*) another is the enormous and accelerating growth of credit. The trend to economic crisis is intensified when such credit rises are accompanied by levels of industrial production and gross national product which are in retreat (see *Map 55: Industrial Droop* and *Map 23: National Income*).

Almost all states and international agencies have participated in the scramble for credit. But while some have been able to borrow on the basis of their conspicuous ability to repay (OPEC member states), others (non-OPEC 'developing' states) have been given further credit because of their very inability to meet current obligations.

Most have been accommodated on the Euro-currency market, the fastest growing international credit market and the one least subject to state surveillance and controls. This map shows recent expansion in Euro-currency bank credits which is measured by the foreign currency liabilities of banks in major European states and in the Bahamas, Cayman

Islands, Bahrain, Panama, Japan, Canada, Hong Kong and Singapore.

The Euro-currency market is essentially the market in money held outside its state of origin. About 75 per cent of this market is in ex-patriate US dollars and the growth in this element has been some ten times the growth in the US domestic money supply during the seventies. This enormous increase in the Euro-dollar sector, with an average annual rate of around 70 per cent in the last decade, has been a primary cause of international credit growth and inflation.

The high and rising cost of credit is shown in the inset map. This is measured as the 'prime rate', or rate of interest charged to best customers, of commercial banks. It is a product of inflation and also a contributory cause, since it often makes borrowing for investment purposes prohibitively expensive and contracts the base of industrial production (see *Map 55: Industrial Droop*).

59. Panic Stations

As a result of the problems depicted in Maps 55–58, there has been an increasing flight from the paper currencies into gold.

The main map shows some of the different features of the gold market: it shows gold producers and levels of gold production; it shows gold holdings of individual states and identified private hoarding; it shows the extent of gold bullion movements throughout the world; and in a graph it shows the annual average increase in the free market price of gold since 1968.

The map indicates the central role played by Switzerland in the world gold market. It is a role essentially supported by special arrangements between leading Swiss banks and the South African Reserve Bank, arrangements which did much to reduce the importance of London, once the centre of the international gold market.

Figures for the Soviet Union's gold production and gold holdings are not made public; but gold production is generally estimated at almost 13 million ounces and holdings have been reported to be over 63 million ounces.

In March 1978, the gold holdings of states within the European Monetary System dropped by almost 20 per cent when corresponding contributions were made to its central pool. Private hoarding is almost invariably secret. We have included estimates by Consolidated Gold Fields for the principal private hoards known to exist in France and India. We have added a Bundesbank estimate for accumulated purchases of Krugerrands (South African gold coins weighing one ounce) in West Germany.

In the United States, it became legal for private citizens to hold and deal in gold at the end of 1974, and this has become a major factor in the international gold market. An even more direct and substantial impact has been made by the New York and Chicago markets in gold futures — contracts to buy or sell specified amounts of gold for a certain price and at a certain date.

Net sales from official monetary gold stocks to private purchasers have consisted in recent years almost entirely of sales from the International Monetary Fund and from the US Treasury. Such sales, at 11.67 million ounces, do not necessarily all find their way into private stocks, since some may have been additions to the gold holdings of certain central banks.

The inset map shows how the flight into gold has been accompanied by a similar movement from the weaker to the stronger currencies.

60. Nuclear Power, No Thanks

By the year 2000, it has been estimated, there will be more than a hundred nuclear power plants which are no longer operational. In addition, there will be hundreds of smaller nuclear installations — research accelerators, fuel enrichment and reprocessing plants, naval reactors, nuclear medical facilities — whose productive lives are at an end. All of them will remain radioactive for hundreds or even thousands of years: an ever-present danger to future generations.

Opposition to nuclear power has taken various forms. In Japan and Yugoslavia, for instance, it is done primarily by law-suit. In some states it has merged into the wider political process. In Sweden, during 1976, it was material in bringing more than four decades of social democratic government to an end. And elsewhere, too, the ballot box has been used to notable effect. In Austria, Denmark, parts of Belgium and parts of the United States, the encroachment of nuclear power has been arrested or slowed by referendum. In other states such as the Soviet Union and Eastern Europe, it is part of a political debate conducted behind closed doors.

The public opposition shown in this map encompasses direct action protests against the whole nuclear energy industry: from uranium mining to the trade in reactors and methods of disposal of nuclear waste. Direct action is shown in all its forms: from industrial strikes and sabotage, demonstrations and festivals, to confrontation and battles with the police. If anything, the extent of such activity is likely to be understated: major West European and American newspapers, which are the source of information for the map, may not have reported many protests which were either small, spontaneous or hidden by authority.

What the map cannot show is the international character of the protest movement: the contingents of Danish protesters in Germany and Sweden; of Germans in France and Switzerland; of French in Germany; of British in France — a character that is a recognition of the degree to which a nuclear facility in one state can affect the environment in another.

Where action has been widespread, as on the Hiroshima–Nagasaki commemoration days of August 1977 in the United States, or the rail transport strike of May 1976 in Australia, symbols have been sited in the appropriate national or regional capital city.

While we had intended to indicate all sites of nuclear accidents grave enough to lead to a shutdown of a nuclear facility, there were so few plants *not* affected that the map would have been rendered meaningless. This strongly confirmed our view that the everyday technical operation of all nuclear facilities is highly dangerous.

61. Nationalism Against the Nation State

One powerful manifestation of dissent against the current world system is the existence of a wide variety of movements seeking to revise either boundaries or allegiances. While they are not all necessarily beneficial, they reflect some of the irrationalities in the world's division into states and in some cases suggest that there may be further proliferation (see *Map 2: The Proliferation of States* and the corresponding note).

Separatist movements seek to create a new state out of one or more already established. Irridentist movements seek a readjustment of state frontiers. Regionalist movements seek to achieve some or more autonomy within their established state. We have been forced to make our own judgements about these movements and have coded the information into easily understood shorthand descriptions.

All movements have been classified as either active or dormant. An active movement is one whose activities have evoked a significant response from authority, usually involving police or army action of some kind. A dormant movement is one considered to have been active within the last ten years or so, which may well become active again, but which was not active at the end of the seventies.

Such definitions inevitably encompass wide variations. The separatist movement in Wales, however serious its intentions, is at present little more than a source of irritation to the government of the United King-dom. Whereas the separatist movements of the Kurds have involved more than one established state in protracted warfare and remain a major source of conflict in the region.

The current armed struggle in Namibia is defined as separatist, since it is primarily directed to ending that country's effective integration with South Africa. But since Namibia has always been a separate territory, whose independence is recognized by the United Nations and its member states, including recently South Africa itself, its struggle is less a manifestation of separatism than a national rebellion against an occupying foreign power.

The government of Taiwan, like the government of China, claims Taiwan to be an integral part of China. In this context, there is a Taiwanese separatist commitment in the Formosan Independence Movement.

We have not attempted to depict the complex situation in the USSR in this map. For this, see *Map 62: Russia's Ununited Republics.*

62. Russia's Ununited Republics

In a state as centralized, diverse and extensive as the USSR, nationalist challenges are inevitable though repressed. Challenge to state control, and to the dominance of the Russian republic within the USSR, date back to the resistance of the Georgian people to incorporation during 1921–22. This event was directly responsible for the conflict between Lenin and Stalin at the end of Lenin's active political life. Stalin won the day and ever since, the Russian government – we use the word 'Russian' advisedly – has reacted with consistent ferocity to crush any movement for or towards national self-determination.

Despite propaganda and education, as well as more brutal methods of repression, nationalist movements have continually emerged, not least among the peoples of the 'annihilated' republics: the five Autonomous Soviet Socialist Republics or ASSRs (Crimean, Chechen-Ingush, Kabardino-Balkar, Kalmyk, and Volga German) and the Karachay Autonomous Region. All of these disappeared from official maps of the Soviet Union in the early years of the second world war and their entire populations were deported to Soviet Central Asia. Four of them (Chechen-Ingush, Kabardino-Balkar and Kalmyk ASSRs and the Karachay AR) were restored in 1957.

Information on resistance movements in the USSR is necessarily scant and uncertain and distinctions between levels of activity must be a matter of judgement. In gathering material for this map, we have called upon a number of experts and a large variety of sources, including oblique references in official reports.

The psychiatric 'hospitals' identified on this map are used for the punishment and control of political dissent. They are administered not by the Ministry of Health but by the Ministry of the Interior.

63. 'Our Bodies Our Selves'

A central theme of the women's liberation movement is the need for women to take charge of their own fates, a right widely denied them by the male-dominated societies of our world. The most satisfactory measure we have found for its success in this respect is contained in this map on abortion rights.

The map shows the spread in legal provisions: from states in which the right to abortion is denied women altogether, to states in which there is some recognition that women should have the right to decide for themselves. In most states there is some right to abortion, but on more or less restricted criteria, and by leave of some, predominantly male, authority.

In no state is the right to abortion a woman's own. Even in the Netherlands, possibly the most liberal in practice, abortion on demand is available only in non-profit clinics; with formal legal sanction for abortion only on narrow medical grounds. In Cuba, another liberal state, abortion on demand is available in government hospitals. Both the Netherlands and Cuba have been put in the most liberal category.

Where abortion is available on demand for certain groups of women only, the criteria differ widely. They include age (usually women over forty); the number of living children (the number varies); and even, in Hungary, whether women have a home of their own. Where abortion is permitted within a specified time limit, that limit is usually the first ten to twelve weeks of pregnancy, as in most of Eastern Europe, but can be as little as eight weeks (Sweden) or as much as twenty-four weeks (Singapore).

Very often, legal provision and social practice are wide apart. France, while fairly liberal in theory, is restrictive in practice; in the Philippines, the opposite is true.

The definitions used need explanation: 'social or social-medical grounds' cover the well-being of the woman and her existing family; 'juridical grounds' cover rape and incest; 'broad medical and eugenic grounds' cover abortion granted to safeguard a woman's physical health and to prevent the transmission of incurable hereditary diseases; 'narrow medical grounds' cover only cases where a woman's life is at stake. We have taken 'social or social-medical grounds' to be a broader category than 'medical, juridical or eugenic grounds' and have adopted it as the determining one where both are given.

In some states with a federal system of government, national legal provisions are moderated by state law and range from extreme liberality (California in the US, Slovenia in Yugoslavia, and South Australia) to extreme restrictiveness (Louisiana in the US, Queensland in Australia).

The inset map shows changing official attitudes to abortion and draws attention to the danger that liberal trends can be reversed where women are not in full control of the decision on abortion. Many East European states, for example, having induced women to enter the labour force by making abortions freely available after the second world war, are now trying to reverse the consequent decline in new entrants to the labour force and the armed services by making abortion more difficult to obtain.

64. The Student Sixties

The student unrest that so spectacularly characterized the closing two years of the sixties was not a new phenomenon. A prominently student opposition to government policy has been endemic in many parts of the world since the second world war; notably in Latin America. Students were in the forefront of the British Campaign for Nuclear Disarmament in the early sixties; were leading militants of the Civil Rights Movement in the United States; and staged, in 1964, on the Berkeley campus of the University of California, a revolt that served as the prototype and pre-cursor of hundreds that took place across the world before the end of the decade.

The student upheavals in each country may be traced to particular conditions or events. In France, it was the sclerotic inflexibility of the Gaullist educational — and political — regime. In West Germany, earlier, in 1967, it was a state visit by the Shah of Iran and the harshness with which his security was protected. In the United States, it was the Vietnam war and the associated demands of the draft. But although there were, everywhere, particular issues and circumstances, there was also a sense of unity that encouraged protest to leap from one campus to another and from one country to another, in a remarkable international movement that was always dramatic and occasionally, as in France and the United States, so important as radically to alter the political scene.

In promoting this sense of unity, an instrument of undoubted influence was the rapid communication of events, by press, radio, and, most vividly, television. But there was too, an underlying unity of dis-content, at educational regimes which processed rather than educated the huge numbers of students resulting from the university expansion of the preceding period, and which provided degrees without acceptable opportunities of employment.

We have defined student disruptions as any student demonstrations that interrupted the normal course of teaching or administration and which led to outside intervention. In a few states, there were disruptions in sites so close together — as at various universities within Tokyo — that they could not be depicted separately on the map. We have identified 89 individual sites in the United States, 37 in Japan, and 32 in Pakistan. Finally, we found no way of singling out sites of repeated student disruption, without causing confusion.

65. Urban Heavings in the Seventies

Urban disorders were no more peculiar to the seventies than student disruptions to the end of the sixties (see *Map 64: The Student Sixties*). But just as student disruption in 1968–69 was remarkable for its extent and its impact, so urban disorder in the seventies reached an unprecedented incidence and intensity.

Some common factors can be identified: both were promoted by improved communications and especially by television; both were prompted by particular incidents, conditions or circumstances in their state of origin; but again, in both there was an underlying unity of impulse, emanating here from increased urbanization (see *Map 50: The Swelling Cities*) alongside a general decline in economic growth. While there was no corresponding increase in employment opportunities (see *Map 55: Industrial Droop* and *Map 52: The Unemployment Time Bomb*), there was an explosive increase in areas of urban deprivation (see *Map 49: Slumland*) accompanied by pressures from inflation (see *Map 56: The First Inflationary Crest, 1974*), especially on the lives of the poor.

An urban upheaval is defined as an urban disorder sufficiently serious in intensity or extent to involve intervention of the authorities by force. Industrial action has been included where it reflects social revolt rather than specific strikes over wages or working conditions. Urban upheavals which have led to a change in government policy or of the government itself are indicated on the site of the national or regional capital.

Subject Index